Designing Computer-Based Learning Materials

NATO ASI Series

Advanced Science Institutes Series

A series presenting the results of activities sponsored by the NATO Science Committee, which aims at the dissemination of advanced scientific and technological knowledge, with a view to strengthening links between scientific communities.

The Series is published by an international board of publishers in conjunction with the NATO Scientific Affairs Division

A Life Sciences **B Physics**	Plenum Publishing Corporation London and New York
C Mathematical and Physical Sciences	D. Reidel Publishing Company Dordrecht, Boston and Lancaster
D Behavioural and Social Sciences **E Applied Sciences**	Martinus Nijhoff Publishers Boston, The Hague, Dordecht and Lancaster
F Computer and Systems Sciences **G Ecological Sciences** **H Cell Biology**	Springer-Verlag Berlin Heidelberg New York London Paris Tokyo

Series F: Computer and Systems Sciences Vol. 23

Designing Computer-Based Learning Materials

Edited by

Harold Weinstock

Air Force Office of Scientific Research
Washington, DC 20332-6448/USA

Alfred Bork

Department of Information and Computer Science
University of California, Irvine, CA 92717/USA

Springer-Verlag
Berlin Heidelberg New York London Paris Tokyo
Published in cooperation with NATO Scientific Affairs Divison

Proceedings of the NATO Advanced Study Institute on Learning Physics and Mathematics via Computers held in San Miniato, Italy, July 15–26, 1985

ISBN-13:978-3-642-82656-6 e-ISBN-13:978-3-642-82654-2
DOI: 10.1007/978-3-642-82654-2

Library of Congress Cataloging in Publication Data. Designing computer-based learning materials. (NATO ASI series. Series F, Computer and systems sciences ; vol. 23) "Proceedings of the NATO Advanced Study Institute on Learning, Physics, and Mathematics Via Computers held in San Miniato, Italy, July 15–26, 1985"—Verso of t.p. 1. Mathematics—Computer-assisted instruction—Congresses. 2. Physics—Computer-assisted instruction—Congresses. 3. Computer-assisted instruction—Congresses. I. Weinstock, Harold, 1934-. II. Bork, Alfred M. III. NATO Advanced Study Institute on Learning, Physics, and Mathematics Via Computers (1985 : San Miniato, Italy) IV. Series: NATO ASI series. Series F, Computer and systems sciences ; no. 23. QA20.C65D47 1986 510'.7'8 86-21902
ISBN-13:978-3-642-82656-6 (U.S.)

Softcover reprint of the hardcover 1st edition 1986

2145/3140-543210

INTRODUCTION

This book should be of value to all those who are considering the use of or have only just begun to use the computer as a learning aid, regardless of the educational level and the discipline being considered. Although the focus is on computer-based instruction in physics and mathematics at the university- and secondary-school levels, the strategies and problems are universally applicable. At the NATO Advanced Study Institute upon which this volume is based, the obstacles encountered by those engaged in such activities were similar in each of the eighteen countries represented.

Despite many false starts by those engaged in applying the computer as a learning aid, we believe unequivocally that the computer presents a unique educational tool yet to be exploited adequately. The reasons for slow development may become obvious as one reads this book: the effort required to achieve measurable success is not trivial. Extensive planning and team efforts are often necessary. Unfortunately, many well-intentioned educators discover this too late.

We emphasize very early that it is the opportunity to engage students as active participants in the learning process which sets computer-based learning apart from the learning potential of other electronic media. In its ideal form, the computer serves the role of an expert instructor engaging a student in individualized dialog. We reinforced this point by devoting about half of the Institute to a workshop activity in which fifteen groups of five or six participants each developed the beginnings of interactive computer dialogs. An example of the product of one such group is presented in the Appendix. Another group, developing a dialog on vector fields, is continuing the effort in an encouraging example of international cooperation, with five countries on both sides of the Atlantic Ocean represented.

While the promise of computer-based learning is high, the subject is still in its infancy. There is a need to recruit many more good teachers into this field of endeavor. As the cost of hardware is reduced, while its capacity and capabilities increase in the light of rising personnel costs and the demands of a more technologically-oriented society, as teachers are in short supply, the computer will play an increasing role in education. It will not eliminate the need for "live" teaching, but it will change the nature of what teachers do and permit them to respond better to individual student problems. First, however, there is a critical need for thoughtful, innovative teachers to design an extensive body of computer-based learning material, transferring their experience and insight into this new and powerful learning medium.

Alfred M. Bork
Irvine, California

Harold Weinstock
Chicago, Illinois

ACKNOWLEDGMENTS

Attending a professional meeting for two weeks in secluded surroundings might create the aura of a religious experience. Never was this more evident than at the Cappucino Study Center at San Miniato, Italy where we directed the NATO Advanced Study Institute "Learning Physics and Mathematics via Computers" from July 15 to 26, 1985, attended by over 80 participants from 18 countries. We emphasize the religious nature because the Center once was a Capuchin monastery. However, the old monks "never had it so good" thanks to the modernization of the facilities by the present owner, the Cassa di Risparmio of San Miniato. We thank the Cassa di Risparmio for making these facilities available to the Institute at no charge and for the gracious hospitality of its staff. Most of all, we want to thank the Scientific Affairs Division of NATO for providing the funding which enabled the Institute to take place.

More personally, we extend our gratitude to Professors Giorgio Olimpo and Elena Sassi, and to Mrs. Giovanna Caviglione, Professor Olimpo's administrative assistant, who served as the local organizing committee. Professor Olimpo's employer, Consiglio Nazionale delle Ricerche (CNR), also must be acknowledged for its generosity in permitting him and Mrs. Caviglione to devote so much of their time to logistical details and in allowing them to utilize its resources. During the Institute itself, Mrs. Caviglione and Ms. Helen McBride served well beyond the call of duty in assisting the participants with logistics and serving as liaisons between the participants and the non-English-speaking Center staff. One of us (H.W.) also wishes to acknowledge the dedicated service of his secretary, Mrs. Irene Malek, for retyping much of this manuscript and other thankless tasks.

Our deep appreciation and thanks go especially to all of our Institute lecturers (whose written contributions appear on the following pages): Arnold Arons, Jef Moonen, Giorgio Olimpo, John Pitre, Peter Ross, Elena Sassi and Lee Shulman. They have been a part of the Institute planning since 1982 and have responded graciously over the past six months or so to the incessant demands of their zealous editors.

TABLE OF CONTENTS

CURRENT RESEARCH IN THE PSYCHOLOGY OF LEARNING AND TEACHING[1]

Lee S. Shulman and Cathy Ringstaff
School of Education
Stanford University, Stanford, CA 94305

The topic of this essay, current research in the psychology of learning and teaching, is itself a model of ill-founded presumption. It exemplifies in its choice of words nearly all the errors of both arrogance and ignorance that an instructor or a designer of instruction can perpetrate. Examine the components of this title to discover the grounds for our claim. We first refer to "current" research. But what does the term "current" imply? Does our audience share our conception of what is already past? Do our readers hold a common understanding of the history of this research domain that would render them equally interested in learning of its current state?

We continue with reference to "research." But is the audience for this paper interested in some esoteric research literature presumably relevant to their respective subject-matter disciplines? More likely, they are curious about how research can inform their classroom practices.

Our question, in general, is: How can we presume to frame a discussion of learning and teaching when we have no idea of the knowledge, orientations, interests or abilities of our readers and audience? We characterized our title as presumptuous because it failed to take account of the likely states of mind of the article's readers. In that sense it made the error most frequently made by educators. Teachers are often so caught up in their own conception of what should be taught and learned that they fail to ask a primary question: What is already in the minds and motives of those whom we presume to teach that will influence the manner in

---

1. We gratefully acknowledge the assistance we have derived from Anderson and Smith's (in press) forthcoming chapter on research on science teaching. Their recent paper provided us with a rich source of information which was helpful in the preparation of this chapter.

NATO ASI Series, Vol. F 23
Designing Computer-Based Learning Materials
Edited by A. Bork and H. Weinstock

which what we teach is apprehended, understood, committed to memory, and subsequently used under new conditions? The fact of the matter is that the learning and teaching of science and mathematics is difficult, more difficult than can be explained merely by the complexity of the topics, concepts, or issues. Indeed, we are coming to understand that a major source of those difficulties lies in what learners already know or fail to know, already understand or think they understand, with respect to many of the scientific and mathematical topics being taught. The rest of this paper discusses examples of such phenomena, and the psychological explanations for their functioning.

Examples of Science Learning

Let us begin with a relatively simple example originally reported by Clement (1982) and subsequently explicated by Anderson and Smith (in press). In a college physics course, engineering majors were presented with a coin toss problem (see Figure 1). The students were told that a coin is tossed straight up into the air from point A, and caught at point E, and were asked to indicate the direction of each force acting on the coin when it is at point B. If air resistance is ignored, the coin is actually subject to only a downward force due to gravity. Most students, however, incorrectly assumed that there is also an upward force acting upon the coin, a belief that Clement calls the "motion implies a force" preconception. Although this coin- toss problem represents a simple application of Newton's laws of motion, only 30% of the students were able to solve the problem correctly after a full year of physics instruction.

The results seem, on the face of it, quite remarkable. How could such an elementary principle of physics be so very difficult for so many students? Moreover, how is it possible that the comprehension of the principle should be so remarkably resistant to instruction? It is as if prior ignorance had conferred upon this population of students a remarkable immunity to instruction.

Figure 1: The Coin Toss Problem*

What are the forces on the coin at Point B, when it is moving upward through the air?

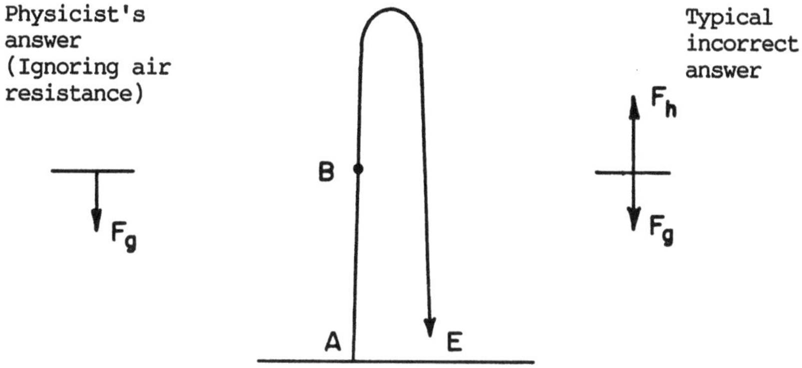

Figure 2: Percentage of students with various pretest answers to the boy and tree problem*

This boy sees the tree. Draw arrows to show how the light travels so that he can see the tree.

Correct answer- arrows from tree to boy - 5%	No arrows between tree and boy - 61%	Arrows from boy to tree - 12%	Other answers - 12%

* From Anderson and Smith, in press.

Consider a second example, also reported by Anderson and Smith (in press). After a five-week unit on light and vision, 5th graders were presented with the question illustrated in Figure 2. To solve this problem correctly, students must understand seeing as detecting reflected light. Before the unit began, only 6% of the 5th graders were able to answer this question. After instruction, only 24% of the students answered the question correctly.

Why is science so hard to learn? What, if anything, can psychology and the other social sciences contribute to our understanding of what makes science and mathematics so resistant to instruction? How can our efforts at the improvement of instruction be guided by the theories and empirical findings of these fields?

Conceptions of Learning

We will begin our discussion with an examination of alternative conceptions of learning. These conceptions correspond closely to alternative approaches to epistemology (at the level of how individuals come to know) and the history and sociology of science (when examining how scientific communities come to know). We shall distinguish among three general approaches to the conceptualization of learning: (a) innate idealism, (b) empiricism, and (c) constructivism or bounded rationality.

Innate Idealism. The view of innate idealism is best reflected in the writings of philosophers such as Plato and Descartes, and linguists such as Noam Chomsky. In this view the problem of how people come to know something is short-circuited by the claim that the ideas are already and always in the mind of the knower and need only the proper conditions or circumstances to be discovered and reflected upon. In the Socratic dialogues such as the *Meno*, the philosopher views his students as already in possession of the important ideas under consideration. They need only the stimulus of his sharp and incessant questions, the shock of his philosophical "torpedo fish," to trigger their recognition and understanding of important definitions, distinctions, or principles. As an example of that kind of principle in instruction, we find the work of the mathematician Robert Davis (1966). He lures his students into generalizing the mathematical rules he has helped them induce to a point where they invariably fall into error. Davis then employs his own form of Socratic method, which he calls "torpedoing." He confronts the students with evidence of the inconsistencies of their own generalizations, thus forcing them to reflect on their own knowledge, criticize it and revise it.

Chomsky (1965) has claimed that the grammar of one's native language is already innately understood by members of the human species. That is, the reason that all known human languages share certain universal syntactic features, even though their lexicons and specific grammatical characteristics may be different, is that all members of our species are born with the capacity to induce a particular form of grammatical structure from the otherwise "blooming, buzzing confusion" of natural human language they hear about them. Chomsky claims that certain aspects of language knowledge are similar to Plato's or Descartes' innate ideas.

Although we, as contemporary cognitive psychologists of instruction, do not believe that many of the concepts and principles we teach about the physical world are innate in the minds of learners, the extreme form of the innate idealist position helps remind us of the likelihood that prior knowledge of some sort always exists. The innate idealist position attacks the key assumption of empiricism, that novice learners approach new situations with their minds as blank slates, devoid of prior knowledge or preconception.

Empiricism. According to empiricists such as Locke and Hume, knowledge depends ultimately on the use of the senses and on what is discovered through them. Locke believed that although the infant is born with a mind completely devoid of content, a "tabula rasa," that he or she will possess certain mental powers or faculties that permit learning to occur. Thus, as the infant begins to experience his environment, he will remember sights, odors, tastes and sounds (in Locke's terms, "simple ideas"), and through his powers of abstraction and combination, will build up "complex ideas."

Empiricists believe, then, that no simple idea is innate, nor can it be invented; it can only result from experience. Ultimately, lack of experience will limit the complex ideas that can be formed. Although Locke's theory may be criticized on a number of grounds, his ideas help remind us of the importance of prerequisite knowledge, that is, the notion that children must often have certain experiences or ideas before they can fully understand new ideas or concepts.

Unlike modern learning theorists, Locke viewed the learner as rather passive, an empty vessel waiting to be filled with information. The third conception of learning we will discuss, that of constructivism, paints a much different picture, one in which the learner is actively processing, simplifying, and reconstructing the information that is presented to him.

<u>Constructivism.</u> This view posits that the human learner is rational in his processes but limited or bounded in his capacity to exercise those processes in a fully logical manner. The source of those limitations is, by and large, a function of the limited capacity of the human short-term memory, the "buffer" within which learners hold those immediate memories with which they work during learning or problem solving.

Perhaps the best way to think about the limitations of immediate memory is to ask how frequently you try to remember a telephone number that you have just looked up only to discover that you had forgotten it by the time you reach the last two digits in the dialing sequence. (This experience will be much more meaningful to the older readers of our article than to the younger ones.) Because of these limitations, it is in principle impossible for human learners or information processers to apprehend the full complexity and richness of "task environments" as they are presented to them.

The world around us is simply more complex than we are capable of representing in our immediate memories prior to comprehension, storage and long-term memory. Therefore, this theory goes on, we have no choice but constantly to be engaged in a simplification and reconstruction of all the information that is presented by the world around us, whether via instruction or our natural encounters with phenomena. This process of construction and reconstruction through simplification is a necessary, universal, and unavoidable feature of all human learning. Due to this process of simplification and reconstruction, we learn not what we have been taught, but what we have <u>come to represent</u> of what we have been taught. In order to understand what and why someone has learned, we must understand the nature of the simplification and reconstruction they have performed, invented, or created, and the form of that representation that has been stored in their memories for future use.

It is not enough merely to claim, however, that all learners transform and reconstruct. On what basis do they engage in the particular form of simplification that they exhibit? We find in our studies of cognitive psychology that the major influence on the form of simplification and reconstruction employed by human learners is the prior knowledge that they already hold, the conceptions or "prototypes" that they already have in memory, and in whose terms they apprehend the new knowledge that they encounter.

Let us discuss three quite different examples of this principle of simplification and reconstruction, for it lies at the very heart of the discussion of current conceptions of teaching and learning. Over the past fifteen years, one of us has engaged with colleagues in a series of studies of the problem-solving processes of physicians, more specifically, specialists in internal medicine (Shulman and Elstein, 1975; Elstein, Shulman, and Sprafka, 1978). We wished to understand how those physicians coped with the potentially unlimited bodies of information that could be brought to bear in the diagnosis of the illnesses of particular patients, and how they selected among those sources as they gathered information for the purpose of solving clinical problems.

A summary of the findings takes the following form: Physicians, contrary to common medical lore, do not gather great amounts of information as a precursor to arriving inductively at a diagnosis. Indeed, this inductive strategy would rapidly overload their limited memory capacities. Instead, they typically generate alternative diagnotistic hypotheses during the first minute or two of the encounter with the patient regarding the most likely causes of illness. Based on the first few questions asked and answers given, usually a recitation of the major features of the patient's chief complaint, the physician begins to erect a conceptual scaffolding, a small set of diagnostic alternatives, among which the physician will subsequently make choices based on the accumulation of evidence. Far from operating in an inductive mode, the physician then begins to generate hypotheses and to test them with new evidence. The physician has simplified the otherwise overwhelming inductive problem by transforming it into a much more limited hypothetico-deductive representation, bounded by no more than two or three working hypotheses considered at any one time. That representation then serves to frame the balance of the medical workup. Thus, experienced physicians perform in a manner consistent with the claim that the world must be simplified and reconstructed in order to be managed effectively by an experienced problem solver.

A second example is taken from the work of our anthropologist colleague, Professor Shirley Brice Heath. Heath (Heath and Mandabach, 1983) studied the manner in which a judge processed the information gathered during a non-jury trial in his courtroom. The question she asked was: How can an individual judge who is simultaneously managing the affairs of the courtroom and listening to the arguments of lawyers and testimonies of multiple witnesses keep track of all the information needed to render a judgment when his only source of memory aid was his own handwritten notes taken during the course of the trial? Clearly, some sort of simplification and organization was underway, but it was unclear what this process entailed.

While working with the judge, Heath discovered that his memory and organization of the facts of the case was highly selective and constructive. Fairly early in the trial, the judge developed a conception of the case and organized his processing of subsequent facts and testimony within the structure of that organization. Moreover, the attorneys for both the plaintiff and the defendant intuitively recognized the importance of the judge's early framing of the case. The opening and closing arguments employed by the attorneys were designed to influence the fundamental ways in which the judge chose to frame the case. When the judge accepted the frame introduced by one of the attorneys, it strongly influenced him to interpret the evidence in a manner consistent with that attorney's position.

Our third example comes from research on reading comprehension. In a series of studies investigating the relationship between a reader's prior knowledge and his reading comprehension and recall, R.C. Anderson and his colleagues have demonstrated that prior knowledge will often serve as a framework for understanding the setting, the mood, the characters and the series of events of a story or other prose passage. In one such study, subjects from the United States and from India read letters about an American and an Indian wedding and were asked to recall as much as possible about each letter (Steffensen, Joag-Dev, and Anderson, 1981). Since American and Indian weddings are profoundly different, the researchers were not surprised to find that subjects most accurately recalled information about the culturally familiar passage. Perhaps the most compelling evidence of the role of background knowledge in reading comprehension and memory, however, comes from an examination of the errors subjects made in recalling the information they had read. These errors can be classified as elaborations, culturally appropriate extensions of the text, or distortions--modifications to the passage that are culturally inappropriate. One example of distortion occurred in relation to the description of the American wedding dress. The text read as follows:

> Did you know that Pam was going to wear her grandmother's wedding dress? That gave her something that was old, and borrowed, too. It was made of lace over satin, with very large puff sleeves and looked absolutely charming on her. The front was decorated with seed pearls (pp. 20-21).

One Indian subject, however, recalled that, "She was looking alright except the dress was too old and out of fashion." In contrast, an American subject "read between the lines," and elaborated upon Pam's choice of her grandmother's wedding gown: "Pam's mother wants Pam's daughter to carry on the tradition of wearing the family wedding gown." These distortions and elaborations again serve to illustrate the role of prior knowledge in the process of restructuring, reorganization, and simplification that is occurring in the mind of the learner as he or she goes about acquiring new knowledge.

Current Views of Learning

What then is our current view of learning? While we shall present a conception of learning that is quite consistent with the perspective of constructivism discussed above, we should point out that, in principle, no single view of cognition is possible. Cognition is context-sensitive. Human beings are remarkably malleable. They have a striking capacity to adapt their performance, their behavior and their thoughts to the task demands and the organizational structure we provide for them.

Cole and Traupmann (1981) offer a striking illustration of how task demands and contextual constraints help to paint different pictures of the same individual. In their study, a 3rd grader, Archie, who was identified as "learning disabled" by the school psychologist, was observed in an after-school cooking club, in an individual testing session, and in a variety of school settings. Archie indeed fit the description of a learning disabled child during the testing situation and when observed in the classroom. He misperceived auditory stimuli, misnamed objects and people, appeared highly distractible, and was reading well below grade level. However, in the cooking club, Archie engaged in "planful, controlled behaviors" that helped him overcome his reading and perceptual difficulties, and enabled him to become a contributing member of the cooking club. In the typical classroom setting, therefore, Archie appears somewhat disabled, but while cooking, he is remarkably competent.

Therefore, as teachers, we must remember that our tasks elicit the forms of cognition we observe. We can make students into memorizing robots or problem solvers or even phenomenologists by virtue of the tasks we set for them and the structures in which we ask them to perform. Thus, it is no accident that when Skinner presents a human subject with a task, that human learner looks remarkably like a pigeon or a white rat. Similarly, when the Gestalt psychologists presented tasks to their research subjects, they observed deliberation, contemplation, and flashes of insight. Any conception of learning that we present or that is presented by other theorists must be understood as both a descriptive theoretical formulation and a normative one. It constitutes a statement of value as well as a statement of fact.

In presenting our conception of human cognition, we shall divide our discussion among three topics:

1. the subject matter of instruction
2. the learner and learning
3. principles of pedagogy

Images of Subject Matter

The central idea in the analysis of the subject matter of instruction from a cognitive perspective is that of structure. The central purpose of any education is to communicate to students a grasp of the essential and central ideas of a subject matter. These are the concepts, principles, and procedures around which the propositions that constitute the knowledge base of the discipline are organized, as well as the rules of procedure for testing the validity of proposed new ideas or adjudicating between competing truth claims in the field. The first of these types of structure, the facts, concepts and principles of the discipline as organized into meaningful and systematic arguments, has been called by Schwab (1978) the substantive structure of the subject matter. The rules of discovery and verification for the discipline are called the syntactic structure. Our goal in teaching is that students come to understand these essential ideas and procedures, recognize why they are central to the discipline under study, and how they can be used to organize knowledge, to discover or invent new knowledge, and to test its validity.

It has long been recognized that teachers have a tendency to ignore or at least give too little attention to the essential structures of subject matter and instead concentrate needlessly on the content of the subject as constituted of long, somewhat disorganized lists of facts, technical terms, or algorithms for problem solution. It is unfortunately atypical for an instructor to take the trouble needed to communicate, in the variety of ways necessary, the underlying structures of his or her discipline. These structures are important precisely because they act both as organizers and as simplifiers of the otherwise endlessly long list of things to know within a given field. It is only through a grasp of these essential structures that experts in the field command their bodies of knowledge. Similarly, the novice first learning a discipline, who has far less sophisticated and powerful tools at his disposal than those of the expert, needs an opportunity to grasp those structures if he or she is to understand and retain significant knowledge in the discipline. Ideas that are not organized by the structure of a discipline will not be well grasped and are probably not worth teaching. Ideas not worth teaching are certainly not worth teaching well.

Modes of Analysis

Given some body of knowledge embodied in a text or lecture notes, it is useful to be able to "parse" the material, to classify it into levels of complexity or difficulty. Given the draft of an examination to assess the quality of student learning, it is useful to analyze the intellectual demands of specific items or parts. We shall examine only two such classification schemes. The first, well-known to most educators, is Benjamin Bloom's (1956) *Taxonomy of Educational Objectives*. Bloom and his colleagues posited six general levels of intellectual complexity in terms of which the subject matter of instruction can be organized and scaled. The lowest level was Knowledge, followed in increasing complexity by Comprehension, Application, Analysis, Synthesis and Evaluation.

The first category, Knowledge, emphasizes the recognition or recall of specific pieces of information, and includes knowledge of specific facts, conventions, principles, and generalizations. For example, the test question, "True or False? Light travels in straight lines," would be classified in this category of educational objectives. The second category, Comprehension, is defined as the ability to understand the literal message of an oral or written communication. Within this category are skills relating to the translation of the communication into other terms, as well as the ability to determine implications and consequences which can be inferred from the communication.

Both the coin toss problem and the light and vision problem require the application of rules, principles, and ideas to particular, concrete situations. Hence, these problems fall within Bloom's third category in the taxonomy, Application.

The ability to recognize relationships, organizational principles, and unstated assumptions represents skills specific to Analysis. For example, a question requiring a student to recognize the point of view or bias in a piece of text is asking the student to analyze information.

Synthesis, the fifth category, is defined as the putting together of elements and parts to create a whole. The ability to produce a unique communication or to create a plan, or the capability of deducing implicit relations, are skills within this category. Finally, Evaluation involves making judgments about the logical accuracy or consistency of an idea, and requires the ability to evaluate material in terms of external criteria.

Bloom's taxonomy has had a substantial impact on the formulation of educational objectives and test items. Few professional educators complete their training without having some exposure to this popular classification system. Although some educators continue to concentrate too heavily on Knowledge objectives, curriculum experts, test developers, as well as teachers, often use this taxonomy as a guide in analyzing cognitive activities so that their students will have the opportunity to engage in more complex, higher-order learning. The full text of the Taxonomy is well worth studying. It is rich in specific examples of both objectives and test items at every level of complexity.

The primary value of such a taxonomy, therefore, is heuristic. As educators, we develop the capacity to characterize and analytically portray the subject matter of instruction in language more general than that of the subject matter itself. These analytic categories, in turn, often relate systematically to principles of learning, of instruction, or of evaluation.

A good example of these relationships is found in yet another approach to the classification of subject matter, that of Robert M. Gagne' (1970). In his now classic Conditions of Learning, already published in its fourth edition, Gagne' argued that the varieties of learning can be classified into five categories. Each of these categories is distinct from the others in that the conditions for its learning, and therefore for teaching within that category, are different. Gagne's five varieties are:

1. Verbal Information
2. Intellectual Skills
3. Cognitive Strategies
4. Attitudes
5. Motor Skills

Gagne' argues that all learning can be classified into one or another of these five varieties. Moreover, it is typical that at the very same moment, more than one kind of learning is going on simultaneously. Much of what a student learns in school takes the form of verbal information, such as names, facts, dates, or sequences of events. Gagne' calls this "verbal" information, not because it is stored in verbal form, but because, when asked to retrieve the information, the student can state it. Modern learning theorists believe that verbal learning is stored in the form of associative networks.

Verbal information becomes organized in memory and is retrieved in a structured manner. For example, if an individual is asked to recall a set of previously memorized words, he will tend to retrieve them in "clusters" belonging to common superordinate categories. Thus, if a person who has memorized a list of vegetables begins by recalling "broccoli" (or another green vegetable), he will most likely continue to retrieve the names of other green vegetables before listing such items as turnips or potatoes.

Research indicates that learners will more easily remember verbal information that is placed within a larger meaningful context. Meaningful material is typically high in familiarity or capable of being organized in some logical fashion. When information to be remembered is meaningful, the learner's associative network will be richer, making the information easier to seek and retrieve.

The retrieval of verbal information is greatly facilitated by providing externally supplied cues to the learner. These cues may take the form of mnemonic devices or mediational strategies. For example, many native speakers of English use the sentence, "Every good boy does fine" to remember the names of the lines on the trebel clef in written music (E,G,B,D,F). The use of this mnemonic device helps in remembering an otherwise meaningless sequence of letters. Similarly, students may engage in mediation, the creating of meaningful links between items or ideas, to aid memory and retrieval. One particularly effective mediator seems to be the use of visual imagery, a technique that has been successfully taught to even very young learners.

Whereas verbal information involves learning "what," intellectual skills require knowing "how." Intellectual skills are acquired hierarchically, and unlike the learning of verbal information, seem to be cumulative in nature. Thus, the learning of intellectual skills requires the combination of simpler rules and concepts. Therefore, teachers must make sure that the prerequisite skills have been learned by the students before attempting to teach a new, more complex skill. Educators can also more effectively teach intellectual skills by providing cues to enable the students to retrieve these prerequisite skills, and by helping students recognize that the combination of these skills will be required to learn successfully more complex intellectual skills.

Cognitive strategies are the essential feature of problem solving. They represent internally organized skills that control an individual's behavior while attending, learning, remembering, and thinking. Since cognitive strategies are used for organizing other cognitive processes into sequences or chains that allow learners to solve problems, they are in a sense more metacognitive than cognitive.

To appreciate the difference between intellectual skills and cognitive strategies, consider the following example. A learner may be capable of adding, subtracting, multiplying and dividing with few errors. He has mastered each of those hierarchically organized intellectual skills. Should he falter, we can prescribe appropriate practice and comprehension activities on the prerequisite of the fully realized skill. But quite frequently we encounter learners who are capable of using the skills in isolation, but are utterly puzzled by a "story problem" that challenges them to select, order, organize and employ those skills in a particular order. Story problems also require the continuous monitoring of one's use of skills to detect errors and to produce cues for employing new skills. This is the province of cognitive strategies. Unlike intellectual skills, they are not hierarchically organized. A poor problem solver cannot merely be trained on specific prerequisites; he must practice applying strategies to new problems with ample opportunites for review and reflection. Thus, of the three most significant cognitive forms of learning, only one--intellectual skills--is organized hierarchically. Although most educators more heavily concentrate on promoting learning within the cognitive domain, formal education always has some effect on student attitudes such as self-concept, self-esteem, honesty, or tolerance. Students can learn to fear mathematics, or to like sports, and these learned dispositions will no doubt influence the choices these children make as they mature.

Gagne' draws upon social learning theory and the work of Albert Bandura (1977) to explicate the processes involved in the learning and teaching of attitudes. Not surprisingly, verbal persuasion, in and of itself, is remarkably ineffective in establishing or modifying attitudes. A more effective way of changing student attitudes involves the use of direct or vicarious reinforcement. For example, when a child successfully completes an assignment in mathematics, she will more likely develop a positive attitude toward this discipline than if she had failed the task. Similarly, observing a human model making the desired choice of action, and subsequently being rewarded for this action, may serve to reinforce vicariously this behavior in the observer. According to social learning theory, models not only convey information to the learner about the nature and predictability of environmental events, but can also teach observers effective strategies for dealing with challenging situations.

Finally, motor skills, prominent in physical education and sports, are learned through a combination of hierarchical training and through the development of an executive process that coordinates and organizes sequences of motor skills. To learn smoothness and timing of motor responses, students must receive feedback from their muscles. Consequently, facilitation of motor learning occurs through reinforced practice of motor responses and practice in envisioning the total sequence of steps in a skill from an "executive" perspective.

In most complex learning tasks, three or four varieties of learning may be occurring simultaneously. A student may be learning both verbal information and intellectual skills for using this information, and will no doubt be developing attitudes toward the learning task as well. Given, therefore, that the conditions for learning each of these varieties differ, the instructor must engage in a complex orchestration of the forms of teaching and the conditions of learning to insure that the proper circumstances are created for the acquisition and retention of each of the varieties of learning. Similarly, an adequate examination of student learning must include a broad array of test items and types to assess the quite different ways in which these different kinds of learning manifest themselves.

Curriculum

In addition to thinking about the subject matter of instruction in terms of structures and analytic modes, for teaching purposes we must also recognize that subject matter to be taught is organized into a curriculum. A curriculum is a carefully structured and sequenced set of topics and their representations designed to facilitate their acquistion and understanding by students. A curriculum is not merely a set of powerfully communicated teaching and learning episodes. In Dewey's apt phrase, the curriculum embodies the "progressive organization of the subject matter." In constructing a curriculum, we build, cumulate and integrate the topics in our field of study much like a novelist or a playwright striving to structure a work of art for optimal impact. Just as the fine dramatist takes great pains to present each scene in turn to build toward the desired effect, the curriculum maker thinks well beyond the dynamics of a single lesson or single topic. Pedagogical design must transcend a focus on individual lessons and portray the full scope of the desired curriculum in a coordinated fashion. The fine curriculum writer, like the fine dramatist or author, always writes his material with a keen sense of the context which it will set and the context in which it will be performed and experienced. That context includes, above all, a clear sense of the characteristics of the audience to which it will be presented and who will actively participate in the construction of its meaning.

Images of Learners and Learning

Let us put our image of the learner in Newtonian terms out of respect for the audience of physicists likely to read this collection of papers. A learner is a body in motion. He is not passive; he is not at rest. She has neither an open mind nor an empty one. With respect to new experiences that a learner encounters, he has framed, he must frame, and he will frame those experiences in terms of the categories and understandings he already possesses. The reorganization of prior understanding to accommodate new knowledge is exceedingly difficult. Because it is difficult it is rational to expect that it will be resisted. Learners will do (unconsciously, of course) nearly anything they can to avoid the necessity for reorganizing or restructuring their prior understandings in the face of new learning.

Moreover, while a student's overt behavior may seem to indicate that he or she comprehends the topics or concepts under study, appearances can be deceiving. Take, for example, the story of Benny (Erlwanger, 1975), a 5th-grade student in a self-paced, individualized mathematics class. From Benny's performance on unit pretests and posttests, one might easily conclude, as his teacher did, that Benny had made substantial progress over the course of the year. However, through a series of intensive clinical interviews,

Erlwanger found that Benny had developed an idiosyncratic, severely flawed set of computational algorithms for solving arithmetic problems. These procedures allowed him to complete his assignments and to pass his tests, but led Benny to conclude that mathematics consists of "magical rules" which often bear little or no relationship to one another. For Benny, mathematics was not an internally consistent system of concepts and rules, but an ad hoc collection of algorithms.

Similarly, Slinger, Anderson and Smith (1983) have found that students can do quite well on certain types of science tests with little conceptual understanding of a topic. For example, in analyzing a unit on light in a 5th-grade science textbook, they found that many students were able to answer correctly questions at the end of the unit that appeared in a section called "Test on Understanding." Questions such as, "True or False? Light travels in straight lines," were easily recognized by the students as identical to statements presented earlier in the textbook, and were of little use in diagnosing student misconceptions or in evaluating student comprehension.

Cuban (1979) uses the metaphor of a hurricane sweeping across a sea to describe changes resulting from new curriculum theories. During a hurricane, the sea is turbulent on the surface, but there is calm on the ocean floor. Like the surface of the ocean during a hurricane, new theories of curriculum will often stir up waves of controversy in professional journals and schools of education. But like the ocean floor, the textbooks are usually left unchanged, and teachers rarely feel the impact of the heated debate. This metaphor can also be used to describe changes in the learner: Overt behavior indicates that the learner has indeed understood the topic or concept, but underlying misrepresentations or misconceptions can easily remain untouched.

Donald Norman (1980) also uses an oceanographic metaphor, "The Iceberg Model," to portray the difference between the simple surface characteristics of learning and the more complex underlying structure. An iceberg has the bulk of its structure hidden beneath the surface, with only a small part above water. According to Norman's model, student behavior is similar to the part of the iceberg that is visible. The teacher must remember, however, that the student has created a huge, underlying structure that must be uncovered if the teacher can successfully understand student difficulties.

One particularly useful way of representing the process of learning is presented in the work of Donald Norman, who classifies the stages of learning in terms of three processes: accretion, structuring, and tuning.

The first stage of learning is accretion, the acquistion and accumulation of new elements of knowledge either via systematic instruction, independent learning, incidental learning or some combination thereof. Much learning in the schools never goes beyond accretion, that is, remaining at the level of acquiring and ordering new bodies of information without necessitating any fundamental reorganization of the structure of prior understanding. Thus, for example, students can learn that the multiplication of fractions by other fractions results in numbers smaller than those with which they began, and that the division of fractions by fractions results in larger numbers. If considered seriously, these attributes of multiplication and division of fractions dramatically violate prior understandings of multiplication as multiple addition and division as making things smaller. Yet, only rarely do students confront this anomaly. In Skemp's (1976) terms, students who are unaware of this seeming contradiction only achieve "instrumental understanding" of the multiplication and division of fractions. That is, they have "rules without reasons." Skemp argues that many students do not understand both what to do, and why, when doing arithmetic. Armed with algorithms, students march through their arithmetic lessons with little or no understanding of the structural relationships underlying the discipline of mathematics. It is reasonable to assert that this characterization is valid for students of the sciences and mathematics more generally--even at the university.

The second stage of learning, structuring, is a process in which a new structure, organization or, in Norman's terms, prototype, is invoked to classify and organize new knowledge. There is little doubt that for cognitive or conceptual learning the process of structuring is the key. Structuring provides the organization and simplification that makes the rough places smooth, that makes possible the retention of large bodies of information despite the fairly limited information-processing capacities of learners. Some learning theorists such as Ausubel (1963) and Novak (1977) conclude that structuring is the most important element of cognitive learning. Ausubel introduced the idea of using "advanced organizers," brief overviews of the structure of the information to be presented and its conceptual connections to what learners already know, before new material is introduced. The advanced organizer serves as a mental scaffolding that provides patterns or anchors for the new information, linking prior understanding to new knowledge.

What are some of the important features of structuring? Norman argues that structuring usually occurs through the use of analogies. We develop new structures by learning that what we are trying to understand at present is "like" something else we already know in some other context. Through the use of analogies, metaphors, examples, and other forms of comparative representation, we tie new structures to old ones. This kind of analogical processing is significantly facilitated by the instructor's ability to provide multiple alternative representations of the new concepts to be acquired. Each of these representations serves as an opportunity for the learner to develop new structures for organizing the learning to be acquired.

Jerome Bruner has suggested a framework for thinking about alternative forms of representation. Based on an interpretation of the developmental theory of Piaget, Bruner (1964) proposed that ideas to be learned may be presented at three levels of representation. The first level is called enactive representation. According to Bruner, giving the child the opportunity to act, touch, see, and manipulate is an important method of helping the child acquire an understanding of relationships and concepts. The second type of representation, where the learner deals directly with figural or spatial images of objects, but does not manipulate them directly, is called ikonic. Finally, symbolic representation involves the manipulation of symbols rather than objects or mental images. Although age and experience allow most older learners to use symbolic representations effectively, the teacher who manages to move back and forth among the three types of representation will provide students with alternative ways to structure the information to be learned.

As Norman points out compellingly, learners have no choice but to make sense, to tell themselves a story within which the new learning becomes coherent and meaningful. If they cannot tell that story in terms of a new prototype or a new set of concepts or of structures, they will inevitably force the new learning to make sense in terms of their old structures. The point is clear and unavoidable. Framing, or structuring, must occur in order to make the simplification and organization of new learning possible. The inertia of old prototypes and existing conceptions will always triumph unless instruction is directed toward facilitating the acquisition of new structures.

Piaget's processes of assimilation and accommodation bear some resemblance to the stages of learning Norman calls accretion and structuring. Assimilation occurs when a learner incorporates input from the environment into his preexisting structures. As the learner is assimilating information, his cognitive structures will influence his perception and interpretation of the information. Since this process involves the accumulation of knowledge into already established structures, it is similar to accretion.

Accommodation, like structuring, requires the creation or modification of the learner's cognitive structures to fit the environment. For accommodation to occur, the learner must be aware of the discrepancy between the information to be learned and his existing cognitive structure.

Even after a new structure has been acquired and put into place, it is unlikely to survive unless a process of tuning occurs. Tuning requires both practice and reflection, both use and deliberation. That is, tuning describes the processes through which new conceptual frameworks become automatized, become habitual ways of thinking, become "familiar furniture of the mind." This occurs through repeated opportunities to practice the use of the new structures in the comprehension of new material or the solving of new problems. It also occurs through providing occasions for discussing with others the significance of these ideas and practicing collective discourse in their use. For example, Tamir (personal communication) has conducted a series of studies of learning in a biology laboratory. He discovered that learning is not adequately consolidated and tuned unless the science students have an opportunity, not only to conduct the laboratory exercises, but to engage in group discussions. They discussed the meanings of these lab exercises and how what they learned relates to what they previously understood or thought they understood. Another example is the observation by Larkin, McDermott, Simon and Simon (1980) who found that experts do not learn from the experience of solving problems, but rather from the experience of looking back on problems they have solved, and reflecting on how they managed to solve them.

We have described how a cognitive perspective leads us to particular ways of conceptualizing the nature of subject matter for instruction. Central to our analysis are the concepts of structures, modes of analysis and curriculum organization, as well as ways of thinking about learners and learning. These involve a restructuring, reorganizing and transformation of knowledge. But we still must look at a third element, principles of pedagogy, which are those principles of instruction or teaching that derive from the conceptions of both subject matter and learning consistent with the cognitive principles we have presented. To that discussion we now turn.

Principles of Pedagogy

The problem of pedagogy, then, becomes the question of identifying presentations and representations of the subject matter that will fit not only the structure of the topics we are teaching and their link to curriculum, but also the structures in the minds of the students we are teaching. Principles of pedagogy must therefore flow out of the analysis of both of these types of structure.

Let us return once again to the coin toss problem. How can a teacher help her students overcome their naive conceptions of motion? Anderson and Smith (in press) suggest that simply presenting information through lecture or from texts is not sufficient to bring about conceptual reorganization in the minds of the students. The coin toss problem illustrates that although students may memorize Newton's first law of motion, they seem to have a persistent belief that motion cannot continue without a force. While the presentation of concepts and facts is a necessary component of successful teaching, it is not, in and of itself, sufficient to induce conceptual change in the learner.

Smith and Anderson found that varying the way the information is presented will strongly influence student learning. For example, 5th graders studying a unit on light were better able to understand seeing as detection of reflected light when the information was given to the students in a way that allowed them to contrast their own answers with the scientific alternatives presented by the teacher. The application of the scientific principle to specific instances (in this case, a boy seeing a tree) further provided the teacher with the chance to diagnose student understanding. Moreover, they found that emphasizing the distinction between the scientific conception and less important, auxiliary information during presentations, along with repetitive application and feedback, contributed to more effective learning.

The teacher's questioning techniques may also serve to increase the likelihood of conceptual reorganization in learners. Since learners are often unaware of their own preconceptions and misconceptions, questions that require students to clarify their own explanations for scientific phenomena and that provide opportunities for students to contrast their explanations with the scientific explanation under study should be provided.

Clement (1982) sees class discussions and arguments between students about alternative conceptions as especially useful in helping learners to articulate and make conscious their own preconceived ideas about scientific phenomena. Clement suggests that Galileo's dialogues, in which he attempts to deal directly with common preconceptions and prevailing theories of his time by using concrete, practical situations to illustrate his theories, might successfully be used as a modern model for scientific pedagogy.

In their discussion of effective science teaching, Anderson and Smith (in press) describe the work of Posner, Strike, Hewson, and Gertzog (1982), who suggest that there are four criteria that must be met before students will successfully change their misconceptions.

1. Students must become dissatisfied with their existing conceptions.

2. Students must achieve a minimal initial understanding of the scientific conception.

3. The scientific conception must appear plausible.

4. Students must see the scientific conception as fruitful or useful in understanding a variety of situations.

Teachers and Teacher Education.

The capacity for designing pedagogy that takes into account the structure of the discipline as well as the structures in the minds of the learners is not a trivial one. Nor is it possible in principle for instructional materials, whether software or hard copy, to be predesigned in a manner that is appropriate for all the likely combinations of topic and student to be encountered. It is therefore absolutely necessary for any of our concepts of pedagogical design to include a conception of teacher role and teacher education, because the teacher will always be the individual who is responsible for tailoring and fitting the pedagogy as designed into the pedagogy as performed. And yet, it is quite typical of most pedagogical designs to be "teacher-proof," if not teacher disdainful.

The most massive curriculum reform in history, that stimulated and funded by the U.S. National Science Foundation during the 1960's and early 1970's, floundered in large measure because it paid far too little attention to the central role of the teacher in <u>all</u> instruction. Curriculum and instructional reform alone is unlikely to result in the enduring improvement of education. As new computer-assisted and augmented forms of teaching are developed, their authors need to design specific roles for teachers in each lesson and unit, as well as the necessary teacher-training materials to ensure that the teacher is adequately prepared to play the needed roles. Without this careful consideration of the teacher's role, and the centrality of human teachers in the computer-augmented classroom, little will be accomplished. In addition to hardware and software, we must design the appropriate teacherware; if not, then beware!

Conclusion

This paper has given an overview of only a small portion of current research in the psychology of learning and teaching. To conclude, we offer our readers five propositions for consideration.

1. Learners are bodies in motion. They actively reconstruct, simplify, and reorganize information. Since it is easier to continue holding on to existing, naive preconceptions or misconceptions, students will frequently engage in psuedolearning, the rote memorization of information with no concurrent restructuring of underlying conceptions. The motivation to engage in real learning,

learning which involves cognitive restructuring, is most likely to come from a deeply felt sense of disequilibrium resulting from learners confronting their own misconceptions.

2. While learning is a process of actively making sense of information, understanding requires retrospection, cumulation, integration, and recapitulation. Since group interaction and discussion can contribute greatly to understanding, individual tutoring cannot serve as the model for ideal education.

3. Units of pedagogy must be seen as part of a whole curriculum. Learning individual pieces of information or isolated concepts does not provide the learner with an understanding of the structures of a discipline.

4. Teachers run classrooms. Since their work is already too difficult, they, like learners, will also resist change. Those developing computer software must think deeply about the implications of their work for teacher education. Computer software cannot be, nor should it be, "teacher-proof."

5. Education is a zero-sum game. If something new is added to the school curriculum, something else must be deleted to make room for this innovation. What is the value added by computer-assisted instruction that should lead an educational institution to undertake the wrenching process of change? In the words of Paul Hurd, it is harder to change the curriculum than to move a cemetery. The argument for the computer as a teaching instrument must be made; it cannot merely be asserted or assumed.

Norman (1980, p. 48) eloquently summarizes the essential message we have attempted to convey in this essay:

> Much goes on in the mind of the learner. Students interpret. They overinterpret. They actively struggle to impose meaning and structure upon new material being presented. To do this, they appear to use a prototype model on which to base future learning. It is something like an iceberg, with the student providing a huge

substructure to account for the small visible parts of the topic matter.

In teaching, it seems best that the instructor provides the prototype models. If the instructor does not do it, the student will, and the student's models are apt to be less fitted for the topic than the instructor's. Different prototypes are needed for different purposes. Each prototype will have strengths and weaknesses. The use of inappropriate prototypes can lead to peril, since the use of a prototype appropriate for one aspect of the task may lead to difficulties in other aspects, unless this is carefully demonstrated to the student.

What goes on in the mind of the learner? More than you might realize; more than you might wish.

REFERENCES

Anderson, C.W. and Smith, E.L. (in press) Teaching science. In V. Koehler (Ed.) The educator's handbook: A research perspective. New York: Longman.

Ausubel, D.P. (1963) The psychology of meaningful verbal learning. New York: Grune and Stratton.

Bandura, A. (1977) Social learning theory. Englewood Cliffs, N.J., Prentice-Hall.

Bloom, B.S., Englehart, M.D., Furst, E.J., Hill, W.H., and Krathwohl, D.R. (Eds.) (1956) Taxonomy of educational objectives: Cognitive domain. New York: David McKay.

Bruner, J.S. (1964) The course of cognitive growth. American Psychologist, 19, 1-15.

Chomsky, N. (1965) Aspects of the theory of syntax. Cambridge: MIT Press.

Clement, J. (1982) Students' preconceptions in introductory mechanics. American Journal of Physics. 50(1), 67-71.

Cole, M. and Traupmann, K. (1981) Comparative cognitive research: Learning from a learning disabled child. Minnesota symposia on child psychology, Vol. 14. Hillsdale, NJ: Erlbaum.

Cuban, L. (1979) Curriculum change and stability. In J. Schaffarzick and G. Sykes (Eds.) Value conflicts and curriculum issues. Berkeley, CA: McCuthan.

Davis, R. (1966) Discovery in the teaching of mathematics. In L.S. Shulman and E.R. Keislar (Eds.) Learning by discovery: A critical appraisal. Chicago: Rand-McNally.

Elstein, A.S., Shulman, L.S. and Sprafka, S.A. (1978) Medical problem solving: The analysis of clinical reasoning. Cambridge: Harvard University Press.

Erlwanger, S.H. (1975) Case studies of children's conceptions of mathematics, Part I. Journal of Children's Mathematical Behavior, 1, 157-283.

Gagne', R.M. (1970) The conditions of learning (2nd edition). New York: Holt, Rinehart and Winston.

Heath, S.B. and Mandabach, F. (1983) Trial by schema: Constructing the story in criminal court trials. Second International Congress on Psychology and Language. University of Bristol.

Larkin, J., McDermott, J., Simon, D., and Simon, H.A. (1980) Expert and novice performance in solving physics problems. Science, 208, 1335-1342.

Norman, D.A. (1980) What goes on in the mind of the learner. In W.J. McKeachie (Ed.) New directions for teaching and learning: Learning, cognition and college teaching. San Francisco: Jossey-Bass, Vol. 2.

Novak, J. (1977) A theory of education. Ithaca, NY: Cornell.

Posner, G.J., Strike, K.A., Hewson, P.W., and Gertzog, W.A. (1982). Accommodation of a scientific conception: Toward a theory of conceptual change. Science Education, 66(2), 211-227.

Schwab, J.J. (1978) Science, curriculum and liberal education: Selected essays. Chicago: University of Chicago Press.

Shulman, L.S. and Elstein, A.S. (1975) Studies of problem solving, judgment and decision making: Implications for educational research. In F.N. Kerlinger (Ed.) Review of Research in Education, Vol. 3. Itasca, IL: Peacock.

Skemp, R.R. (1976) Relational understanding and instrumental understanding. Journal of Mathematics Teaching. December, 1976.

Slinger, L., Anderson, C.W., and Smith, E.L. (1982) Studying light in the fifth grade: A case study of text-based science teaching. (Research Series No. 129) East Lansing, MI, Institute for Research on Teaching, Michigan State University.

Steffensen, M.S., Joag-Dev, C., and Anderson, R.C. (1979) A cross-cultural perspective on reading comprehension. Reading Research Quarterly. 15, 10-29.

Tamir, P. Personal communication.

Norman, D.A. (1980) What goes on in the mind of the learner. In W.J. McKeachie (Ed.) New directions for teaching and learning: cognition, and college teaching. San Francisco: Jossey-Bass, Vol. [illegible]

[illegible]

Overcoming Conceptual Difficulties in Physical Science Through Computer-Based Socratic Dialogs

A. B. Arons
Department of Physics FM-15
University of Washington
Seattle, WA 98195/USA

1 INTRODUCTION

Research in physics education continues to develop compelling evidence that many students emerge from introductory physics courses with inadequate mastery of some of the most basic concepts and fundamental modes of reasoning. [McDermott (1984); Trowbridge and McDermott (1980), (1981); Arons (1983), (1984a), (1984b); Clement (1982); Fredette and Clement (1981); Minstrell (1982); Viennot (1979)]. Explanation, exposition, presentation, however lucid, are not sufficient to generate grasp and understanding (except, perhaps, in the upper few percent of the students), and conventional end-of-chapter problems and laboratory exercises do not provide adequate help. They leave too many students in a passive intellectual mode, expecting to learn through inculcation, and they fail to generate the kind of active mental engagement essential for learning. Many students, in fact, fail to break through to mastery of certain concepts and reasoning processes unless they are led to articulate the ideas in their own words in a sequence of Socratic dialog.

NATO ASI Series, Vol. F 23
Designing Computer-Based Learning Materials
Edited by A. Bork and H. Weinstock

Although it is clearly impossible to provide enough teachers to allow one-on-one interaction for all students who would benefit from it, I am convinced that the computer has evolved to the point where it can become an effective substitute in many instances.

To produce effective instructional material of this variety, it is necessary for authors to be aware of the specific learning problems revealed in research and to be aware of how students actually respond to various specific questions. (A priori conjectures about how students are likely to respond are more frequently wrong than right.)

This paper will illustrate efforts at such Socratic instruction by describing, and giving excerpts from, dialogs which have been generated and used with various groups of students. Suggestions are also made concerning areas in which many students have severe difficulty and in which dialogs, not yet generated, would be very desirable.

2 DRILL

One very primitive obstacle impeding learning in introductory physics courses is lack of sufficient drill to embed a definition, a procedure, or a physical phenomenon in the student's memory to such a degree that it becomes second nature and no longer stands in the way of the next level of utilization or reasoning. Space in textbooks is costly and limited, and adequate drill, with immediate feedback and reinforcement, can rarely be provided. This is something which can readily be provided, however, on the computer, and, although this instructional mode may seem to be pedestrian and unsophisticated, the results for the student are far from trivial.

Specific areas in which availability of such drill is currently inadequate and would be highly desirable are:

(1) Drill on definitions of sine, cosine, and tangent: Recognize each function when the right triangle is presented in a variety of orientations on the screen. Given labelled sides on triangles in various orientations, set up the ratio with the specified name. Given (symbollicaly) the ratio of two sides in a depicted triangle, recognize the trigonometric name. Recognize directly what the products $c \times \sin\theta$ and $c \times \cos\theta$ (where c is the length of the hypotenuse) mean without going through algebraic manipulation of the ratios.

(2) Drill on calculating numerical values of torque (or setting up algebraic expressions): Forces should be presented in random orientations on the screen, differing from the original figure used in the textbook. Different angles should be labelled, not always the same one (e.g. sometimes the angle between the force and the line to the axis; sometimes the angle between the force and the normal to the radius arm). Forces should occasionally be directed through the axis of rotation to lead students to recognize situations of zero torque. Net torques should be calculated when several are imposed simultaneously.

(3) Drill on addition and subtraction of vectors in <u>one</u> dimension, both numerically and graphically.

(4) Drill on addition and subtraction of vectors in two dimensions both graphically and numerically (with the use of components).

(5) Drill on the basic electromagnetic phenomena: magnetic field directions around various configurations and orientations of current carrying conductors. Exercises with the Lorentz force: given $\vec{F}$, $\vec{v}$, and $\vec{B}$, what must have

been the sign of the charge on the moving particle? given the charge, $\vec{v}$, and $\vec{B}$, what must be the direction of the force. Similar exercises with induced emf.

(6) Drill on significant figures in numerical calculations.

3 INSTRUCTIONAL SOCRATIC DIALOGS

A less well known use of the computer, but one which, to my mind, has particularly high educational potential, is that of instructional (or Socratic) dialog. The bulk of this paper will be devoted to discussion of this mode. In this context, the term "Socratic dialog" is used in its classical sense: leading a learner to the articulation of conclusions, insights, or lines of reasoning by a series of questions.

Exemplars of effective Socratic dialogs exist, but they are not very numerous and not widely known. The ones with which I am personally acquainted (and some of which I have collaborated in writing) have been generated at the Educational Technology Center, directed by Alfred Bork, at the University of California, Irvine.

The dialogs to which I refer are <u>not</u>, in general, conducted via a series of multiple choice questions or yes-no answers, although such forms may arise occasionally. Most questions require response in words, symbols, or numbers chosen by the student. The computer recognizes verbal response by searching for specified combinations of key words or phrases. Graphic displays are used throughout: graphs are formed and interpreted; objects move across the screen; flashlight bulbs burn with various degrees of brightness; the moon exhibits various phases. The student uses the built-in pointer to point to places in diagrams in answer to some of the questions or to indicate how to construct appropriate graphs.

Analysis of verbal response is prepared for in the writing and editing of the dialog. Prior knowledge of student response, accumulated in real person-to-person dialogs, is used to anticipate the general course of the dialog; additional unanticipated answers are collected and edited into the program through trial runs. A correct answer allows the student to continue in the main sequence of questioning; an incorrect answer is dealt with in a remedial branch applicable to the error or misconception revealed. Dialogs frequently end with a test, a number of questions being chosen randomly from a large bank, and the student is given an assessment of level of performance.

From the point of view of the user, these dialogs are, in some ways, similar to what researchers in artificial intelligence are calling "expert systems" [Duda and Shortliffe (1983)], e.g. programs that lead a medical student through relevant symptoms and test results to diagnosis of an illness. In this case, however, the intelligence of the expert teachers who design the dialog is reflected in the sequence rather than in any built-in intelligence in the program.

Key word analysis, although fairly powerful when the questions are well phrased and student response well anticipated, nevertheless does not allow as much freedom as one would like. Graphics confined to line drawings are also highly restrictive. Future developments in parsing sentences and understanding natural language, as well as utilization of the "intelligent" video disk, are likely to improve this situation substantially.

4 EXAMPLES OF INSTRUCTIONAL DIALOGS

To illustrate more specifically the nature of the dialogs described in the preceding section, I offer a few examples which have been generated at Irvine:

(1) LUNA [Bork (1981)]. A dialog which exploits graphics to lead students into forming a mental picture of the configurations assumed by sun, moon, and earth and to use the model to deal with questions such as: Would you expect to see a full moon rising at midnight? Why or why not? At what time of day or night would you expect to see a new crescent moon setting? A half-illuminated moon crossing the local celestial meridian?

(2) TERRA [Bork (1981)]. A dialog which provides remediation for users of LUNA who fail to exhibit adequate comprehension of the meaning of terms such as north and south, noon and midnight, vertical and horizontal, latitude and longitude, terrestrial and celestial poles and equators, etc.

(3) HEAT [Bork (1980,1981)]. Many college and university students in the USA, even those in technical courses, use the terms "heat" and "temperature" synonymously, showing little or no awareness of an operational distinction between them. This weakness originates in the fact that few textbooks or teachers elaborate the distinction. Terms such as "heat" and "transfer of heat" are brought into the discourse without explicit definition as though they were commonplace primitives, understood by everyone because of their occurrence in everyday language. Such an approach is, in fact, just as fallacious as would be the introduction of the terms "force" and "energy" in physics without recognition of the necessity of operational definition and without attention to the profound change in meaning associated with

the shift from everyday speech to technical usage.

The HEAT dialog is designed to lead students to an operational definition of "transfer of heat". It starts with acceptance of the thermometer and its readings as primitives. It then leads the student to articulate everyday experience with the trend to thermal equilibrium between bodies initially at different temperatures. The thermometer in a pan of hot water placed in a room drops to the same reading as the wall thermometer; the thermometer in a pan of cold water rises to the same level. Exactly the same temperature changes, from the same initial to the same final values, take place more slowly if the same samples of water are encased in vacuum insulated bottles. Since the rates of change are altered without alteration of any thermometer readings, the interactions apparently involve a process which the thermometer readings alone do not reveal.

Other familiar situations reinforce this perception: two different quantities of water, each heated from 20 C to 80 C over identical burners require different amounts of time and fuel -- both larger for the larger mass of water. As ice cubes melt in a beaker of water, a change is continually taking place, involving interaction with the warmer air in the room, without any change in the reading of the thermometer in the beaker. In each case, we encounter additional evidence of a process of interaction which the thermometer readings alone do not reveal. Having articulated awareness of existence of such a process, we give it the name "transfer of heat." The dialog then goes on to complete the operational sequence by leading the student to the idea of measuring "quantity of heat transferred" through observation of temperature changes occurring in the mixing of known masses of water and to invention of the concept of "specific heat" of other substances.

Figure 1, which follows, shows excerpts from authors' initial flow sheets from the dialog HEAT. Quantities of hot and cold water are exposed in a room in open pans, and the same quantities of water at the same initial temperatures are placed in thermos bottles in the same room. The student is asked to compare the behavior of the thermometers in the open pans with the behavior of thermometers inserted in the thermos bottles.

Unbracketed statements are the ones that appear on the screen. Statements within curly brackets are directions to the coder. The student responds at the point marked "await student input". Key words in boxes are those for which the computer searches the student response. An exit to the side of a box shows computer response if the given key word is found. The numbers 1, 2, 3 indicate the response made the first, second, third time an exit is made at that location. An exit from the bottom of a box shows the computer's response if none of the boxed responses is recognized.

AGAIN, TAKE THE CONTAINERS OF HOT AND COLD WATER, EACH AT THE SAME INITIAL TEMPERATURE AS BEFORE.

{ DRAW AND LABEL PANS OF HOT AND COLD WATER. }

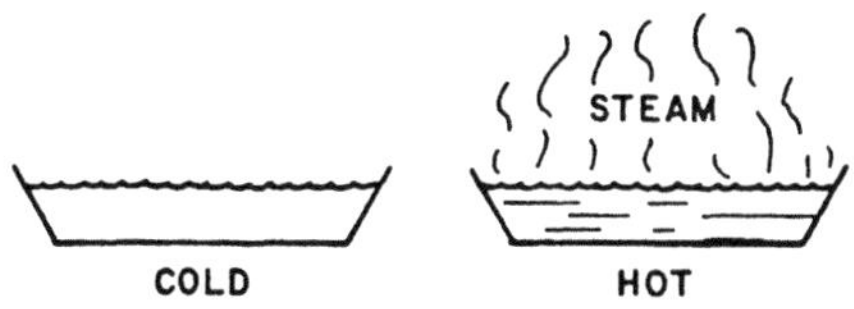

PUT THE SAME QUANTITY OF HOT AND COLD WATER INTO TWO THERMOS BOTTLES.

{ DRAW THERMOS BOTTLES. }

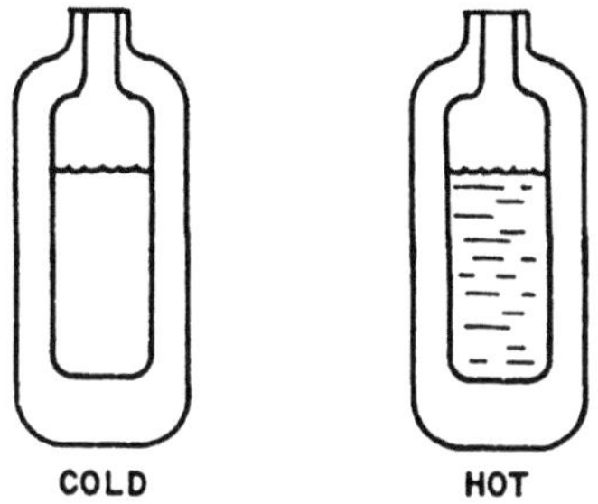

NOW WE INSERT A THERMOMETER THROUGH EACH STOPPER.

{ ADD STOPPERS AND THERMOMETERS TO PRECEDING PICTURE. }

WHAT IS THE DIFFERENCE BETWEEN THIS SITUATION (WITH THE THERMOS BOTTLES) AND THE PRECEDING ONE (WITH THE OPEN PANS)? HOW DO THE THERMOMETERS BEHAVE IN THIS CASE COMPARED TO THEIR BEHAVIOR IN THE PREVIOUS ONE?

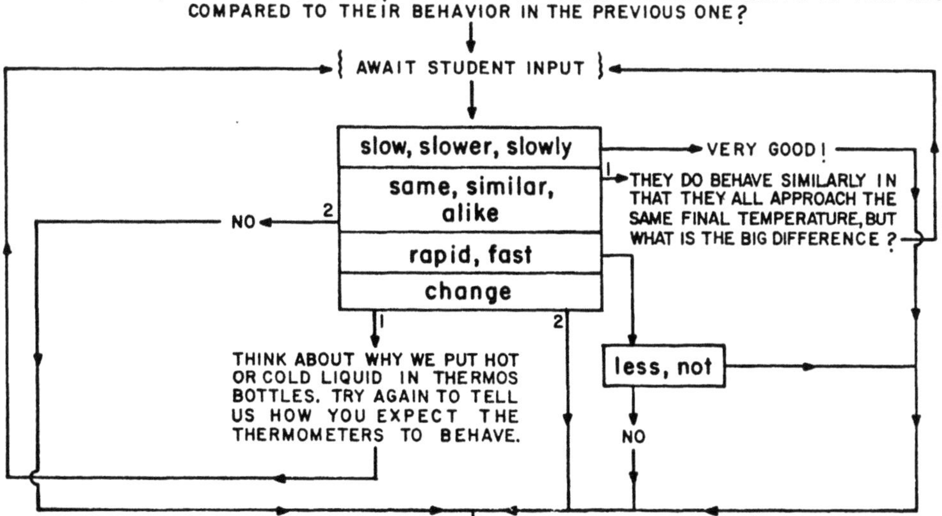

THE TEMPERATURE CHANGES VERY MUCH MORE SLOWLY.

BUT THE INITIAL AND FINAL TEMPERATURES ARE JUST WHAT THEY WERE WITHOUT THE THERMOS BOTTLES. THERE IS A DIFFERENCE IN BEHAVIOR WHICH THE THERMOMETER <u>READINGS</u> ALONE DO NOT REVEAL.

The preceding is an outline of the logical flow of the dialog. Since one is, in this case, organizing familiar experience into synthesis of a new concept, the sequence is relatively linear. There is little to remediate in the way of misconceptions and faulty reasoning, and there is consequently relatively little branching for remedial purposes. Figure 1 illustrates a brief segment of this dialog and shows how various responses are handled.

(4) BATTERIES AND BULBS [Arons, Bork, Franklin, Kurtz, and Collea (1981)]. The computer screen presents fairly realistic pictures of a flashlight bulb, battery, and two wires. The student is asked to use the pointer to show where the ends of the wires should be connected in order to light the bulb. The computer draws the wires connected between points indicated. The space inside the bulb remains dark if the connections are not properly indicated to the battery terminals and to the tip and screw base of the bulb. If correct connections are indicated, the bulb "lights" as brightness appears within the envelope.

It is noted that the bulb does not light unless the "two-endedness" of both the battery and the bulb is exploited to form a closed loop. Such a closed loop is given the technical name "electric circuit."

The circuit is then "opened" by showing a gap in one of the wires; the bulb goes out. Various familiar objects (coin, pencil, key, shoe, etc.) are then shown inserted in the gap in simulated experiments. Those which allow the bulb to light are classified as "conductors" and the others as "non-conductors," and a growing list is retained on the screen. The student is led to observe that air is present in the gap in the absence of other objects and thus must be classified as a non-conductor. Recognition is then elicited that the conductors are all metallic.

The "model" or mental picture of an invisible flow or "current" within the circuit -- terms such as "charge," "electrons," etc. are not injected and are set aside if the student volunteers them -- is now synthesized by appeal to the preceding observations and additional simulated experiments: bulbs do not light, wires do not get hot, unless the twoendedness of each object is exploited to form a continuous closed loop. When wires glow (as they do in stove elements and toasters), they glow uniformly over their entire length from one source terminal to the other. When a wire is connected directly across the terminal of the flashlight battery, it gets warm uniformly over its entire length. A bulb connected to the battery glows equally brightly whether the connecting wires place it near one battery terminal or the other.

All these observations combine to suggest an invisible flow which continues <u>uniformly</u> all the way around the system without being "used up" in the portion of the loop outside the battery and which is interrupted by any non-conducting break in the loop. (Many students, including those in technical courses, have a deeply held misconception that current is "used up" in an electrical circuit and decreases from one terminal to the other. They are not distinguishing between current on the one hand and energy transformations on the other.)

Simulated experiments then show that the brightness of a bulb decreases as additional bulbs are inserted end-to-end, i.e. in series. This observation is reinforced by exhibiting increasing and decreasing brightness of the bulb as the length of a "special" (e.g. nichrome) wire is decreased or increased in series with the bulb. The student "controls" the length of wire by moving the pointer along the wire shown on the screen, thus showing where the connection is to be made. The brightness of the bulb increases or decreases accordingly.

Observation that the brightness of the bulb decreases as additional material is inserted in series is used to suggest that the brightness of the bulb might be used as a measure of the intensity or strength of the current and that such material, in increasing length, "impedes" or offers an "obstacle" to the flow. This motivates invention of the concept of "resistance."

The dialog then goes on to elaborate the concepts of "current" and "resistance" into a model with predictive capacity. Combinations of resistors in series are shown to lead to lower brightness of a bulb used as an indicator of intensity of current and to slower "running down" of a battery. Combinations of resistors in parallel are shown to run a battery down more rapidly and to higher brightness of the indicator bulb. The student is led to articulate the physical conclusion (without formulas or Ohm's Law) that effective resistance increases in series combinations and decreases in parallel ones. Many students, including those in technical courses, fail to comprehend the latter idea regardless of the formulas which they study and the numerical problems they "solve" (without interpretation) in end-of-chapter exercises. The concept of "short circuit" and the point and purpose of fuses or circuit breakers are introduced in further simulated experiments.

Toward the end of the dialog, students deal with various new series and parallel configurations of several identical bulbs connected to a battery. They are asked to use the currentresistance model to predict how the brightnesses of the bulbs will compare with each other initially; to predict what will happen to the brightnesses of the remaining bulbs if one particular bulb is removed; to predict what will happen to the brightnesses of the bulbs and to the current at some indicated point if a wire is connected (as a short circuit) between two specified points in the system; etc. After the concept of potential difference is invented, students can be asked to predict what will happen to potential differences between various points in the circuit when some of the above changes are made. (It is my experience that college and university students, even those in physics-engineering courses, have very much greater difficulty with these apparently simple, phenomenological questions than they have with the conventional mathematically formal ones [Arons (1982)]. Yet this kind of qualitative thinking is exactly what they must engage in when dealing with troubles in real electrical circuits.)

Figure 2 presents a short excerpt from the BATTERIES AND BULBS dialog showing the logical flow of question and response at one point.

(5) OBSERVATION AND INFERENCE [Bork, Trowbridge, and Arons (1983)]. The dialog begins with presentation on the screen of the following statement:

> In one of the Sherlock Holmes stories by Arthur Conan Doyle, Holmes and his brother Mycroft are watching a man dressed in black with several packages under his arm. Mycroft says:
>
> "Of course, his complete mourning shows that he has lost someone very dear. The fact that he is doing his own shopping looks as though it were his wife. He has been buying things for children. There is a rattle, which shows that one of them is very young. The wife probably died in childbirth. The fact that he has a picture book under his arm shows that there is another child to be thought of."

The computer then draws a box around the phrase "dressed in black" and classifies it in the category "Mycroft sees." The phrase "lost someone very dear" is

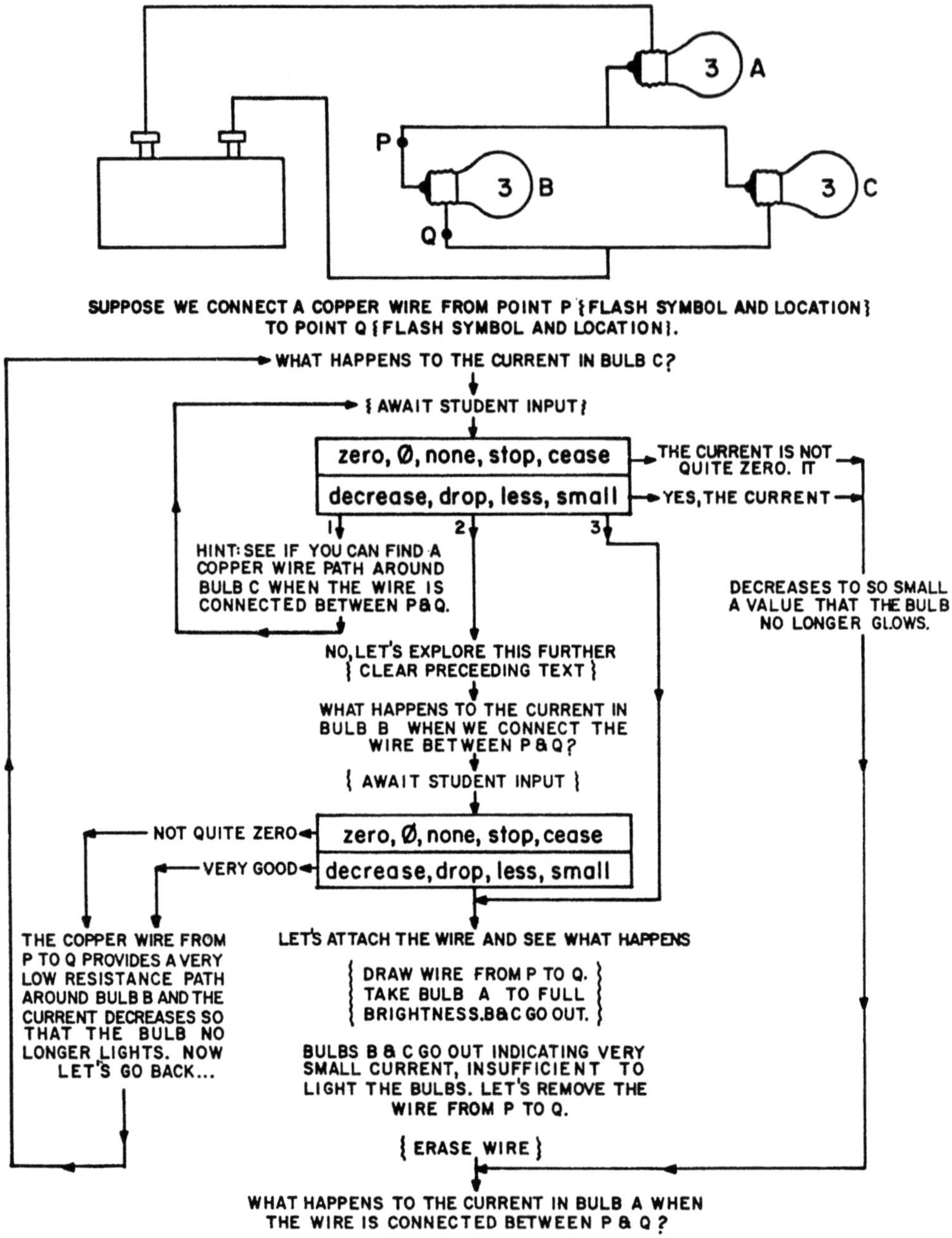

Figure 2

Excerpt from authors' initial flow sheets from dialog BATTERIES AND BULBS: A wire is to be connected between two points P and Q in the series-parallel configuration, and the student is asked to predict what will happen to the current in bulb C. (See caption of Figure 1 for explanation of notation.)

classified as "Mycroft reasons." A few more phrases are classified for illustration, and the student is then asked to classify the remaining phrases and is corrected if he makes mistakes. The two classes are given the names "observation" and "inference."

If several mistakes are made, the student is branched into another exercise in which the distance away from a lightning stroke is determined by measurement of the time interval between seeing the flash and hearing the thunder, and then applying the known velocity of sound. The process is examined to classify observations and inferences. From this branch, the student rejoins the main sequence which is being followed by those who made very few mistakes in analyzing the "Sherlock Holmes" passage.

The screen shows a sketch of a large rectangular field teeming with grasshoppers. The problem is to estimate the number of grasshoppers in the field. The computer zooms in on a one square meter patch in which grasshoppers (represented by bright dots) come and go. The student must watch the fluctuating spots and estimate the average number of grasshoppers -- 5 or 6 -- present in the sample square. The sides of the rectangular field are then paced off, and the number of grasshoppers in the entire field is calculated. Steps of the sequence are classified as observations and inferences. The opportunity is also taken to inject the comment that, in science, estimating is not a matter of wild guesswork but is a matter of careful reasoning, however uncertain or imprecise the results.

The motivation behind the generation of this dialog is the fact that students have very great difficulty when confronted with questions requiring them to discriminate between observation and inference in their own laboratory experiments and in the evolution of accepted models such as the heliocentric system or the wave nature of light.

6) AREA. This dialog leads students to articulate the operational definition of "area" as a counting of unit squares within a figure of arbitrary shape and provides exercises in such counting, including estimating fractional squares around the periphery. (This may strike sophisticated readers as a trivial matter. It is a fact, however, that a very great proportion of U.S. college students, both science and non-science majors, when asked what "area" means or how it is assigned numerical values, respond with "length times width" rather than with a general and meaningful operational definition.)

The dialog then leads the student to derive the formulas (or short cuts to counting unit squares) for simple figures such as rectangles, parallelograms, and triangles. From here the sequence goes into the scaling of areas when a figure is scaled up or down by a given length factor. Finally it develops the operational definition of "volume" and leads the student through exercises in scaling both area and volume and in calculating length and area scale factors when a volume ratio is given. A brief excerpt concerning area scaling is shown in Figure 3.

We regard this as a very important, basic dialog since a great majority of U.S. college students, regardless of area of concentration, have great difficulty with such ratio reasoning when they do not have formulas into which to substitute actual dimensions [Arons (1983)].

Other dialogs in existence or in preparation at the Irvine Educational Technology Center deal with matters such as: discrimination between position and velocity and between velocity and acceleration in rectilinear kinematics (these dialogs are motivated by the research of Trowbridge and McDermott (1980,1981); forming and interpreting position-clockreading and velocity-clockreading graphs for rectilinear motions; enhancing understanding of the law of

Figure 3

Excerpt from authors' initial flow sheets from dialog on SCALING: Student has previously been led to perceive that areas scale as the square of the length factor when the factor is an integer. In this excerpt, the student is led to verify that the area still scales as the square of the length factor when the latter is non-integer, namely 1.5 in this special case. (See caption of Fig. 1 for explanation of notation.)

HERE IS THE ORIGINAL SQUARE.

{ DRAW INITIAL SQUARE 1.0 ON EACH SIDE }

NOW WATCH THE LENGTH OF EACH SIDE INCREASE BY A FACTOR OF 1.5:

{ ANIMATE THE EXPANDING SQUARE BY SHOWING

SEQUENCE OF LINES THAT MAKE SQUARE APPEAR TO GROW ON THE TWO SIDES INDICATED. LEAVE HEAVILY OUTLINED INITIAL SQUARE THROUGH THE WHOLE SEQUENCE.

FINAL PICTURE AFTER ANIMATED EXPANSION:

}

NOW LET US COUNT THE NUMBER OF UNIT SQUARES IN THE LARGER FIGURE:

{ ADD TO THE PRECEDING PICTURE AS FOLLOWS:

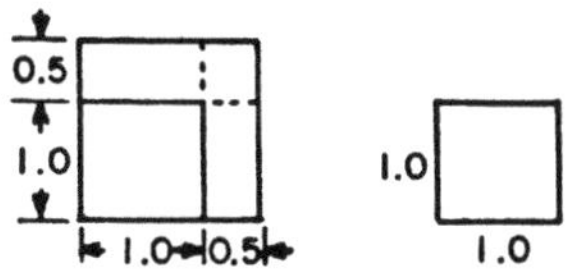

}

HERE IS ONE WHOLE UNIT SQUARE

{ BLINK OUTLINE OF BOTH UNIT SQUARES____THE ONE INSIDE THE LARGER SQUARE AND THE ONE ON THE RIGHT. }

WATCH WHAT HAPPENS TO THE TWO SMALL RECTANGLES

{ TRANSPORT THE TWO SMALL RECTANGLES FROM THE LARGER FIGURE TO THE REFERENCE SQUARE ON THE RIGHT, SHOWING THAT THE TWO RECTANGLES COMBINE TO FILL THE UNIT SQUARE. }

[SEQUENCE GOES ON, LEADING STUDENT TO PERCEIVE THAT THE SMALL SQUARE IN THE CORNER HAS AN AREA EQUAL TO 0.25 UNIT SQUARE AND THAT THE TOTAL ADDS UP TO 2.25.]

WE HAVE SO FAR THOUGHT ONLY ABOUT INTEGER SCALE FACTORS n=2,3,4, etc., BUT WHAT HAPPENS IF WE INCREASE THE LENGTH OF SIDE BY A NON INTEGER FACTOR SUCH AS 1.5?

DRAW TWO SQUARES SIDE BY SIDE, ONE WITH LENGTH OF SIDE 1.0 AND THE OTHER WITH LENGTH OF SIDE 1.5.

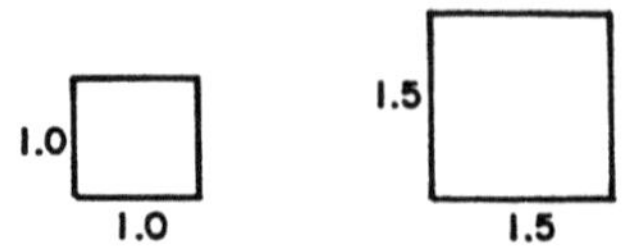

LABEL SIDES AS INDICATED

THE AREA THEN INCREASES BY A FACTOR OF_____. (PLEASE FILL IN THE BLANK WITH A NUMERICAL VALUE.)

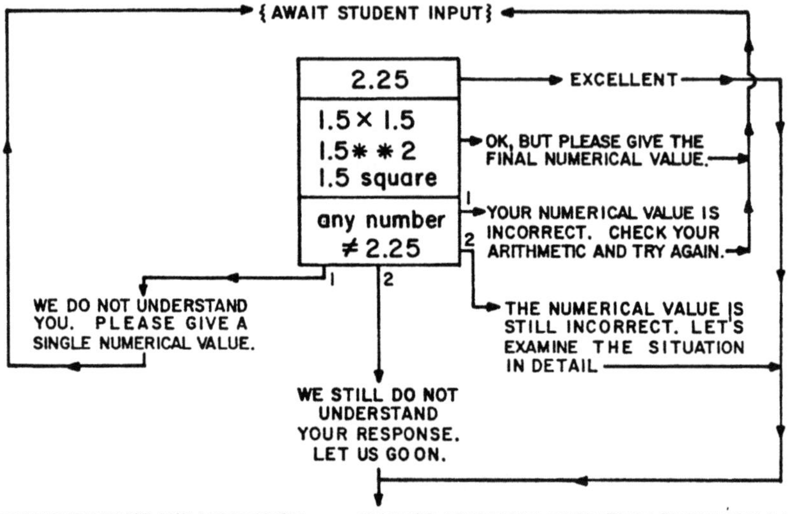

WE FOUND PREVIOUSLY THAT THE EXPRESSION n × n WORKED CORRECTLY WHEN THE LENGTH SCALE FACTOR n WAS AN INTEGER. IF WE EXTEND THIS TO OUR NEW CASE, IT SUGGESTS 1.5 × 1.5=2.25 FOR THE FACTOR BY WHICH THE AREA INCREASES. LET US DRAW THE PICTURE AND COUNT THE SQUARES TO MAKE SURE THAT THE EXPRESSION n×n STILL GIVES THE CORRECT RESULT FOR THIS NON-INTEGER CASE.

{CLEAR SCREEN}

inertia; cultivating a systematic approach to solving end-of-chapter kinematics and dynamics problems.

A system for generating such dialogs, coding them, and making them operational is described by Bork (1981).

5 REQUIREMENTS FOR THE GENERATION OF GOOD INSTRUCTIONAL DIALOGS.

There are several prerequisites for the writing of good instructional dialogs:

(1) The authors must have a clear perception of the basic thinking and reasoning processes which will be invoked and cultivated in the dialog, and they should know whether or not the students being addressed have achieved command of these processes [Arons (1984c)].

(2) The logical structure of the subject matter sequence must be carefully thought through at the given level of instruction. Motivation and plausibility must be carefully built in. The learner's prior experience must be evoked to every extent possible. Drift away from the basic plan of the dialog tends to occur during writing and needs to be firmly controlled. (Much writing is undertaken without careful preparation in these aspects, and the result then tends to be an ex-cathedra presentation, more in textbook style than a genuine Socratic dialog.)

(3) Authors must cultivate excellent command of the language being used in order to insure precise and lucid framing of questions. Such careful framing is critical for the extraction of fruitful responses from the learner. (The same requirement applies to the framing of clear, unambiguous questions in ordinary testing, and the questions

must be checked and refined in a similar way.)

(4) Authors must have prior knowledge of student difficulties in the given area -- not just with basic reasoning processes but with the specific subject matter itself. Unfortunately such knowledge is not acquired simply through good will, or experience in lecturing, or by conjecture, however thoughtful. The necessary knowledge is acquired only through personal dialogs with students [in the style of Jean Piaget (1958)] and through the careful examination of responses on well designed test questions which probe for lines of reasoning and for understanding rather than for calculational procedures and end results (as do the majority of conventional end-of-chapter homework problems).

My own experience has been that the large majority of my conjectures as to "what students are thinking" and how they will answer a certain probing question (in a field I have not previously explored) are simply wrong. The answer which emerges, if incorrect, is usually quite plausible, however unanticipated. Its roots and origins can be traced, and remediation, still through Socratic dialog rather than by assertion, can be provided.

It is easy to anticipate the right answers. The real problem is to provide effective remediation for the wrong ones, and this is possible only if the wrong ones are properly anticipated and understood.

Thus, writers of instructional dialogs must acquire substantial empirical knowledge of student response. Results of modern cognitive researches (such as those exemplified in many of the references cited below) will, of course, be very helpful in this respect. The saving grace with respect to all this effort on the part of authors is the fact that every individual is, in fact, <u>not</u> different from every other individual as some egalitarians would like to have it. Incorrect responses to a particular Socratic question invariably cluster around a relatively small and ascertainable number of answers, and the answers are frequently given in almost identical words. Acquiring the necessary empirical background is, therefore, not an attempt to grasp infinity; the situation is not so diffuse as might initially appear.

(5) Experience in generating Socratic dialogs indicates that it is not a good idea for one individual to write alone; two or three working together and checking each others' logic and phraseology is more nearly optimum. When one writes alone, one tends to leave logical errors in the flow sheet. This refers not to errors in the subject matter, but to the logic of the instructions to be programmed into the computer. One also tends to overlook ambiguities and alternative interpretations of one's own phraseology. Working in groups is obviously more costly than working individually, but it is considerably more efficient, and the group product is of considerably higher quality. (It is interesting to note that, in parallel to the preceding remarks, there is some evidence it is better to have two students running a dialog than one alone. Their arguments and discussions preceding the answering of a question are conducive to learning.)

6 POTENTIAL EDUCATIONAL IMPACT OF INSTRUCTIONAL DIALOGS

Given the generation of significant numbers of well designed Socratic dialogs, substantial impact can be anticipated on learning and intellectual development at both secondary and tertiary school levels:

(1) It is well established in the U.S. that up to three quarters of our college and university students perform poorly on rudimentary tasks of abstract logical reasoning [Chiappetta (1976)] such as: almost any kind of ratio reasoning, including scaling and estimating; solving arithmetical problems involving division; controlling variables; forming and understanding propositional statements; doing elementary correlational reasoning; translating symbols into words and words into symbols (as in the verbal interpretation of graphs, other visual presentations, in the translation of verbal statements into graphs, or into arithmetical or algebraic operations [Arons (1983, 1984a,b)]. There is good reason to believe that such very basic skills, lack of which causes many students to fall hopelessly behind at early stages of physics courses, can be enhanced, at least statistically, in large numbers of individuals [Arons (1983,1984a,b); Lawson (1980)], given sufficient repetitive practice in a wide variety of increasingly richer contexts. Few individuals who have difficulty with such kinds of reasoning benefit significantly, however, from exposition, illustration, and explanation imparted, however lucidly, by a text or teacher, while they themselves remain passive readers or listeners. It is essential to engage their minds in the activity. These individuals do begin to show significant progress, not after one single remedial episode, but only after a temporally spaced series of episodes in which they are led to articulate explanations and lines of reasoning in their own words through the help of Socratic dialog.

There are far too few teachers to reach huge numbers of students in such one-on-one dialog, but the availability of numerous computer dialogs, carefully designed to provide the necessary practice, could make a significant statistical impact on a serious educational problem. This problem could, of course, be almost entirely removed from the realm of tertiary education if adequate help and instruction of this variety were provided in earlier schooling. Dialogs currently needed for this purpose at tertiary level would probably serve equally well in most instances at the secondary level.

(2) Many students perform badly, drop out, or learn very little beyond memorizing technical jargon and calculational procedures in our introductory physics courses. This applies both to "professional" courses for science majors and engineers and to "general education" courses for non-majors. A substantial fraction of this weak performance stems from failure to grasp the concepts and lines of reasoning at a few very crucial points early in the respective courses . Again, many students break through to grasp these issues only if they receive timely help through one-on-one dialog. Availability of appropriate dialogs at early stages of development of kinematics, dynamics, momentum, energy, electric, and magnetic concepts could significantly reduce these unnecessary losses. This would be especially true of many disadvantaged students who do not now survive the early stages of our physics courses.

(3) The last decade has seen the emergence of vigorous studies of cognitive processes associated with the learning and understanding of specific areas of scientific subject matter [Resnick (1983)], and, because of its very fundamental role, physics has been a leading subject. Such studies deal directly with preconceptions, misconceptions, and impediments affecting students' penetration and mastery of abstract scientific concepts, models, laws, and principles. The insights being gained are not rapidly assimilated into textbooks, and, even if they were, few of the learning difficulties lend themselves to remediation through didactic presentation to a reader who suffers from the impediment. Again, the most effective pathway for many learners is that of Socratic dialog. Thus appropriately designed dialogs offer a promising avenue to more rapid

incorporation into day-to-day instruction of the best insights being gained in current cognitive research.

7 SUGGESTIONS FOR ADDITIONAL DIALOGS: UNDERPINNINGS

In addition to the drill dialogs suggested in Section 2, there are a number of other concepts and modes of reasoning which underpin the learning of physics and with which many students have substantial difficulty. Dialogs assisting in the enhancement of these capacities do not exist (at least in the U.S.) at the present time, and their development would be highly desirable.

(1) Verbal interpretation of ratios: What is the meaning of the number obtained when one length is divided by another length or one mass by another mass? (Here one is comparing two numbers by finding how many times one is contained in the other. Many students fail to recognize division as counting how many times one number can be subtracted from the other because they have never had to say something to this effect in their own words.) What is the meaning of the number obtained when the mass of an object in grams is divided by its volume in cubic centimeters? (Here one is finding how many grams are present in, or associated with, <u>one</u> cubic cm. (Many students fail to articulate this aspect of division and hence fail to take the next steps necessary in a sequence of arithmetical reasoning.) It is also necessary to deal explicitly with the reciprocals, e.g. what is the meaning of the number obtained if the volume is divided by the mass? A very important number to consider explicitly and interpret in concrete terms is the number obtained when the circumference of a circle is divided by its diameter (i.e. the meaning of pi).

Many students have great difficulty with such interpretations in unfamiliar scientific contexts. Such students benefit from being carried back to more familiar situations (e.g. what is the meaning of the number obtained if the cost of an item is divided by its mass in kg? if the mass in kg is divided by the cost? if a total amount of money earned is divided by the time required to earn it?) One can then return to the parallel scientific situations and lead students to articulate the similarities.

(2) Arithmetical reasoning involving division: Given the question "We have 800 g of material which has 2.3 g/cc . What must be the volume occupied by the sample?" Students should be led to argue the solution without recourse to manipulation of the density formula (e.g., what does 2.3 g/cc mean? 2.3 is the number of grams in one cubic cm; we can think of 2.3 g as a clump or package; if we find how many such packages there are in 800 g of the material, we obtain the total number of cc's since each such package is associated with one cc.)

(3) Coupling arithmetical reasoning with graphical representation in cases of simple linear relationship: e.g., associating density with slope of a graph of total mass M vs total volume V ; interpreting an arithmetical calculation by representing it on the graph and vice versa; interpreting the difference between finding the total V , given the density and a total M on the one hand, and finding the change in volume when the same M is added to a given block on the other. Many students see these as entirely different calculations and subtract the final and initial total volumes, not recognizing that they can calculate the change directly.

For students having difficulty, similar exercises, including graphical interpretation, are necessary with the meaning of pi and the relation between changes in circumference and changes in diameter of circles; with concentration of solutions; with graphs of position vs clockreading and velocity vs clockreading in kinematics; with graphs of net force vs acceleration imparted to objects of different mass (Newton's Second Law); etc. [See Arons (1983)].

(4) Distinction between linear relationship and direct proportionality. Many students fail to register this distinction in earlier experience and must be helped to articulate it in their own words.

(5) Ratio reasoning involving the scaling of various physical effects when functional relations are known: When a bob revolves on a string in uniform circular motion, by what ratio does the centripetal force change if the angular velocity is increased by a factor of 2.6 while the radius is decreased by a factor of 1.7 ? What happens to the intensity of light falling on a film if the diameter of a camera lens is increased by a factor of 1.5 and the focal length is increased by a factor of 5.3 ? If both electrical point charges are increased by a factor of 8.0 in an electrostatic interaction, by what factor must the separation be changed to keep the force of interaction unaltered? Many students have an overwhelming inclination to substitute numbers in the formulas. They show strong resistance to thinking in terms of the ratios, and they benefit from Socratic help.

(6) Radian measure: Relatively few students have acquired any genuine understanding of the reasons for introduction of radian measure in place of degrees; they have simply memorized a ritual more or less successfully. They should be led to see <u>why</u> radian measure is introduced, how it differs from measure in degrees, and in what sense it is to be regarded as "natural." The examination should not be confined to the relation among angle, arc length, and

radius; it should extend to the observation that the sine and tangent of an angle become more nearly equal to the angle itself for decreasing angles, providing one uses radian measure, and, for students taking calculus, it should extend to examination of the limits of the relevant ratios underlying the derivation of the derivatives of the sine and cosine functions.

8 SUGGESTIONS FOR ADDITIONAL DIALOGS: PHYSICS CONCEPTS AND REASONING MODES

Following is a list of subjects in which many students encounter serious conceptual difficulty at introductory levels and thus fall irretrievably behind. Dialogs helping them surmount the difficulties early on are much to be desired.

(1) Trowbridge and McDermott [(1980), (1981)] have shown that many students at the introductory level tend to confuse very primitive constructs and do not discriminate clearly between position and velocity or between velocity and acceleration. Clarification could be provided through dialogs that present simulated experiments of the kind Trowbridge and McDermott used in the laboratory.

(2) Given an acceleration vs clockreading graph consisting of abrupt "steps" (i.e. successive different intervals of uniform positive, negative, zero acceleration), have the student sketch the corresponding velocity vs clockreading graph immediately above the acceleration graph. This exercise is very helpful in improving student grasp of the acceleration concept and distinguishing it from velocity.

(3) Given a swinging pendulum, ask a student to predict the trajectory of the bob after the instant the string is cut at various points in the swing, including the end points.

(4) Show velocity, acceleration, and force vectors (in separate diagrams, never on the same diagram) for:

a) An object thrown vertically upward while rising, falling, and at the top of its flight. b) At various points in projectile motion. c) A car at various points in a roller-coaster ride. d) A pendulum at various points in its swing, including the end points. e) A bob on a spring in horizontal simple harmonic motion. f) A bob in circular motion. g) A pendulum bob suspended from the roof of an accelerating car.

(5) Distinction between gravitational and inertial mass using appropriate gedanken experiments. [See, for example, Arons (1965), Section 7.13]

(6) Frictional force. Many students tend to memorize the formula $f = \mu N$ and regard this as the size of the frictional force acting on a stationary block in all cases. They need to be led through a sequence in which they must recognize that the frictional force increases from <u>zero</u> to f as the external force applied to the block increases.

In connection with another facet of frictional effects, many students acquire the misapprehension that frictional forces always oppose the motion of the entire body on which they act. Although it is true that frictional force always opposes the <u>sliding</u> of one surface over another, it does not always oppose the motion of the entire body: witness the frictional force exerted by the road on the wheels of an accelerating car.

(7) Tension in strings. Many textbooks introduce the term "tension" as though it were a primitive with obvious meaning to everyone. Since "tension" is actually a subtle concept which requires careful and explicit operational definition, many students become seriously confused. A dialog leading students through the formation of such a definition and identifying the magnitude of tension in various simple cases frequently invoked in textbooks would be very useful.

(8) Massless strings. Most textbooks introduce the "massless" string as though it also were an obvious concept that requires no special introduction or discussion and as though it were immediately clear to everyone that forces at the opposite ends would have the same magnitude even when the system is accelerating. An effective dialog would lead students to consider first a simple case (e.g., a block being pulled on a horizontal surface by a massive string) in which a string with appreciable mass is being accelerated, establish the fact that the forces at opposite ends of the string would not be equal in magnitude, and then examine what happens to the forces as the mass of the string is made smaller and smaller.

(9) Free body force diagrams. Many students fail to develop the capacity to draw correct force diagrams when limited to conventional textbook problems. They tend to fiddle with the algebraic manipulations until they get the "right answer," and the correctness of the force diagrams is rarely checked. There is also a strong tendency to follow the space-saving pattern in the majority of texts and not separate the diagrams of the interacting objects. Hence, forces exerted by a car on the road are not distinguished from forces exerted by the road on the car.

We need dialogs that would lead students to draw force diagrams for various simple situations, as many as possible from everyday experience: one's own body and the ground while walking or running; one's own body, the seat of the car, the car, and the road surface when the car is speeding up, or slowing down, or going around a curve; one's own body sitting on a box resting on a merry-go-round (carousel); a balloon, electrically charged by rubbing, sticks to a wall, etc.

(10) Consider the following two situations: (a) A ball rests on the floor of a stationary cart. The student accelerates the cart. (b) The student holds a bob on a string. He accelerates the end of the string he is holding.

In each case many students say that the ball or the bob are "thrown backwards" when the acceleration occurs. They need help in straightening out the confusion of frames of reference and in recognizing explicitly that neither the ball nor the bob is thrown backward relative to the ground.

(11) Many students labor under the misapprehension that <u>any</u> centrally directed force in circular motion is a "centripetal" force regardless of magnitude. They must be led to recognize that if a centrally directed force is larger than the quantity mv^2/R, the object will tend to spiral inward; that if the centrally directed force is less than mv^2/R, the object will tend to spiral outward; that the term "centripetal force" denotes that <u>net</u> force which imparts the particular value of acceleration equal to v^2/R.

Because the discussion of centripetal force usually starts with the bob on a string moving in a horizontal plane, many students acquire the misapprehension that the tension in the string is invariably the centripetal force. They will, for example, identify the tension in the string with the centripetal force when the motion takes place in a vertical circle.

A still more subtle situation, which gives difficulty even to many of the better students, is that of the definition of the local vertical (or the direction of g) at various points on the surface of the earth as this direction is affected by the earth's rotation. A dialog on this subject would help many students deepen their grasp of the centripetal force concept.

(12) Visualizing effects transcending direct sense perception. Many students have great difficulty accepting the proposition that the table exerts an upward force on the book resting on it [Minstrell (1982)]. They need to be led to the perception that the upward force is made possible by the deformation of the table, a deformation which is not zero even if it is a sheet of paper that is supported by the table. The recoil of objects in elastic collisions also involves deformations which the students fail to visualize unless explicitly led to do so.

A long rod is laid on the table, and a force is applied to one end. If asked whether the opposite end moves at exactly the same instant that the first end moves, most students will say "yes". They do not visualize the passage of the elastic wave which precedes motion of the object as a whole. Visualizing such effects consciously and explicitly, however, is an important prelude to the introduction of time delays and propagation effects in electromagnetic phenomena; it helps students understand the very basic phenomenological questions which Faraday and Maxwell were asking and prepares them for recognition of the failure of action-at-a distance (Newton's Third law) and the motivation for the invention of field theory.

(13) Qualitative (what will happen if....?) questions regarding simple electrical circuits consisting of batteries and bulbs going beyond the dialog available at Irvine. Similar questions for simple R, L, C circuits.

(14) What happens to the diameter of the hole in a metal plate when the plate expands on increase in temperature? What happens to the pressure at the base of a vertical column resting on a table when the column expands with an increase in temperature?

(15) Force diagrams for cases in which unequal point charges interact with each other. (Many students ignore Newton's Third Law and show a larger force acting on the smaller charge than on the larger charge.)

9 CONCLUDING REMARKS

The preceding suggestions are essentially illustrative. Many other such dialogs, with similar objectives, are needed in other introductory subject matter areas. With the availability and judicious use of sensitively prepared materials, I believe that effectiveness of instruction could be enormously enhanced, freeing teachers to deal more successfully with the development of more sophisticated levels of knowledge and understanding.

Not only would this improve the education we provide future scientific and engineering professionals, it would significantly improve the science competence of school teachers in precisely those areas of subject matter in which we currently find their greatest deficiencies; and it would make a significant contribution to achievement of wider public understanding of science.

All of this is wishful thinking, however, pending the development of a very much larger volume of competently written Socratic material and its testing in actual instructional context.

References

Arons, A. B. (1965). Development of Concepts of Physics. Addison-Wesley Publishing Co., Reading, MA. USA.

Arons, A. B. (1982). Phenomenology and Logical Reasoning in Introductory Physics Courses. Am. J. Phys. 50, 13.

Arons, A. B. (1983). Student Patterns of Thinking and Reasoning, Part One. The Physics Teacher. 21, 576.

Arons, A. B. (1984a). Student Patterns of Thinking and Reasoning, Part Two. The Physics Teacher. 22, 21.

Arons, A. B. (1984b). Student Patterns of Thinking and Reasoning, Part Three. The Physics Teacher. 22, 88.

Arons, A. B. (1984c). Education Through Science. Jour. Coll. Sci. Teaching. 13, 210.

Arons, A., Bork, A., Franklin, S., Kurtz, B., and Collea, F. (1981) Science Literacy in the Public Library -- Batteries and Bulbs. in Proceedings of the National Educational computing Conference, June 17 - 19, 1981 in Denton, TX, USA. Published by University of Iowa Weeg Computing Center. Iowa City, IO, USA.

Bork, A. (1980). in Computers and Education, Vol. 4. Pergamon Press Ltd. Oxford, UK.

Bork, A. (1981). Learning with Computers. Digital Press. Bedford, MA. USA.

Bork, A., Trowbridge, D., and Arons, A. (1983). Observation and Inference -- A Computer-Based Learning Module. in Proceedings of the National Educational Computing Conference at Baltimore, MD, USA, June 8, 1983. Published by IEEE Computer Society Press, Silver Spring, MD, USA.

Chiappetta, E. L. (1976). A Review of Piagetian Studies Relevant to Science Instruction at Secondary and College Level. Sci. Ed. 60, 253.

Clement, J. (1982). Students' Preconceptions in Introductory Mechanics. Am. J. Phys. 50, 66.

Duda, R. O. and Shortliffe, E. H. (1983). Expert Systems Research. Science. 220, 261.

Fredette, N. H. and Clement, J. (1981). Student Misconceptions of an Electric Circuit: What Do They Mean? J. Coll. Sci. Teach. 10, 280.

McDermott, L. C. (1984). Research on Conceptual Understanding in Mechanics. Physics Today. 37, 24.

Lawson, A. E. (1980). Relationships Among Level of Intellectual Development, Cognitive Style, and Grades in a College Biology Course. Sci. Ed. 64, 95.

Minstrell, J. (1982). Explaining the "At Rest" Condition of an Object. The Physics Teacher. 20, 10.

Piaget, J. and Inhelder, B. Growth of Logical Thinking. Basic Books. New York. USA. 1958.

Resnick, L. B. (1983). Mathematics and Science Learning: A New Conception. Science 220, 477.

Trowbridge, D. E. and McDermott, L. C. (1980). Investigation of Student Understanding of the Concept of Velocity in One Dimension. Am. J. Phys. 48, 1020.

Trowbridge, D. E. and McDermott, L. C. (1981). Investigation of Student Understanding of the Concept of Acceleration in One Dimension. Am. J. Phys. 49, 242.

Viennot, L. (1979). Spontaneous Reasoning in Elementary Dynamics. Euro. J. of Sci. Ed. 1, 205.

PEDAGOGICAL DEVELOPMENT OF COMPUTER-BASED LEARNING MATERIAL

Alfred Bork

Educational Technology Center

Information and Computer Science

University of California

Irvine, California 92717 USA

This paper is addressed to the serious producer (either present or future) of computer-based or interactive videodisc learning material. It is not aimed at the casual producer. Very few individuals can develop good computer-based learning material, in any substantial quantity, as a casual activity. It is a serious activity demanding time, effort and resources. The low quality of much of the existing commercial and non-commercial material shows the difficulty of trying to view such production as a "spare time" activity. I will use "computer" in this paper to include interactive videodisc, the combination of the computer and the videodisc or compact disk player.

These remarks are particularly directed to pedagogical developers. Little will be said about programming or other technical details, because the pedagogical developers should not, I argue, be involved in details of technical implementation. Other books and papers discuss this aspect of the computer in education, as well as the important role of formative evaluation in the development of high quality learning material.

NATO ASI Series, Vol. F 23
Designing Computer-Based Learning Materials
Edited by A. Bork and H. Weinstock

Different talents are needed in these different stages of production. I am concerned in this paper with the pedagogical talents.

The system described in this paper has been developed at the Educational Technology Center during the last 17 years. The "proof" of any system for producing learning materials should not be an abstract argument for that system, or elegant prose describing it, but rather it should be in the products it generates.

Hence the supporting "evidence" that I offer to support the views presented in this paper is not contained within the paper. Rather it is to be seen in the materials my colleagues and I have developed at the Educational Technology Center. Appendix 1 lists these materials. Readers should examine some of this material, such as the recently produced material in the Scientific Reasoning series, that illustrates many of the points raised in this paper.

PRECODING STAGES

Within pedagogical design I am particularly concerned in this paper with the detailed design stage, the full specification of an individual computer-based learning module. It is assumed that the group is working from a specification or description in general terms of the context of the module.

I will not describe the earlier stages in detail. They involve the overall design of the full set of modules to be developed, perhaps a course or a segment of learning materials. Other media beside computers and videodiscs may be specified or suggested in this top-level design.

Several stages of top-level design may be involved. First, the nature of the overall project may be determined. This determination may come in the form of a proposal for funding. A series of proposals of increasing complexity may be involved. The proposals may have tentative suggestions for modules, and will specify the goal and objectives of the project. I do not mean to imply a behavioral specification; the guiding pedagogical philosophy may be very different in different projects.

When funding is available, an early stage should be a full-scale planning meeting. It is in this session that individual modules are specified. Research input is important in this planning stage.

This diagram illustrates the process:

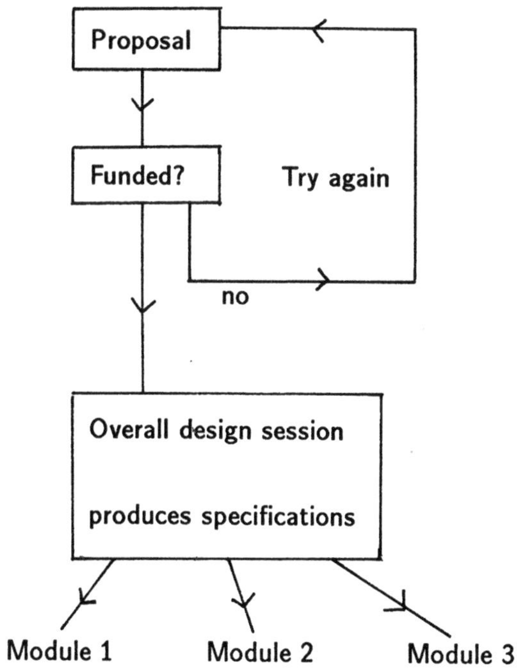

Further information relevant to these early stages are in the Lee Shulman and Arnold Arons papers in this volume. The references at the end of this paper provide additional details.

Now I return to the discussion of detailed pedagogical sessions, the main topic of this paper.

WHO ARE THE AUTHORS?

The first consideration is who will be the authors of a series of computer-based learning modules, the participants in the detailed design groups? It is critical to pick the best possible teachers. The important thing, I stress, is NOT subject matter expertise - that is usually relatively easy to find - but rather expertise in helping students to learn about the subject matter. We want teachers and faculty members who normally teach in a highly interactive fashion. It is the insights of these very good teachers that we hope to capture in good computer-based learning material, their understanding of the student problems that occur in the learning process. So a teacher who is particularly skillful at lecturing, or at writing textbooks, does not necessarily reflect the kind of attitude toward the learning process that we would like to stress. We want teachers who talk to students and who also carefully listen to what is being said by students. Not all teachers listen to students!

Saying that we want the best possible teachers is, unfortunately, a long way from identifying such teachers. No sure mechanism is available for choosing these teachers; we must rely on trial and error. I emphasize again that we want teachers who work interactively with students, and teachers who are accustomed to listening to students. They have the insights into typical student learning problems, and often have developed tactics for dealing with these learning problems.

These good teachers may come from almost anywhere in the world. Indeed, it seems to me to be a serious mistake to believe that all the people who are best in teaching X, happen to be in a particular geographical location, no matter what that location is! Good teachers from distant locations can be brought together for these relatively brief design sessions.

In addition to these good teachers, another desirable individual in the design is a person who has done research regarding learning in the particular area involved. Often such research is available, particularly in areas of science education. We want to employ the results of the best available research in creating learning units, with and without the computer.

A third essential person is someone who has had previous experience with the development of technology-based learning material. This person might be thought of as a media expert, the person who brings to the development process a rich background in how to use the computer as a learning device. Just as a film or video expert is needed in designing educational films, an expert on computer-based learning is also needed in the design process. If video is involved, a video expert will also be important.

It is not at all critical that all the people developing computer-based learning material have previous computer experience, or previous experience developing computer-based learning material; only the media specialist needs this experience. We find, on the contrary, that such previous experience is often a handicap. A teacher who has used the computer, but in highly limited ways, often has fixed, but inadequate, views as to the most effective way the computer can be used in education. Such a person does not work well in the environment to be suggested. In particular, acquaintance with simple-minded programming languages such as BASIC or PILOT is very likely to be a negative factor; teachers with such experience may already have developed bad habits that are difficult to overcome.

A bright teacher with no previous computer experience, but one who understands the student problems, will be a much more valuable participant than someone who has been puttering around without support on a home computer for a year or so.

GROUP VS SINGLE DEVELOPMENT

It will be noted that in the last section I have already talked about three types of people who should be involved in the pedagogical design of computer-based learning material; excellent, interactive teachers; researchers in this specific learning area; and individuals experienced with computer-based learning, media specialists. The implication is that a GROUP should be involved in development.

A typical group might involve about four people: two or three teachers, one researcher (if such a person is available), and one media specialist. Group development leads to a much better product than individual development, particularly with regard to interaction.

WHAT WORKING ENVIRONMENTS ARE DESIRABLE?

The process of working together in groups of four or so, as just suggested, is difficult to arrange if one has to do this in the normal working environment. Furthermore, the usual environment is full of interruptions - phones ring, students need help, visitors arrive, your colleagues talk with you. Since the people in the group are excellent, they are in great demand, and their time is valuable. Some may come from a great distance.

These considerations suggest that the group should work for a relatively brief intensive period, away from the usual work environment. We usually have a group work for a week or two; in large projects several groups may work simultaneously.

We seek pleasant environments for development. Since this is to be the full-time activity for a week or two, and since the activity is not an easy one, the more relaxing the environment, the better. Much of our recent work has been done in the Southern California mountains. We also have worked in a "hot tub" - a type of thermal bath - for relaxation, particularly when the group was stuck on a difficult issue. Large cities present too many distractions, particularly in the evenings.

THE FIRST MORNING

The first morning of the design session (in a pleasant environment) is devoted to a brief intense workshop, stressing the benefits of the computer in learning environments, and also stressing the pitfalls for the beginner, the things to be avoided. If computers are available, it is useful to have this half-day session as a hands-on workshop, basing it on examples of good and bad computer-based learning material to illustrate the points being made.

I stress that this initial training workshop is NOT concerned with teaching people about any programming languages or authoring systems, or in giving them any details about the technical aspects of the computer. (The last thing a writer of computer-based learning material needs to know is what a bit, byte, or CPU is! The fact that so many books about computer-based learning start with this information is a strong indication of how young and inexperienced this area is.) The following topics are stressed in this initial workshop.

1. Overcoming Previous Media Sets

One of the first issues discussed in this workshop is overcoming habits useful in developing learning material in other media, but that are definite handicaps with the computer. A developer who comes into the group with extensive experience in lecturing or writing textbooks, is already accustomed to a noninteractive mode of working with students. Lectures and books are seldom interactive. Someone with little interactive experience often wants to start with several dense screens of text at the beginning, allowing perhaps one or more trivial student interactions. This person is really writing a book, or giving a lecture, and needs to understand that this is not an effective way of using the computer.

Likewise, people entering computer-based learning with a film or video background often are primarily concerned with visual material. They develop elaborate animation sequences or other pictorial information, using a medium that is at the present time only marginal with regard to its graphic capabilities! The key problem is that they neglect the principal merit of the computer, its interactive capability.

Computer-based learning units are not books or films. This is not to say that text and graphics are not needed in computer- based learning material. They certainly are! But the instructional developer must learn to use them in ways that are appropriate for the computer as the learning medium. Putting a book or movie on the screen is not desirable. Developers need to understand this potential problem.

2. Important Aspects of the Computer Interaction and Individualization

We stress in the initial workshop two extremely important aspects of the computer, its interactive nature, and its ability to individualize learning experiences to the needs of each student. Unless the developer realizes the full potential of the computer in this regard and works toward using it, the materials produced are not likely to be of acceptable quality. Unfortunately, many existing materials do not provide adequate interaction.

Interaction has several aspects. First, I consider the frequency of interaction. Our informal studies indicate that there should be an interaction approximately every fifteen to twenty seconds. Time is measured in this fashion:

1) After the student has completed one interaction, RETURN is pressed. The clock starts at that point.

2) When the computer ultimately has asked another question and is waiting for student input, the clock stops.

Remember that the fifteen or twenty-second interval suggested between interactions is a goal for an average time, not something to be measured carefully at each interaction.

You easily can see that the brief time between interactions does not allow for elaborate displays of text or pictures. A student cannot read several screens of text, or watch long animation or video sequences, and still preserve an interactive environment. This is not to say that occasionally one might not have considerable text or graphics. But this should be rare. Designers should be particularly concerned about this potential problem at the beginning of the dialog.

Another aspect of interaction is the quality of each interaction. Some interactions can be entirely trivial, some can be weak, and others can be of quite high quality.

At least three factors play a role in determining quality of interaction. First, we must consider what type of interaction is used. Interactions involving multiple-choice questions seem to me to be beneath contempt. There is very seldom any reason for using multiple choice in technology-based learning material, since it is a highly user-unfriendly approach, and one that does not correspond to the real world. Would the user desire brain surgery performed by a doctor whose skills were verified by multiple choice?

Typically the best interactions are those that are natural to the area. Thus, in science numerical answers might be frequent. But in many areas, questions in the user's language, with the student answering in a free-form fashion in the language, are the best choices. Contrary to popular belief, it is not difficult, technologically, to use free input within computer- based learning material. We do not need the elaborate analysis techniques of artificial intelligence, parsing natural language in many situations, although they may eventually prove to be useful in some specialized environments.

A second aspect of the quality of interaction concerns the immediate consequences of interaction. That is, what does one "say" at once to the user. We need not say anything immediately! In particular, computer-based learning material is often too anxious to tell students that they are right or wrong in their responses. If it is possible to point out briefly why a particular answer in not an appropriate one, it is probably good to do that right away. A good role is to reply as you would if you were working individually with the student. In some cases the entire intent of a question may be only to have the student spend time thinking about the issues.

The third aspect concerning the quality of interaction concerns the long-range consequences of a student response. Here, we reach one of the most important aspects of student-computer dialogs, the fact that we can direct appropriate learning material to each student.

One of the tremendous advantages of the computer as a learning device is that we can individualize the learning experience to the needs of the student. That is, unlike a book or a lecture, the experience can be different for each individual, reflecting the student's background, capabilities, performance, and desires. This individualization can be achieved without computers if the instructor is only working with one, or very few, students. But this is prohibitive in most learning situations.

We can individualize technology-based learning material. Our excellent teachers have good intuition on the kinds of student problems likely to occur. The program can wait for just these situations, and offer specific help relevant to most student problems. Formative evaluation also can improve the material in this regard.

One common technique, used before the introduction of computers, that makes individualization possible, is the use of pretesting and post-testing in connection with the learning material. Thus, a module can start by checking interactively to see whether the student is familiar with all or some of the ideas to be presented. Those topics that the student already knows, need not be touched, so the student can work directly only in the areas in which help is needed. Hence, we can save student learning time, and we can treat the student in a more mature manner.

It may be possible, through carefully chosen questions, to determine the nature of the problems that arise. Then we can help students to learn what they do not know, with some understanding of the student's learning problems. We can gain considerable time by individualizing the material to the needs of each student. We need not "teach" something the student already knows!

Another mode of individualization is also important. Suppose that an attempt is made to help a student learn a particular concept or capability, but the attempt fails. Perhaps the particular approach to learning may not be ideal for that particular student; perhaps another medium may be better. In that case another approach to learning this concept can be presented. The mastery-based learning enthusiasts, such as Benjamin Bloom, have argued that an appropriate mode of learning can be found for each student, for each task. Thus, everyone should be able to learn everything! But at the present time, we may not know how to find such an appropriate mode, although we try different ones.

I also should mention a possible danger in attempting to individualize learning. A design group too interested in individualization may spend vast amounts of time on a particularly narrow topic, and so produce little material. A design group should not look for every possible mistake, but only for the ones that seem likely with the students that will use the program. In the testing part of the development process (or formative evaluation), other unanticipated student difficulties may appear, and then the material can be extended to include those. The design group should behave in a rational manner in the development of the materials.

3. Graphics

We stress in this early design-group workshop the importance of graphics, the use of pictorial information of a variety of different types to aid the learning process.

Traditional education in the United States, particularly university education, has been highly verbal. Relatively few graphic learning aids are used. But in almost all subject matter, some use of this visual material is introduced by experienced teachers. In creating technology-based learning material, we want to increase graphic use in such a way that it is directly relevant to the learning process.

Since many of the people participating in the design sessions will be relatively inexperienced in using pictorial forms for learning, it is necessary in the initial workshop to emphasize the usefulness of iconic information. Again, as with many of the other details, examples are very helpful. In addition to its direct role in the learning process, pictures are important as an alternate way of displaying information, or as a way of helping those who learn early through visual information. Iconics also is important from a motivational point of view, since the media that surround us today use many elegant pictures.

On the other hand, as already mentioned, we find, with some individuals, the tendency to overuse graphics just as others have a tendency to overuse text. This is encouraged by systems that make it relatively easy to create fancy pictures, but make it difficult to do anything else. A key issue always is whether the graphics is intrinsically connected with the learning process, or whether it is simply there for entertainment. Entertainment is not equivalent to motivation.

4. Group Dynamics

The workshop also should consider how the group is to interact. It should be emphasized that the group is truly intended to be a group, with everyone working together, and with each group member playing a role. There is to be no leader in the group. Everyone is to be equal. Some design groups tend to have the person with experience in computer-based education serve as a leader. This should be the case only in the early stages of the design activity, if at all. We want active groups. Everyone should participate in the design process.

We can illustrate two types of group interaction. In the following figures, the circles represent people, and the lines indicate the flow of communication. The figure is an example of a group with poor dynamics:

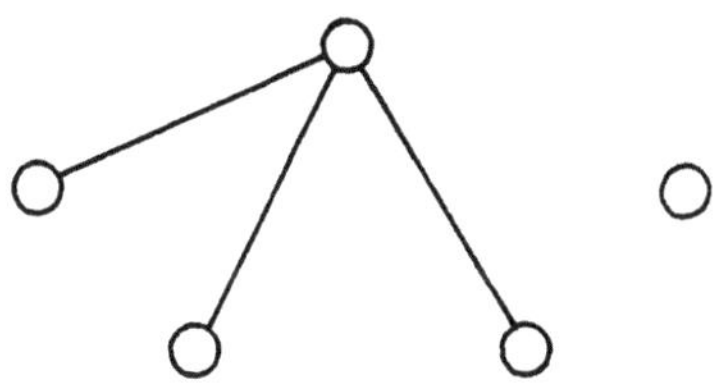

One person dominates this group, and one person does not communicate with the others. A better situation is illustrated in this figure, because the group really is working as a group.

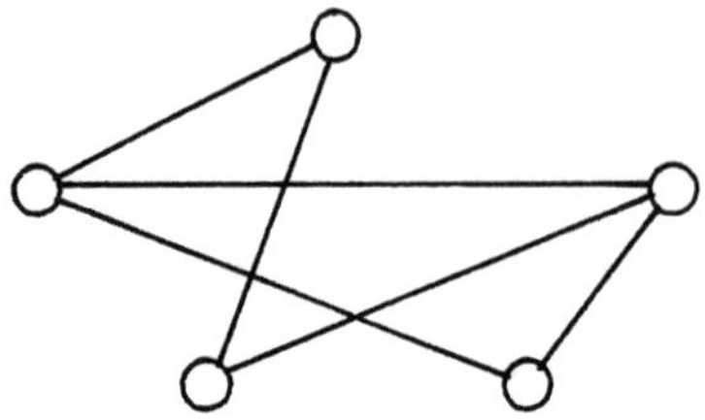

Participants must also be prepared for the likelihood that the group will not be in perfect accord! That is, they should understand that quarrels, even heated disputes, will occur. Teachers are often not prepared for the fact that different teachers will have very different views about how to approach a given topic, or about how students will react to that topic. The group should come to a consensus on each point, and the group members should not let their own egos become involved in the process.

5. Language

Many questions concerning language arise in developing computer-based learning material. Most students are not good readers, so the users should be concerned with making the language clear and understandable. In particular, it is not necessary to be verbose. On the other hand, too much simplification of language probably will have deleterious long-range effects on student development.

The way one addresses students inevitably should be polite and considerate to the student. A certain degree of humility is needed even in telling students that they are wrong. There is some chance that the program may not have been clever enough to recognize a right answer! In any case, we want the student to have a positive attitude toward learning, even if there are a few missteps along the way. Students should develop confidence that they can learn.

We prefer at Irvine to make the language somewhat intermediate between the informal language of common speech and the more formal language in textbooks. It is not, for example, always necessary to have complete sentences on the screen. In some cases outline forms with phrases may be useful. Humor is useful if carefully used.

6. Other Comments for Initial Workshop

An important design principle is that decisions should be made on pedagogical grounds. The designers in the group should not be concerned with how easy or difficult it will be to program the material, but rather only with considerations of what is the best possibility for learning. Technical implementation should follow design, rather than the reverse.

The designers should avoid the use of gimmicks of a variety of types. It is not necessary to make the materials extremely simplistic, or to make them essentially comic strips. This is often insulting to the user. While motivational issues are certainly important to increase time on task, computer dialogs can be motivating without being a game.

I emphasize again that the purpose of this initial workshop is to get the designers to understand the advantages, and the pitfalls, of the computer in a learning environment. Other topics might be discussed in addition to those mentioned, some specific to a particular area.

HOW ARE THE DESIGN DECISIONS RECORDED?

Working together in groups producing computer-based learning material, we need a way of recording decisions made by that group. These decisions must reflect a complete pedagogical specification, suitable as the basis for a later technical production stage that will involve such issues as screen design and programming. All messages appearing on the screen must be fully stated, and sketches must be given of all the pictures. A complete description of how the student input is to be analyzed, and what decisions are to be made based on student inputs, must be on the recording document. I prefer to call such a document a SCRIPT.

The question of how to write scripts for computer-based learning does not need to be part of the initial workshop. Since one person in the group will be experienced with computer-based learning material and has prepared such scripts before, that person can be the initial writer.

Our experience is that quickly all the people in the group learn the strategy, simply by seeing it in action. By the end of the first day we usually have everyone in the group having spent some time in the writing activity. Indeed, we find it is best to make certain that everyone does this, since then everyone will feel fully acquainted with the process involved.

The exact details of the reporting process are not terribly important, provided that they offer a clear specification to the graphic designers and programmers who will implement the scripts. We have developed a series of strategies over the years at Irvine that serve the purpose well, in that they are easy to learn by design groups and teachers, and are easy to understand for the people involved in technical implementation. The script can even be inserted directly into a computer, although we do not find this the most convenient way to proceed. Ordinary handwriting is more than sufficient, and can be done quickly.

To further elucidate the notion of the script, with complete specification from a didactic point of view of the learning material, I enumerate the ingredients of the script, with some discussion.

1. Text to appear on the screen.

Messages are to be displayed to students. These are shown directly on the script.

Some comments about language have already been made. Designers may want to pay attention, however, to other features. For example, it is often desirable to split a sentence at a natural phrase boundary, or at a major mark of punctuation, such as a period or a comma. This can be indicated simply by writing the messages in the script in this fashion. Also, designers may want to indicate special timing considerations, such as pausing after a period, or before and after a critical word, or emphasizing a word or phrase in some way. (See the section on comments for further information.) Short lines usually aid readability, as does blank space.

Textual material should be kept to a minimum. Long messages begin to make the unit resemble a book or a lecture. As indicated, this is a source of difficulty for many literate developers of computer-based learning material who tend to teach in a noninteractive, heavily text-based form. Design groups should police this internally. Topics that at first look as if they "must" be done as long messages, can be converted into forms in which the student plays a more active role in learning.

2. Pictures.

Pictures can be shown as sketches, usually with some accompanying comments. It is useful to sketch not just the picture, but the entire screen, showing how the text and pictures fit together. The designers should view the screen as a unit, not simply something that has text, and incidentally, perhaps, also has pictures. Area for text and graphics can be indicated by rectangular boxes, called ports or windows.

Pictures and text need to be interwoven, with some lines drawn on the picture, then some text, then other parts of the picture, etc. Ordering of pictures in this form can be specified in a variety of ways. Designers can attach numbers to individual lines, and comment on the order in which these numbered lines should appear. One can even use color for this; comments might say, for example, "draw the red part on the diagram." The problem with this latter approach is that it is often useful to copy scripts, since one does not like to give the original scripts to the technical production people. Hence, a numbering scheme for order or specification in comments is probably better.

3. Analysis of student input.

The heart of any piece of computer-based learning material is the ability to respond individually to students in a wide variety of situations. This is where the skills of the group are particularly needed, and this is where we are most likely to determine the quality of the eventual computer-based learning modules. We want dialog, so we must pay attention to what the students "say" as they are using the programs.

We want to spot not only the "correct" responses, but, much more importantly, we want the responses that solicit specific help for the student. Any time we can tell the student, immediately, why a particular response is not the best one, we are giving highly desirable individualized aid to the student. We want to gather information on student difficulties to use later in the dialog.

The design group should understand clearly that they will not be able to put on paper every possible response that someone might make. If the designers can succeed, as a result of the initial design sessions, in responding reasonably to eighty or ninety percent of the student answers, that would be (I would argue) a very good situation. Later formative evaluation will pick up some missing responses. In any case, we cannot expect complete success in dealing with student input. Even a person working directly with a student does not attain that. The program does not need to respond to professionals in the area; only students count!

Interaction arises when the student or students running the program respond to a question from the computer. The design group must both formulate the question and decide on the student answers that are to be sought. Thus, the design group will end up with a series of likely answers to the questions, some correct, some showing the need for help. Then they must determine how they will check the student answers for these responses.

In most situations we find that simple string matching applied to student answers will work. Often it is a question of logic, i.e., testing the student answer for several strings. Does the answer, for example, contain any of several specific words, and in addition contain any of other specific words. Looking for fragments of words, rather than whole words, makes the program more flexible in responding to typing and spelling problems.

A convenient notation for such an analysis might be as follows:

$$\left\{\begin{matrix} \text{litt} \\ \text{smal} \\ \text{tiny} \\ \text{minu} \end{matrix}\right\} + \left\{\begin{matrix} \text{boy} \\ \text{girl} \\ \text{child} \\ \text{pers} \end{matrix}\right\}$$

We require that the student input little, small, or tiny, plus boy, girl, child or person. Then, if the student types "It must be a little green person," the match is successful; if the student types "little elephant," it is not successful. Note that we often test on fragments of words, thus overcoming some typing and spelling errors.

At another point we may want to specify that a numerical input be within some range, or specify that it should have only a certain number of decimal places. The matching process may occur in several stages. If the student response requires a number plus associated units, the testing for the units might come first, and be followed by the testing for the number.

Usually a series of tests, not just one, will be specified for each input. The authors typically want order to these tests. That is, the authors will specify which tests should be done first, which second, etc. We find a convenient notation to be one that lists these tests in a series of descending boxes. A successful exit occurs when the test matches the student input, and the exit is by way of the box to either side, with a control line to the left or right. (Control lines are discussed below.) If the match was not successful, the program is designed to go to the box below, and try the match indicated in that box.

The following figure illustrates this notation:

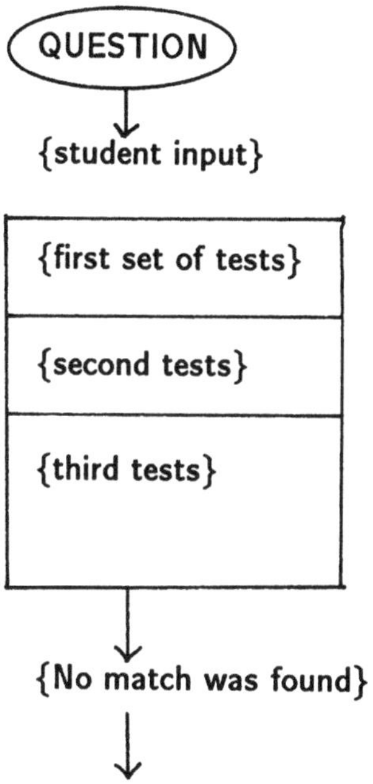

One obvious measure of the degree of interaction is simply to note how many tests are made on a particular page. A page of the script that is almost all text and pictures does not represent good use of the medium!

No matter how many tests are made, unless the tests are logically exclusive, the designers also must ask themselves what will happen if NONE OF THE TESTS MATCH. This case, that might be referred to as the "drop through" situation, is shown by control lines coming out of the bottom of the set of testing boxes just indicated.

4. Control.

Another factor is regard to interaction and individualization is the idea that different people will be treated in different ways. This is shown on the script by the flow of control, information primarily used by the programmer. Again this information must be specified by the design group.

Control interaction can be specified through a variety of features. First we have directed lines, lines that say "after this is done, then do this." Arrows on these lines can show directions. The group also must consider conditional control aspects, control that depends on the history of the student's progress up to this time. Some of these need to be specified with comments, a subject discussed in the next section. That is, the student who has already been through a given routine may be shunted along a path that is different from the one for a student who has not been through the routine. The comments need to be clear enough to indicate this. In other cases, numbers such as 1, 2, 3, etc. will indicate what should be done the first time at this point, the second time at this point, the third time at this point, etc. These numbers will be close to the corresponding directed control lines.

One aspect of sophisticated control is the ability of the computer to gather data about student progress, to keep fairly detailed information to indicate just what has happened so far. One may want to give students some help if they have repeatedly had difficulty with a particular concept. An internal "counter" can gather data as to how often the student has a problem at a given point, and this information can be used in later control statements.

5. Comments.

We have on several occasions mentioned that not everything can be indicated formally. Often we need to make comments either to the graphic designers or to the coders who will be involved in implementation. Comments also may specify goals and objectives of a section, or they may indicate possible lines for future development of the modules.

The concept of comments can perhaps best be indicated by a few examples.

{Input}

{Input at blank}

{Pick a random number here between 1 and 10, an integer}

{Draw the circle, display message, draw the straight line}

These examples are probably self explanatory. The bracket, {...}, is a convenient notation for comments. The issue is to give clear directions to the graphic designers and coders. Comments should be freely used.

REVIEW WITHIN GROUPS

If several groups are working simultaneously, toward the end of a session the scripts produced by each group can be interchanged, and the groups can offer constructive criticism of the other materials. If only a single group is working, the material can be sent for review to some appropriate individual who is not in the group. It should be noted that at this stage nothing is running. We only have a paper and pencil design to consider.

In any case, whether at the design session itself, or later, review of the script is an essential feature of careful development. The script can be copied and sent to other teachers and researchers who were not part of the project. If these individuals have not seen scripts before, it may be necessary to give them some help in how to read scripts.

The changes suggested by reviews, either at the design sessions or elsewhere, need to be considered. In some cases they will find errors in the script. They may suggest new pedagogical approaches, question the language used, or suggest additional tests. If the design group, or part of it, is still available, they can review these suggestions and make appropriate changes in the scripts. If they are not available, the project managers will need to make these decisions.

Such review is tricky. As with the editing of a textbook, different reviewers will not agree. The project managers must resolve these differences.

This completes our study of the pedagogical aspects of producing computer-based learning units. Details about later stages in the production process can be found in the following references.

References

Bork, Alfred. "Production Systems for Computer-Based Learning." Instructional Software, Principles and Perspectives for Design and Use. Decker Walker and Robert Hess editors. Belmont, CA: Wadsworth Publishing Company. 1984.

Bork, Alfred. "Producing Computer Based Learning Material at the Educational Technology Center." Journal of Computer Based Instruction. Spring. 1984.

Bork, Alfred. Learning with Computers. Bedford: Digital Press. 1981.

Bork, Alfred. Personal Computers for Education. New York: Harper and Row Publishers, Inc. 1985.

Bork, Alfred. Learning with Personal Computers, New York: Harper and Row Publishers, Inc. In press.

Appendix 1

COMPUTER DIALOGS DEVELOPED AT IRVINE

I. Mechanics course

- Quiz based (over 100,000 quizzes given)
- Two different courses, 27 quizzes WITH help
- Still on timesharing system

II. Other university-level physics

- Electricity, relativity, astronomy
- Still on timesharing system

III. Newton

- Versatile F=ma simulation for improving student intuition
- Needs associated workbook
- Timesharing and personal computer

IV. Waves quizzes

- Personal computer (older)

V. Teacher training about educational technology

- Two modules (prototypes)
- Personal computer

VI. Scientific Reasoning Series

- 12 modules, 20 hours
- Wide variation in age
- Help students to reason like scientists
- Critical thinking and problem solving
- Personal computer - color on some
- part of the Series is commercially available

VII. Getting started in physics

- 6 modules, 12 hours
- Wide variation in age
- Aids students at the beginning of a physics course
- Problem solving, naive worldviews, mathematics
- Personal computer

VIII. Self-teaching spreadsheet

- Joint project with University of Geneva
- Online instruction replaces manual
- Personal computer

IX. Dialog versions in other languages

- Joint project with University of Geneva
- Personal computer

X. Beginning programming with young children

- Student project
- Personal computer

MODELLING AS A METHOD OF LEARNING PHYSICAL SCIENCE AND MATHEMATICS

Peter Ross
Department of Artificial Intelligence
University of Edinburgh
Forrest Hill
Edinburgh EH1 2QL
Scotland

1. INTRODUCTION

Computer programs to aid learning, in which the aim is not to emulate a teacher carrying on a tutorial dialogue, can very commonly be classified as either simulation or modelling programs. For the purposes of this paper the difference is this:

- in a simulation program, the principles to be learned are encoded within the software. The user's aim is typically to "discover" the rules by some kind of scientific investigation or to acquire a gut feeling for how the encoded principles control various situations. For example, in a program (developed at the University of California, Irvine) that simulates planetary motion, the user sees a plane view of the path of a planet about a sun. He or she can shrink or enlarge the view, change the initial location and velocity of the planet, change the masses of the planet and sun, and even change the exponent of the law of force. If users make good use of this program, they can "discover" the elliptical paths associated with an inverse square law of force, the concept of "escape velocity" and the unstable or non-periodic paths associated with some other laws of force.

- in a modelling program, the user builds a

NATO ASI Series, Vol. F 23
Designing Computer-Based Learning Materials
Edited by A. Bork and H. Weinstock

simulation, and then either uses it to see if his understanding agrees with what "ought to happen" or uses it to acquire the kind of gut feelings mentioned above.

Some authors use the terms in another sense, for example, Hinton [12] uses the term "modelling" in a situation where the users work with several different simulations of one problem, and compare the results of these with real experimental data. Others use the terms in the above sense - see e.g., Tawney [19].

The division between these classifications is not as sharp as this may suggest. For example, imagine a program that allows the user to experiment with matrix algebra. This might contain code to generate the inner product of a row and a column of two matrices and to ensure that only matrices whose dimensions satisfy the normal constraint can ever be multiplied, but allows the user freedom to redefine matrix multiplication so that it is always commutative. For some purposes this program might be regarded as a simulation, since it contains constraints whose effect the user definitely sees; yet for other purposes it might be regarded as a modelling system since it allows the user to create "matrix worlds" whose worth and sense only a user can judge. For example, the user's new multiplication rule might not allow the existence of an identity element; a program might not be able to verify this important characteristic automatically.

This paper discusses the advantages and disadvantages of modelling as a method of learning. Much of the experimental work on this at Edinburgh has employed LOGO as the modelling language.

2. GENERAL CONSIDERATIONS

Modelling makes more demands on a user than simulation. There are several aspects to the task:

(a) defining what is to be modelled. Students often do a bad job of this, because they have no way of immediately checking their assumptions, even if they are aware of them. When flaws do appear at a later stage, they may not attribute them to mistakes in definition. On the other hand, spotting and correcting definition mistakes can be a good experience in learning both about the topic and about formal ways of thinking.

(b) designing the model. This is also demanding, since they must be able to describe, at least to themselves, the important features and how they interrelate. Students often handicap themselves by limiting their designs to what they envisage can be implemented, so they tend not to use their design requirements as a motive for learning more about implementation.

(c) creating the model. Students need to know a computer modelling language and have some programming skills. A modelling language must be fairly general, and only general kinds of support tools can be provided. Research into creating computer programs which can automatically analyse incorrect programs and find the bugs has not, as yet, made very much progress. Learning a modelling language is done "on the job," which increases the cognitive load, or beforehand in isolation, without much motivation.

(d) testing the model. This can be the most difficult aspect. Assuming that they do adequate testing, students need to be able to judge what ought to happen. They need to be able to classify surprising results as the consequence of a design flaw, the consequence of an implementation flaw or as not a flaw at all, but merely outside their present understanding of the task. The first two ought to trigger design or implementation changes with further testing. The third possibility may also trigger a change of goals.

The literature suggests that students be encouraged to work through cycles of (a)-(d), or perhaps (b)-(d). This orderly approach must usually be taught and only applies when the overall goal is clear. If the goal is not well defined, then not much can usefully be said about the ordering or relative importance of these aspects.

Clearly there are many further caveats. Students learn to do modelling only by experience and need to see benefits to persevere. The domain being modelled often poses its own special problems. Consider the modelling of water flow. Students may be taught that the flow of water down a channel of rectangular cross-section is "governed" by an equation of the form

$$\frac{dy}{dx} = \frac{u(x,y)}{1 - v(x,y)} \quad \text{(x is distance along the channel, y is depth)}$$

Someone might choose to encode a numerical algorithm which approximates the solution of this to plot a graph of depth against distance, without ever worrying about the possible singularity on the right-hand side. If one does worry, one may fail to appreciate that this equation does not capture the whole reality, that a singularity does not occur in practice - a hydraulic jump is the worst case - and that it is adequate in modelling to set v(x,y) to some suitable value if it gets too close to 1. Equally, one's software experience may prompt one to include a trap for this, but one may never ask whether there is any good physical basis for this. Intuition may, on the other hand, guide a student well in this case, but let him or her down when considering water flow over an edge because he or she lacks an intuitive grasp of the possibly dominating effects of viscosity in this situation.

Computer modelling has many possible disadvantages as a method of learning, but great advantages are also possible. Learning by discovery, it is often claimed, is very effective. The use of a computer forces students to be precise about their understanding, and the computer can provide at least indirect feedback to help them locate mistakes in their models. This methodology, of testing understanding by making and experimenting with computer models, is one of the mainstays of the subject of Artificial Intelligence (AI). To quote Carl Hewitt [11]:

> "AI deals with systems that lie somewhere in the spectrum between problem solving and algorithmic. For the most part AI does not produce completely algorithmic systems in which applications decide things themselves. Rather AI takes problems that are not well understood (hence require problem solving capability) and attempts to move them towards the algorithmic end of the spectrum."

Much work in AI has been devoted to the creation of languages, tools and environments specifically to support modelling work. It is possible to capitalise on this effort for specifically educational ends. For instance, the development of the LOGO language has been strongly influenced by AI work on LISP environments.

Modelling is a kind of discovery learning, and there is a good deal of educational research on the latter. Much of this was stimulated by the Piagetian school of developmental psychologists with its emphasis on the stages in development of thinking abilities - see [3] for a good summary. Some people cast doubts on this view. For example, Pascual-Leone [15] and Case [4] suggest that the development of memory capacity would lead to surface effects equivalent to Piaget's stages. A substantial literature argues for and against the Piagetian view. Other factors also affect the outcome. Anthony [2] and Scandura [17] have suggested that discovery learning surpasses expositional kinds of learning, as measured by long-term recall and problem-solving abilities, only if the process of discovery is successful. Trown [21,22] and others have shown that extrovert personalities profit more from discovery learning and that the reverse is true of highly anxious personalities. The basic conclusions for learning by modelling are that it is good to try to ensure, somehow, that students' modelling efforts do have some ultimate success; it is important to cater to a wide variety of learning styles when designing the management of the learning.

3. THE REQUIREMENTS OF A MODELLING LANGUAGE

In modelling work the student not only has to have some knowledge of the particular subject, but also has to know how to use the computer for modelling. This usually means that he has to know a suitable language, either a general-purpose programming language or a general-purpose language within a certain domain, such as two- and three-dimensional geometry. The language ought to be chosen or tailored to minimise the extra cognitive loading that this entails.

Unfortunately, as yet no good theories of learnability can guide the choice or design of such a language, although this is an active research question (see e.g. [1], [10]).

Experiment and experience are still the guides, although general design principles apply. One such principle arises from the distinction between structure and function in design. Defining characteristics which are independent of specific use, for example, those which could be called class properties rather than instance properties, are called structural. Characteristics specific to use, those which could be called instance properties, are called functional. To give an example, consider a procedure in Pascal which computes the factorial of a given number. Structural characteristics include the general syntax - a title line, optional parameter declarations, and a body which is a compound statement in the language. Functional characteristics might include the fact that the single input is a number whose factorial is to be found, the output is a number, and any side effects triggered by unreasonable values of the input, such as the printing of an error message.

Functional characteristics are by nature specialised, and the user ought not to be asked to remember too many of them. For example, the editor may have a sequence for deleting a selected word. It makes sense to change this from being a functional characteristic of the editor to being a characteristic of the entire system; the user can employ it whenever entering input. It is also a sound principle to make the set of structural properties of a modelling language as small as is convenient and as uniform as possible. For example, the syntax of a command should not depend on its context. The structural characteristics should allow specific functional characteristics to be built out of them. For instance, a language which does not allow you to build new operations out of the provided set is limited in scope. This suggests a serious constraint on a modelling language, since most novices can only compose fairly simple combinations of the basic structures. A good environment and tools can ease the load on the user. For example, in the Cornell Program Synthesizer [20], the editor only allows the user to type syntactically correct programs. But, it is not clear what the best tradeoffs are.

Is it a better investment for students to learn one general-purpose language which they can then use for several years, or to learn several languages each cognitively relatively undemanding, but of limited use? In the former case, they will eventually need to learn how to design their own, albeit simpler, languages to be implemented in the original. For an interesting discussion of these issues and how they affected the early design of BOXER, see reference 7.

The student using a modelling language needs an overall model of how the system works, a model which may omit some details as long as it does not contradict the reality and has useful predictive powers. An awkward question for the designer of a language is "how does the user acquire this model?" Often the answer has to be "by a combination of analogies with already familiar systems." The basic analogies must be ones very familiar to the whole spectrum of intended users so that incremental cognitive development is possible and, in the early stages of use, very easy. The language LOGO offers a good example.

4. SPECIFIC STUDIES: USING LOGO TO AID MATHEMATICAL LEARNING

GO is an interactive, list-processing and graphics-handling language. Its best known feature is "turtle graphics," a set of graphics commands that even children as young as 5 or 6 can use without much difficulty. This is essentially a simple command interface for graphics that demands no computing or mathematical knowledge at the start, just an awareness of the concepts "forward," "backward," "left" and "right." Various features make it a useful modelling language for school use:

- "turtle graphics" makes it possible for a new user to get appreciable rewards for very little initial effort or commitment.

- it is interactive. The user is not forced to work through the common cycle of edit-compile-test operations which can encourage him to create systems in chunks too large for convenient testing and debugging.

- it is extensible. The language initially provides between one hundred and two hundred basic operations, but the user can define new ones syntactically indistinguishable from them.

- the list-handling procedures allow the user to represent and manipulate data structured in almost any way.

LOGO was first created in the late 1960s at Bolt Beranek and Newman Inc. (BB&N), a non-profit research laboratory in Boston, as part of a contract funded by the U. S. Office of Naval Research. It was basically a simplified version of the artificial intelligenc language LISP; LOGO's designers were Wallace Feurzeig, Seymour Papert and Daniel Bobrow. In 1968 BB&N began a research project to investigate the merits of learning programming as an aid to understanding ideas in mathematics. The work was funded by the U.S. National Science Foundation, where there was considerab interest in C.A.I. at the time; the language chosen was LOGO. There were a number of hypotheses to be tested by the work:

- Programming can help children acquire habits of rigourous thinking and expression by trying to make the computer understand and perform their algorithms.

- Programming provides a realistic framework for the introduction of problems that often seem irrelevent to previous experience when taught by more conventional means.

- The vocabulary and concepts of programming form a useful language for talking about concepts in mathematics and in problem-solving generally. Such language has the great virtue of being free of confusing overtones and emotional values because children have little or no previous experience that might cloud their grasp of it.

- A suitably programmed computer could be a wonderful laboratory to foster an experimental approach to math notions.

In over a decade of research, none of these has been refuted. Indeed, there is now a large body of evidence that suggests there is some truth in each, although these claims may need to be qualified somewhat - see below. However, none of these claims have been demonstrated convincingly. These ideas guided the first tailoring of LOGO as a language to be used by school children themselves for experimenting in mathematics. The project reported a large measure of success by the end of its first funding in 1969. It was so promising that the Artificial Intelligence Laboratory at MIT, where Seymour Papert was a professor of mathematics, started another LOGO research project, while BB&N continued its own research efforts. Papert was responsible for adding "turtle graphics" to LOGO. This feature of LOGO has been such a tremendous success that many people now imagine it to be synonymous with LOGO, even though it forms only a small part of the language.

In 1972 Daniel Bobrow from MIT spent a sabbatical year at the Department of Artificial Intelligence in Edinburgh and created a version of LOGO written in the AI language POP-2. This aroused much interest and provided a seed for subsequent work there. Educational research based on LOGO has been going on at these three sites (BB&N, MIT, Edinburgh) ever since and has spread to many other locations.

The research with LOGO, both at MIT and at Edinburgh, started using small numbers of volunteers and went on to take LOGO to schools, once suitable equipment was available. At MIT their dialect of LOGO was almost fully defined and changed very little after the PDP-11/45 version of LOGO appeared in 1974. This dialect has been implemented on a variety of microcomputers such as the Apple II and IBM PC, mainly by specialist companies such as Krell Inc. and LOGO Computer Systems Inc. of Boston.

At Edinburgh the language changed in important ways almost from the start. In 1973-74, the POP-2 based LOGO system was mounted on a DEC-10 machine at Edinburgh, and used from teletypes. Special hardware was built to drive plotters and displays to provide children with graphical output for their procedures. However, in parallel with this a new system was written for Edinburgh University's ICL 4/75 mainframe computer, under the EMAS operating system. This version was "experimental" in that the strategy was to build a system which could be modified readily as experience demanded. Two versions evolved: AI2LOGO, which supported work by undergraduates taking a course in Artificial Intelligence, and ELOGO, used for work with children and novice programmers. Both were very heavily used until 1980, and were very extensively developed in that time - by the end of its life AI2LOGO had reached version 9.10, having had nearly forty upgrades.

Edinburgh's initial practical experiments with LOGO in the early 1970s were equivocal about the supposed benefits. Like the work at BB&N, the aim was to use LOGO as a means of enriching the teaching of classroom mathematics. The experiments involved forty 11-13 year old boys of average and below average ability. They came in groups of four to a laboratory at Edinburgh to work with LOGO outside normal school hours. At the start, the aim was to teach them what seemed to be useful programming concepts and techniques as recommended by Papert.

However, they needed so much time and so much individual help that it rapidly became clear that the unstructured approach suggested by Papert could probably not be managed in a UK classroom with one teacher and perhaps thirty pupils. The Edinburgh group therefore turned its attention to the problem of making LOGO manageable in a normal classroom setting. The work proceeded on two fronts: making the language easier to learn, and developing written materials to guide children's explorations with LOGO within the prevailing math syllabus. Rather than replace the existing syllabus with a new LOGO-based one, the Edinburgh group chose to introduce LOGO as a tool in a specific part of the existing syllabus, and to let the syllabus and LOGO shape each other.

The reservations about introducing LOGO in a fairly unstructured way have been recently confirmed by studies done at Bank Street College. Pea and Kurland [14,16] observed the effects on social interaction within a classroom, children's understanding of programming and the possible transfer of cognitive skills to other areas. They worked mainly with two classes, of 8-9 year olds and 11-12 year olds, who spent a year using a discovery learning approach to LOGO. Among other interesting results, it was found that many children acquired a wrong model of recursion, which persisted in many cases even after they were shown examples which disproved their beliefs. Pea and Kurland also found no difference in performance between those who had used LOGO for one year and a control group, on a planning task not directly related to programming. Their study recommended the use of guided instruction as well as discovery learning in using LOGO to impart thinking skills.

Between 1976 and 1978 in Edinburgh, the mainframe ELOGO system was used for a formal educational evaluation study, to investigate the benefits of LOGO for teaching mathematics to secondary school children. This study compared the changes in mathematical maturity of two groups drawn from a nearby school. Other studies, between 1976 and 1980, investigated whether LOGO could help trainee primary school teachers having mathematical difficulties to re-learn the concepts that caused them problems. In the main study, eleven boys aged 11-13 from a neighbouring school came to a special programming classroom in the AI department during normal school hours. The group was selected from the lowest achievers in mathematics; a control group was selected from among the somewhat higher achievers. The performance of the members of both groups was measured at the beginning, during, and at the end of the two-year experiment. Nationally standardised tests of such facets as "general scholastic ability," "basic mathematical knowledge" and "mathematical skills" were the basic instruments. During the first year the experimental group learned to program in LOGO. The aim was to make the boys feel comfortable with building and understanding programs, and to give them an adequate mental model of how the LOGO system worked. To do this, they worked through 33 self-paced worksheets on computational ideas such as procedures and recursion, problem-solving tactics such as top-down and bottom-up analysis, and debugging skills. In the second year they used their programming knowledge to explore selected topics in arithmetic, algebra and geometry, again with self-paced worksheets. The worksheets used two basic strategies:

(1) suggestions to construct LOGO procedures that could model certain aspects of the topic in question or could be used as tools in the topic under study. The suggestions had to be fairly specific, given the age and abilities of the boys. For example, "..Try to build a procedure called (name) which takes inputs (details). These should be (more details). The procedure should do (task specification). Try to use it to find out (problem statement). To help you, (list of hints).

(2) suggestions for the use of LOGO procedures created by project staff, if it would cost the boys too much effort to construct these themselves. The procedures again were tailored to the topic in question. For example, "..In this worksheet you will use the procedure (name) which you can load by (method). Here is an example of its use: (details). First use it to do (task 1),..."

This kind of worksheet used simple kinds of simulation written in LOGO, but sometimes went on to have the boys look at how the simulations were implemented by examining the code. The unstated aim was to give the experimental group a gentle introduction to computer modelling of suitably selected topics. The test results suggested that the gap between the groups had all but vanished by the end of the study. Attitude tests suggested that the experimental group had a much more positive attitude toward mathematics. This was independently confirmed by their school teachers and a school inspector. Further details of this project can be found in reference 13. The encouraging results were only suggestive; the groups were too small to allow convincing statistical analysis, and the experimental group was working in highly abnormal circumstances.

In contrast, the study mentioned above which aimed to help student teachers tackle their own weaknesses in mathematics before being required to teach the subject, highlighted some of the problems of the modelling approach to learning. In that study [8], although the teachers benefitted to the extent that the modelling activity showed many of them the need for clear and explicit reasoning in mathematics, they also met difficulties. Some failed to see how the programming work could be relevant to attacking their own weaknesses, and it proved hard to design projects directed towards the right areas of mathematics and within their programming competence. Often too much time had to be spent on programming, leaving too little time for applying their efforts. A more traditional "concept demonstration" approach using procedures created by project staff, but never even studied by the teachers, proved more successful.

In 1978 the AI department started a new project to see how things would work out in a secondary school classroom, with teachers managing the use of LOGO in normal math classes. Microcomputers were used, and a new version of LOGO was specially created during 1978-80. Among its many novel features, this version recorded all keyboard input, with timings, and stored it for later analysis. By the end of the project several megabytes of data had been accumulated. During 1979-80, teachers from a local secondary school that had volunteered to take part in the study came to the AI department to learn to program in LOGO, mainly by using the existing sets of worksheets. This proved far from ideal; they had no other computing experience and the worksheets were aimed at a considerably lower level of general maturity. The teachers offered valuable criticisms of the learning style those sheets embodied. The worksheets were redesigned with their aid.

The actual study was carried out during 1980-81, using 155 12-13 year old children in six undifferentiated mathematics classes. The numbers were divided 48%:52% between the three control classes and the three experimental classes. Six microcomputers with printing facilities were installed in a normal classroom, and the pupils in the experimental classes spent a portion of their normal mathematics lessons working in pairs at the computers. In the earlier study, the boys had averaged 40 hours of hands-on time during a year; in this study it was not possible for any class to average much more than 12 hours of actual hands-on time during a year, though they spent rather more than that in preparation away from the computer. Given six computers, a class size of around 30, and a weekly math allocation of 4 hours, the maximum hands-on time was about 15 hours.

The worksheets focused on a few topics judged by the teachers and project staff to be suitable for a LOGO modelling approach. Since the children had no computer experience, yet needed to feel that they were making progress in mathematics in the same way as the control group receiving more conventional teaching, it was necessary to teach them programming concepts and techniques at the same time as introducing them to LOGO modelling of those selected topics. Doing this was difficult and not wholly successful since the teachers were concerned with ensuring that each pair of pupils had a fair share of computing time, and so were forced to limit the time any pair could spend at a machine at one session. Fortunately, the children were already familiar with the notion of using worksheets, since the school already used structured sets of worksheets for teaching mathematics - the LOGO worksheets only needed to be integrated into the "flow pattern" of the existing set.

To illustrate the kind of modelling approach advocated by the worksheets, consider the topic of simple 2-D geometric transformations - rotation about a point, reflection in a line, and so on. Two methods were tried in this case. In one, the pupils were first encouraged to use the basic commands (FORWARD, RIGHT, etc.) to draw shapes and then to "transform" these line by line as necessary (so RIGHT becomes LEFT in reflections). Then they went on to devise procedures to draw the shapes, and were encouraged to experiment to see how, for example, variations in the variables affected the shapes. In the second approach, pupils were given an appropriate kit of procedures suitable for basic modelling of transformations. The kit included procedures such as REFLECT, which affected how AHEAD and TURN behaved. This allowed a somewhat higher level of modelling - a pupil who had devised a shape only had to give the command REFLECT and then draw it again without change in order to see its reflection. Both methods of presentation of the topic have their advantages. Which is the better will depend on issues such as how obtrusive the pupils find it to do the actual process of modifying their procedures. Details of the actual worksheets can be found in reference 9.

This study was designed as a psychometric evaluation again; though case-study methods have great benefits, they require considerably more manpower to use. Also, there is a limit to the amount of disruption of normal classroom practice that teachers will tolerate and that experimental design can allow. To have people "looking over the teachers shoulder" too much could have prejudiced the results of the project. Project staff did attend math lessons frequently, but only to serve as extra resources for the teacher when needed, for instance, to sort out operational problems with the microcomputers for individual pairs of children.

Nationally standardised tests were used again for "before" and "after" measurements. The results were striking and are given in detail in reference 13. One particularly interesting case is reproduced below. It compares the average scores on nationally standardised Mathematics Attainment tests at the start of the classroom phase with those at the end. A different test was used at the end from that used at the start, with the tests designed for specific age groups. The sample size was 129 rather than 155, since pupils who missed one or more of the tests were discounted.

CM: control group males (34) LM: LOGO group males (35)
CF: control group females (30) LF: LOGO group females (30)

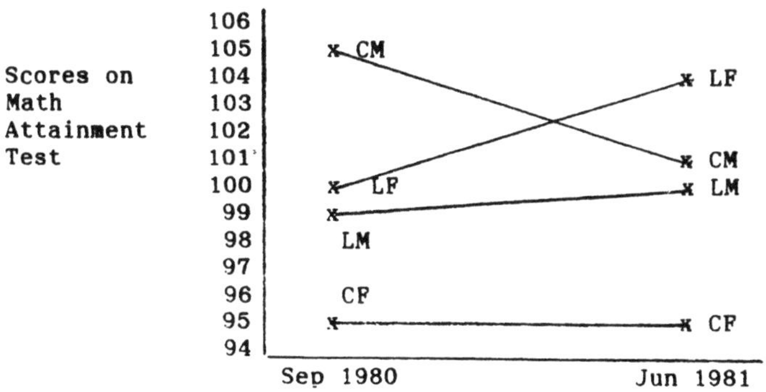

A test using eleven questions from material developed by the Chelsea College Project on Concepts in Secondary Math and Science showed a similar trend. The LOGO group average on each question equalled or exceeded that of the control group, except for the single control question whose topic had been taught to both groups by the same means. On that question there was no significant difference in performance.

These two results were the most striking, but they are only suggestive rather than conclusive. To put it in perspective, no pupil spent more than 10% of his math lessons on LOGO-related work. It would be interesting to see what effects might appear if it were possible for pupils to continue with LOGO-related work for several years. In later years the cognitive load imposed by having to know how to make use of LOGO would decrease dramatically relative to the load imposed by the new mathematical concepts they would meet.

5. SPECIFIC STUDIES: USING LOGO TO TEACH CONCEPTS OF PROCESS CONTROL

This section gives an account of recent work done by Paul Chung at Edinburgh for his Ph.D. thesis.

As the structure-vs-function discussion above suggests, LOGO is not always a good choice of language to support modelling work. One domain where standard LOGOs prove inadequate is in modelling the control of processes and machinery, one of the topics highlighted as vital by the Schools Working Party of the British Computer Society in 1980 [18]. At present this topic is taught to 11-13 year olds as part of a technology awareness course and to older pupils as part of electronics or computer science courses. In the former, the emphasis is on what control devices can do, rather than on how; in the latter it is on aspects of electronics and microprocessors. Neither stresses the analysis of questions such as what functionality is needed, how can it be achieved, and what kinds of information are needed for that. Chung developed a language called Concurrent-LOGO and experimental learning materials (principally worksheets) to fill this gap. Details of the language can be found in reference 5; details of a successful but small-scale study of its use by twelve 14-16 year old pupils in an Edinburgh secondary school over two school terms are to be published [6].

A language to let users model control algorithms and systems must provide convenient metaphors for entities such as sensors and actuators, and must provide control structures at the right structural level to allow users to experiment without becoming overburdened by computational issues. To this end, in Concurrent-LOGO sensors and actuators connected to the computer are viewed as objects in a sense similar to that used in Smalltalk. Each object has associated state and procedural information, for example, a simple electric lock has a state of "locked" or "open" and procedural information about how to lock or open. Each object is an instance of a general class of device and the user defines the properties of the class of device rather than that of each instance of the device. Thus, in an experiment to control a mechanical model of a lift, relevant classes might be DC-MOTOR (with one instance, the lift drive motor), BUTTON (with one at each floor) and SENSOR (with one at each floor to detect the arrival of the lift). Since a simple DC motor can at best be set turning only clockwise or anti-clockwise, the user can define only properties to make one turn in one direction or the other, make it stop, or find out in which of these states it is. The definitions are expressed in terms of fundamental classes called SWITCH and RECEIVER, which are in reality output and input bits on parallel ports on the computer. The user who wants to be involved in the lowest level of control that Concurrent-LOGO allows thus needs to know what each SWITCH controls and what each RECEIVER shows about the external devices.

Pupils who take courses in microelectronics and microprocessing need to learn about interrupts, polling and timing considerations before doing serious control experiments. To package this kind of detail in a comprehensible and useful way for pupils, Concurrent-LOGO provides several extra computing constructs beyond those offered by LOGO. These include:

WHEN condition action

- do the action when the condition becomes true, e.g.,
  WHEN RECEIVER 1' ON (PRINT [SOMEONE HAS ARRIVED])

WHENEVER condition action

- do the action whenever the condition is true, e.g.,
  WHENEVER :X > 200 (TURN 180)
  to make a robot platform turn round when it has gone too far.

FOREVER action

- do the action forever, till the user stops it by keyboard action.

action1 // action2

- do the actions in parallel, e.g.,
  FOREVER (BEEP) // OBEY.USER
  might be the command to make a robot platform beep continually while obeying the user's typed commands.

SWITCHes will obey a specialised command, ONUNTIL (condition) in addition to the basic commands such as ON and OFF. RECEIVERs will obey a specialised command, KEEPCOUNT, to keep count of the number of times the input signal has changed state. There are, of course, commands to examine and reset this count.

As a simple illustration, the LOGO command FORWARD can be redefined to command a robot platform:

```
FORWARD :X
     MOTOR 1   TURN.CLOCKWISE :X // MOTOR 2
     TURN.ANTICLOCKWISE :X
```

In the initial evaluation study, the pupils were able to do some non-trivial experiments with various external systems:

(1) a windmill, with one DC motor.

(2) a mechanical turtle with two DC motors which could be driven in either direction. One pupil was able to devise a method of controlling speed by pulsing the motors in parallel.

(3) a model lift with one DC motor and detector switches at each of three floors.

(4) a model house with burglar switches on each window, a front door bell switch, a DC motor for controlling the front door and two switches for limit sensing of the door.

(5) a mechanical turtle with stepping motors.

(6) a five-degree-of-freedom robot arm controlled by stepping motors. Prewritten procedures were provided to allow the pupils to tackle a higher level of control modelling with this more sophisticated device.

Success was measured by a specially designed test given afterwards and by case study methods, both looking for evidence of understanding of basic control concepts that would suggest how the course was working. Some details are available in reference 6. The main features of Concurrent-LOGO have excited interest to such an extent that they have been incorporated in a commercially available LOGO system, RM LOGO, designed to run on Research Machines Nimbus computers (which are 80186-based micros).

6. CONCLUSIONS

The research outlined has shown that computer modelling can be successful as a method of learning, but that it is certainly no less demanding on pupils and on teachers than simulation or other kinds of computer-assisted instruction. There is some suggestive evidence that the extra benefits are worth the extra efforts, although it is essential to design the software and materials very carefully. Our experience has been that a controlled discovery learning approach is practicable, in the context of certain Scottish schools at least. It is not clear whether the results reported could be repeated in schools of other educational systems, nor is it clear whether the recent flurry of interest in school computing in the UK would alter the results, were these experiments to be repeated now.

7. REFERENCES

[1] Anderson, J.R. (ed), Cognitive Skills and Their Acquisition, Lawrence Erlbaum, 1981.

[2] Anthony, W.S., "Learning to discover rules by discovery," Journal of Educational Psychology, 64, 325-8, 1973.

[3] Boden, M., Piaget, Fontana, 1979.

[4] Case, R., "General developmental influences on the acquisition of elementary concepts and algorithms in arithmetic," in Carpenter, Moser and Rombey (eds). Addition And Subtraction: A Cognitive Perspective, Lawrence Erlbaum, 1982.

[5] Chung, P., "Concurrent-LOGO: a language for teaching control applications," DAI Research paper no. 243, Dept. of AI, Edinburgh 1984.

[6] Chung, P., in Robotics in Education, ed. Colin Terry, Croom Helm, 1985 (to appear).

[7] diSessa, A., "A Principled Design for an Integrated Computational Environment,: MIT AI Memo ?? 1982.

[8] du Boulay, J.B.H., "Teaching teachers mathematics through programming" International Journal of Math Education in Science and Technology, 11 (3), 347-360, 1982.

[9] Edinburgh LOGO Group, "Teaching Mathematics Through LOGO Programming: Teacher's Notes and Example Pupil Worksheets," DAI Occasional Paper Nos. 38-41, Dept. of AI, Edinburgh, 1984.

[10] Gentner, D. and Stevens, A. (eds), Mental Models, Lawrence Erlbaum, 1982.

[11] Hewitt, C., "An Artificial Intelligence Perspective," in Brody et al (eds.), On Conceptual Modelling, Springer-Verlag 1984.

[12] Hinton, T., Computer Education, 2, 71-88, 1978.

[13] Howe, J.A.M., Ross, P.M., Johnson, K.R., Plane, F and Inglis, R., "Learning Mathematics through LOGO Programming: the transition from laboratory to classroom," DAI working paper 118(b), Dept. of AI, University of Edinburgh, 1982.

[14] Kurland, D.M. and Pea, R.D., "Children's mental models of recursive LOGO programs," Technical Report No. 10, New York: Center for Children and Technology, Bank Street College of Education, 1983.

[15] Pascual-Leone, J., "A mathematical model for the transition rule in Piaget's developmental stages," Acta Psychologica 32, 301-345, 1970.

[16] Pea, R.D. and Kurland, D.M., "Logo programming and the development of planning skills," Technical Report No. 16, New York: Center for Children and Technology, Bank Street College of Education, 1983.

[17] Scandura, J.M., et al, "An unexpected relationship between failure and subsequent mathematics learning," Educational Studies in Mathematics 1, 247-151, 1969.

[18] Schools Committee Working Party, "Syllabuses for the future," London: British Computer Society, 1980.

[19] Tawney, D.A., Simulation and Modelling in Science Computer Assisted Learning, C.E.T., London, 1976.

[20] Teitelbaum, T. and Reps, T., "The Cornell Program Synthesizer: A Syntax Directed Programming Environment," Dept. of Computer Science Technical Report TR 80-421, Cornell University, 1980.

[21] Trown, E.A., "Some evidence on the interaction between teaching strategy and personality," British Journal of Educational Psychology, 40, 209-211, 1970.

[22] Trown, E.A. and Leith, G.O.M., "Decision rules for teaching strategies in primary schools: Personality - treatment interactions," British Journal of Educational Psychology, 45, 130-140, 1975.

TOWARD AN INDUSTRIAL APPROACH TO EDUCATIONAL SOFTWARE DEVELOPMENT

Jef Moonen
Centre for Education & Information Technology
Enschede, Netherlands

1. THE DEVELOPMENT OF EDUCATIONAL SOFTWARE IN THE NETHERLANDS

Educational software is defined as software which is developed for use in or applied to education. The production of educational software is a new activity. Until recently, experience in the Netherlands was mainly concentrated within university education and in projects in primary and secondary education supported by universities. These developments were mostly achieved with the aid of mainframe computers. Generally, the final product did not comprise a single lesson, but instead more or less it contained a number of coherent lessons.

The introduction of the microcomputer has brought changes to education. Individuals and organizations with more limited computer facilities now have the opportunity to produce educational software. This production is carried out on non-complex microcomputers and generally results in individual lessons. These small lessons are made available only on the microcomputers on which they are developed. The expertise, which until recently could only be achieved through close cooperation of teams of academics supported by university computing centres, with advanced hardware and software at their disposal, is now available to individuals with only very limited facilities as far as application software and equipment is concerned.

Currently many teacher/programmers are working with enthusiasm in their free time to produce much educational software.

NATO ASI Series, Vol. F 23
Designing Computer-Based Learning Materials
Edited by A. Bork and H. Weinstock

The publishers of educational materials now accept this procedure, although some facilitate the distribution of tasks between (teams of) teachers and programmers.

Several illustrative examples follow:

a. <u>Development in a University Environment</u>

In early 1974, a start was made at the Department of Psychology of the University of Leiden with the development of computer-aided modules in support of a course in Statistics. The package entitled LEISTAT was intended as a (partial) substitute for practical exercises and a part of the examination in Statistics. Originally, it was only a "one-man-project"; the statistics lecturer determined the content of the modules and also developed the programs. He was assisted by the use of a main-frame computer provided by the university's computing centre - generally an IBM 370/158 type.

The program was developed in APL, since this was the only interactive programming language then available. After the first modules had been written, and after an evaluational assessment, the broad structure of the package was established. Further activities were then delegated to a number of assistants. These assistants too, determined, in their own manner, the content of the modules, and finalized the programming. In this way, 62 lessons could be programmed. At a later stage conversion to a computer of the IBM 5100 type and the PLATO system was carried out. Modifications became necessary because of new releases of operating systems and programming languages. These activities were carried out by programmers specially recruited for that purpose. Changes in curricula also necessitated the continuous modification of the content of the modules.

The LEISTAT package has been operational for more than 10 years, and is used by more than 200 to 300 students per year. During it's operation, it has been continuously adapted to changing circumstances. On the basis of these experiences, a number of conclusions can be drawn.

- It is rather difficult for a teacher - but not impossible - to specialize both in the pedagogical design and in the programming of those designs. As far as the latter is concerned, this only can be carried out for a limited period of time. The evolution of operating systems and programming languages makes it impossible for him or her to remain a specialist in that field.

- The construction of a pedagogical design is a difficult task which requires both a detailed knowledge of the subject in itself, as well as wide experience in the didactic approach toward students. This task is hardly one to be entrusted to newly trained teachers.

- As soon as one entrusts specific programming activities to specialists, problems in communication arise between them and the teacher who carried out the pedagogical design. Well thought out selections in the pedagogical design are not always assessed by the programmer according to their true value, and therefore are sometimes considered less relevant than are less complex solutions from a programming point of view. At later stages, this results in a time-consuming process of review and change.

- Programmers are apt to maintain the wrong priorities with relation to the desired objective. It is difficult for them to keep to tight schedules, since the developed product - in their opinion - can always be further modified and programmed much more perfectly and efficiently.

- During the initial stages of the design of LEISTAT, insufficient attention was paid to the careful registration of student data. When, at a later stage, it was necessary to produce practical surveys of the registered data and to process these data, much time had to be invested in the adaptation of the software.

- The effective use of the work station and the system by the student was stressed in a demonstration session. Subsequently, each student had to carry out an interactive introductory lesson using the system. Finally, a written set of guidelines on the use of the system was distributed. Nevertheless, a number of students did not really master working with the system.

- In general, universities do not follow an organized and systematic approach in the development of educational software. This is due to lack of experience in this field, and also due to the fact that such activities are mainly carried out within or in relation to research projects. The need to work within budgets and time schedules also generally plays an insignificant role in university environments.

b. Development in a "Higher Education Environment"

At the beginning of 1980, a joint project was initiated to develop computer-aided learning modules in mathematics: participants included the University of Leiden (Department of Psychology) and two Schools for Higher Economic and Administrative Education (Management Schools) in the Hague. This project was aimed at yielding a large number of computer-aided learning modules for the support of students who, in the transition from higher education to university education, were deficient in knowledge of mathematics, and who were required to supplement that knowledge. The project was also initiated to carry out research on a number of organizational problems: the project was to be developed for two different groups (university students and students following higher educational training courses), for two different computer configurations (a TERAK microcomputer and a PDP 11/34), and with two different operating systems (UCSD-PASCAL and UNIX). For the programming language, two versions of PASCAL were chosen. The project organization proposed distribution of the tasks to be carried out: the construction of a pedagogical design, the system design, and the progrmaming of the lessons. A project coordinator, five experienced mathematics teachers, and two small teams of programmers at both the Hague and Leiden were employed.

Budgetary restrictions and the desire to appoint experienced personnel resulted in the fact that several of those appointed were only able to fulfill tasks on a part-time basis, working several hours per week on the project.

In the initial stages of the project, the basic context could be determined - choice, sequence and individual coherence of the various subjects - and the broad structure of the system design established. Subsequently, an agreement was reached with regard to the schedule to be followed in the further development of the pedagogical design of each module, the distribution of individual activities, and consultation between teachers, project coordinator and programming teams, the compilation of the entire documentation, and the manner in which it was to be implemented. The project was planned for 2 years, after which prolongation was permitted.

With regard to this project, several conclusions can be drawn:

- The appointment of project personnel in part-time positions was disastrous. In the search for experienced personnel, one is dependent on persons involved in the project on a part-time basis. It is extremely difficult for them to establish priorities and to keep to set schedules. One must appoint a staff which either involves specific full-time positions, or - if restricted by available budgets or existing appointments - which involves "detached personnel" on a full-time basis for limited durations of time. Only then can their full effort and devotion to the project be expected, and only then can there be time for necessary consultation.

- Although experienced mathematics teachers had been appointed, it appeared that their experience could hardly be translated in terms of good pedagogical design of computer-aided material. Proposals were generally restricted to the automation of classical written exercises. True originality, in which the capabilities of the computer were applied functionally, was hardly ever achieved.

- Two teams of programmers worked on the project: one at the Hague, and the other at Leiden (at some 15 km distance). Although it was intended that the teams maintained continuous contact for purposes of consultation and that developments made by one team could be employed by the other, this did not work in practice. Both teams worked entirely on an individual basis, even up to the level of system design.

- PASCAL was the selected programming language. Reasons for this choice were to increase compatibility between, and to simplify, the conversion of code to other computers at a later stage. At the Hague, it appeared that the PASCAL version on the PDP 11/34 did not meet set requirements, which necessitated the transfer to the language C. At Leiden, the programmer was not familiar with PASCAL, and could not feel comfortable with the editing capacity on the TERAK. To speed work, it was decided that a transfer should be made to a GIGI terminal, connected to a main frame of the university's computer centre, so that APL could be used as the programming language. This made communication between the two teams of programmers even more difficult, and led to stagnation of the exchange of the developed lesson modules.

- Great problems in communication resulted between programmers and teachers, firstly due to the fact that part-time assignment to the project made consultations at agreed times difficult. Furthermore, there was little understanding of someone else's "language" and intentions.

- Teachers doing project work part time were often forced to discontinue their work. Subsequently, other teachers were assigned to their tasks, and this often led to renewed discussion on agreements already reached with the previously assigned teachers with regard to the content, sequence, design, etc., of the lessons to be developed.

- Insufficient account was taken of the organizational problems associated with implementation. Within the university environment this did not lead to immense problems, since the students themselves were less committed to set schedules for their lessons, and could follow computer training at times which were more conveniently suited to their needs. This could not be said for the 2 schools at the Hague. One was a day School for Higher Economic and Administrative Education, the other open only in the evenings. Although both schools used the same computer, programs were kept separate. Day students, therefore, could not work during the evenings, and the opposite was the case for those following evening classes. Also, students were committed to strict schedules which left relatively little time for computer lessons to be done on an experimental basis.

- The broad conclusion which can be drawn from the results of this project is that it lacked a systematic approach, as well as good coordination. The latter partly resulted from the fact that the coordination of the project had to be carried out on a part-time basis. Furthermore, insufficient attention was paid to good documentation and to the problems encountered with the implementation in the educational sector for which the project was intended.

c. Development in a Primary and Secondary School Environment.

After the microcomputer had appeared on the market at the end of the 1970's, and schools could acquire such equipment, many enthusiastic teachers throughout the Netherlands started the development of educational software. The computers available to them were Commodore (4032 and 8032), Tandy (TRS models I & III), and Apple II. These were later supplemented with Commodore 64, the BBC computer, the New Brain, the Philips P 2000T, and the Aster CT-80. Enthusiastic teachers attempted to do all development work without assistance from others. BASIC was the principal language used for programming, since only this was available on those computers. Many, with or without the support of hobby-computer groups became specialists in the use of these microcomputers.

Then, it was rapidly discovered that the memory capacity of the computers used was restricted (first to some 8 K, later to 32 and 48 K bytes capacity). This led to even more inventiveness in solving some of the technical problems.

Later the concentration of user groups in the Netherlands led to an agreement with regard to the use of the BASICODE-protocol, so that the exchange of programs between various computers could be enhanced. A user's association entitled DIDACOM published a guide for the uniform use of BASIC in education.

Small scale, non-subsidized projects developed; those involved were enthusiastically devoted to their work, convinced that they were engaged in something entirely new. At a later stage they became frustrated because time and equipment constraints prevented them from developing their promising ideas. Personal (financial) investments only led to increased costs and no prospect for extra income. Requests to publishing companies to market the courseware which had been developed were hardly ever granted. Exploitation on a personal basis, or through computer groups, often resulted in disappointment due to the illegal practice of copying software.

Several general remarks also can be made with regard to these developments:

- Ignoring limited exceptions, many of the programs developed lacked the originality relevant to use in education. Good ideas were introduced in endless variations: these included such material as spelling exercises,

exercises in foreign language word games, arithmetic exercises in all possible forms and grades and exercises in place names.

- Successful implementation often remains restricted to one's own school environment and is therefore largely dependent on existing enthusiasm. Those programs offered no contribution to structural changes, let alone to the improvement of education itself.

- The experience just described still continues. For each frustrated teacher who gives up such activity, three others are diligently waiting to attempt the impossible. This inevitably results in an enormous waste of enthusiasm and effort.

d. Development through Educational Publishers

While adopting a "wait-and-see" policy, together with the basic attitude of investigating market potential, for several years a limited number of publishers in the Netherlands have been active in the development of educational software. At first, attempts were made by those publishers to develop software by introducing a cooperative, government-subsidized corporation. However, these plans were discontinued because of the diverse interests of each publishing company. A number of these companies had already laid the foundation for their own development projects, and were not willing to share with others the advances they had made.

The procedures followed by publishers still show no coherent pattern. Much of the educational software published is foreign software which has been translated. Most of the published educational software does not correspond to the learning materials (mainly text-books) previously published by the same companies. The translation of such material is mostly done by small teams of programmers. These programs are intended to investigate the market potential of educational software. A few publishers attempt to publish products more systematically, so that the software will correspond to other products previously introduced. This development is assisted by the use of teacher/authors, responsible for both the texts and the coordination of the software development. In other situations, teams of teachers work together in a pedagogical design coherent with existing textbooks, to be coded by programmers to produce the end product.

Although based on limited experience, the following can be said of this development:

- Problems arise because publishers are forced to specify a given computer. If that given computer fails to develop a strong market, the market potential for that software is reduced. The rapid change in the computer market puts the publishers at risk. In the Netherlands some computer manufacturers have gone bankrupt despite controlling a large fraction of the market in educational products.

- Schools (especially) in the Netherlands have a large diversity of equipment at their disposal. A recent inquiry to secondary schools (March 1985) by the COI shows that 52% of these schools have two types of computers, the Commodore C-64 and the Philips 2000 T. The remaining 48% is distributed among more than 30 types. Unless compatible software can be developed for a larger number of microcomputer types, the market share that can be acquired remains too restricted. Software development can be made a profitable enterprise only if the software is developed for many different types of computers at reasonable prices, or if it is developed for the most popular computers.

- There are signals - especially from the United States and Great Britain - that publishers will discontinue their contributions to educational software if the outlook for profitability of these activities does not take a turn for the better.

e. Development of Government-Subsidized Projects.

There is great need for educational software. It is for this reason that the Netherlands government has subsidized projects developing educational software. One of these projects is currently being developed by the "Stichting voor de Leerplanontwikkeling" (SLO) (National Institute for Curriculum Development). In this project, educational software is being developed for information technology in secondary education.

This software is being developed for two types of computer: the Philips 2000T and the Aster CT-80. These are 8-bit computers which have been selected by the government as standard equipment within the framework of the "100-Schools Project." In this project - which has taken place between August 1983 and June 1985, 100 schools had been provided with 8 computers on loan from the government, in support of the introduction of information technology in education.

Initially a concept curriculum for information technology was developed. In consultation with a team of teachers, specially formed for this objective, content and accompanying computer programs were developed. Subsequently, a team programmed the educational software.

Problems were caused by the limited computer capability, both in relation to the development of the software, and in relation to the usefulness of that software for the lessons.

It also was known that the selected computers could remain up to date for a limited time only. The question then arose: What should be done with the previously developed software? If it was decided that the previously developed software was to be adapted, how were the attendant costs to be supported?

Another project is being undertaken by the Centre for Education and Information Technology (COI) and the Netherlands Institute for Audio-Visual Aids (NIAM). This entails the translation of selected programs from the Scottish Micro-Electronics Development Program (SMDP). These are mainly computer-aided learning programs. Here, one is faced with the problem of the selection of the computers to be applied, and the software to be translated for those computers. Of significance here are the financial difficulties met, and the conditions set by the government. The government is prepared only to finance this project for a limited period, which means that after the finalization of the project by the NIAM which is also entrusted with product distribution, that the project must be profitable to the NIAM. So the translation and adaptation should be carried out for the greatest possible number of computers and at the lowest possible costs.

One conclusion which can be drawn from these examples is that there is a particular need for very powerful development and conversion aids. In this way, conversion and development for the benefit of a greater number of machines can be carried out much quicker. This also means that the price of the final product will probably be kept within acceptable budgetary limits, and that a reasonable profit can be made by the producers.

Yet another project has been set up by IBM and a number of secondary schools, which were granted computer hardware by IBM. The aim of the project is to develop courseware, especially for mathematics and the Dutch language. The development approach is team-oriented; phases of pedagogical design, system design, coding and review are involved. The problems encountered can be summarized as follows:

- Teachers are not accustomed to work out in detail the steps in the development of a pedagogical analysis, nor are they concerned with how something put down on paper will appear on the screen.

- From the limited number of trails with students, it is already clear that a great number of proposals for changes in the courseware will be made.

- The organizational aspect of producing the pedagogical design is very difficult: one must look for a balanced view between strong leadership and real influence of the teachers who are involved in the work.

- At first, the project participants chose an authoring language to code the programs. This was not a success because of the constraints of both the language and the hardware. A decision was taken to switch to PASCAL. Subsequently, they were confronted with the fact that one has to create all the required subroutines.

f. <u>Summary</u>

The projects illustrated are a random sample of the development activities carried out in the Netherlands in the field of educational software.

A number of broad conclusions can be drawn:

1 - A great number of projects have been initiated from a research point of view. The result is that a product and a research-oriented procedure are hardly compatible.

2 - Single-individual efforts eventually must incorporate more people, or else fail as a result of the frustrations of insufficient recognition, insufficient compensation for the investment made or insufficient perspectives with regard to the work which is to be carried out.

3 - There is a considerable shortage of professional designers of educational software. Even experienced teachers have great difficulty in achieving originality in the pedagogical design, whereas, in general, it is considered that wide experience in education is a necessary condition for its success. It is also apparent that this characteristic is not sufficient in itself.

4 - In a team-oriented approach, it appears that communication between teams of teachers and teams of programmers forms a large obstacle. Both groups speak different "languages" and do not readily understand the problems of the other.

5 - It also appears that, within a team of teachers, it is difficult (but not impossible) to reach agreements in relation to a common pedagogical approach.

6 - Although it is conceived that the production of educational software must involve a multidisciplinary approach between subject-area specialists, one hardly takes account of experience already known for years in the computing profession, and from what is known as essential in a project approach.

7 - The direct development of educational software on target machines is hindered, at least as far as the limited capacity of those (8-bit) target machines is concerned. This restriction affects the quality of the final product, the time investment

necessary, and the possibilities to convert to other target machines. [Editorial note: Currently 8-bit machines are relatively unimportant.]

8 - Discussions on the use of general programming languages, authoring languages or authoring systems are still going on.

9 - Publishers need support from the government (financially, or through policy decisions) in order to reduce the risks they encounter when introducing their educational software into the commercial market. Because of the uncertainty about the profitability of these kinds of activities, there is some question as to whether this support will become necessary on a permanent basis.

10 - Educational software is like any other educational material: it becomes obsolete. None of these materials will remain available for an indefinite period of time. It will be necessary to adapt or modify this material, forced by changing circumstances in curricula and new technical developments. In the software industry, it is known that 30-60% of the total cost of the products comprise the "maintenance" of programs.

g. Consequences

Neither a strict individual approach, nor a strictly separated procedure of teachers and programmers, offers the real solution. The individual approach is impossible to maintain if one aims at large-scale and professional production. The other approach has the disadvantage that the communication between teams, in relation to the nature of the desired product, becomes extremely difficult. This results mainly from a lack of standards and concrete forms in relation to educational software.

Because educational software is a relatively new entity in education itself, it is not easy to determine in advance, the actual desires of the potential user. When the completion of the final product is almost reached, the potential user then realizes which parts are desirable and which are not. This means that, during development, evaluation must be done continuously.

At this time (in the Netherlands), production strategies are as follows:

	higher education	secondary education	primary education
Individual approach	x	x	x
Team approach	x	x	
Project approach	x		
Industrial approach			

In the individual approach, the whole project is carried out by one individual. In the team approach, different teams are responsible for the pedagogical design, the system design, the coding, and the evaluation. The project approach lays emphasis on the use of professional project-management techniques. In the industrial approach, the production of educational software must become profitable for the book publishers, software houses, and computer manufacturers. As seen in the table above, none of the educational sectors have achieved an industrial approach toward educational software.

From an educational point of view, publishers must produce educational software that can be integrated into existing curricula. This can be achieved, for example, by presenting software as a content-oriented supplement to different parts of textbooks.

It is common to be able to choose from among different textbooks. This also should be the case for educational software. Because of the high cost involved, one can question whether the opportunity to select specific software will ever occur. A solution to this problem is to make educational software easily adaptable to new situations, by creating possibilities for teachers/users to modify existing software. This kind of solution led to two complications:

- Who owns the copyright of the product after it has been modified?

- There are major technical problems involved in making it possible for teachers, with no programming experience, to be able to modify complex software to meet their needs.

Concerning the second complication, a number of strategies can be followed:

- Creating so-called "semi-products"; these are programs with a fixed general structure and which must be supplemented with relevant text, graphics, and illustrative material by the teacher.

- Products which can be modified by teachers using specialized user-friendly software tools.

At the same time, this approach could offer a solution in situations in which educational software has become outdated. Developments of this kind must be devised in laboratory situations. At a later stage in this article, this will be referred to as "level 1 development."

One must realize that it is necessary to push developments toward the industrial approach. This means that the development of educational software must become more project oriented, based on economic considerations. Only in this way can educational software be made affordable to schools. This situation has not yet been achieved. Meanwhile, development is in a transitional phase, from "grassroot activities" to industrial approaches. This is an extremely critical phase.

Because of financial reasons, there will be some pressure to accelerate the process of development. On the other hand, it is essential that both teachers and students remain involved in this development process. Organizing this process in a practical manageable manner, is the principal problem with which one is confronted.

2. METHODOLOGY

2.1 Introduction

Educational software has been developed and applied for more than 20 years. This has led to numerous proposals with regard to the methodological approach to the development of educational software. One of these proposals is the "Author's Guide" by Peters and Johnson (CONDUIT, 1978). This guide was first intended as an aid to those authors who wished to distribute their material through CONDUIT. Here, the following distribution of tasks and activities was illustrated:

- design:
  - learn about the media
  - consider a systematic approach

- development:
  - using the computer to reach your objectives
  - developing your materials

- style
  - writing style
  - computer-student communication
  - programming style

- packaging
  - organization
  - student guide
  - instructor's guide
  - installation guide
  - abstract
  - review

This guide was published at a time when the development of educational software was carried out exclusively on mainframe computers. One characteristic here was the direct feedback for the commercial publication of the product. This is especially apparent from the stage entitled "packaging."

This approach was proposed by CONDUIT when the development of educational software on mainframes had been carried out for more than 10 years. It was in about this time that it became even more apparent that the subsidization of the development of educational software would become even more difficult. This resulted in an increasing interest and desire to follow a more commercial pattern. The introduction of the microcomputer called an early halt to this process, and as though nothing had been learned from past experience, the process of learning and experiencing started anew. Now, after many years, again there is a general tendency to realize that the use of educational software will survive only if it can become a commercial success. This is one of the reasons for the present interest in its commercialization and the more industrially-oriented approach. Meanwhile, one is growing increasingly convinced of the fact that, with the more industrially-oriented approach, an explicit distinction should be made between the various phases in the development of educational software.

It is in particular Alfred Bork who has carried out pioneering work in this area. In all proposed software developments, one or more of the following procedures are followed:

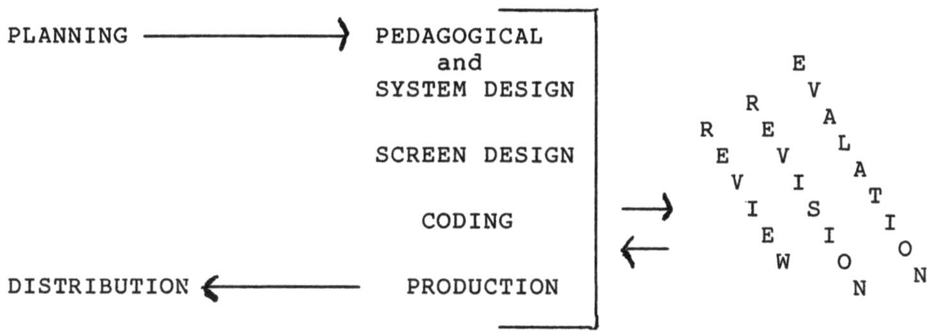

Figure 1

2.2. An Ideal Solution?

What is the ideal solution to the development of educational software? What are the obstacles to the solution to this problem? Have there been systems in the past which could be considered as the ideal solution?

From the discussion earlier in this paper, three separate aspects may be considered which form obstacles in the development of educational software:

- pedagogical developers must have a powerful development environment available;

- during the process of development, it is necessary to have continual interaction between developers and the target group (teachers and students);

- one should note the large variety of computers so that development for a single system is insufficient.

In the past, the PLATO system marketed by Control Data Corporation (CDC) offered the best possible solution. During the period from 1978 until 1981, the Universities of Amsterdam and Leiden experimented with the PLATO system. They intended that this system be made available to all Dutch universities. The advantages of this system were that the developers had the availability of a powerful development environment. That environment was continually extended and maintained by CDC. Also, provisions were made for a continuously increasing series of auxiliary routines. With these development aids, it was possible to provide for the on-line consultation of programming experts. There was also the availability of a worldwide network, partly on-line, for communication with colleagues. Finally, one had at one's disposal an on-line consultancy with a very extensive library of educational software, in which the initiation of ideas through one's own development effort was considered as quite relevant.

Despite these advantages, the PLATO system was not a success, due partially to financial factors. The high cost occurred because students used terminals connected to a large mainframe computer. Not only was this an inherently expensive operation, but there were high additional costs due to telephone charges for geographically scattered terminals linked to a single mainframe computer. Later, CDC introduced a decentralized PLATO microcomputer. Even so, the cost of this system was exceptionally high in comparison to other microcomputers. The PLATO concept should be thoroughly investigated and subsequently translated in terms of present computer technology, with its attendant reduction in cost.

In the search for an ideal solution, it is important to consider not only technical, but also organizational problems. Further, it should be established that the development of educational software should take place at three different levels:

Level 1: Development of an experimental program carried out in a laboratory environment;

Level 2: Development of a prototype carried out in specialized institutes adapted for that purpose, and capable of organizing consultations in an efficient manner with the target group of the product.

Level 3: Production of educational programs for various target-machines by following an industrial procedure within which the relation between cost and income plays an essential role.

a. Level 1 Development

The development of experimental programs occurs in laboratory environments, using computers in new types of applications. These developments occur without direct feedback to the potential target groups. The development generally comprises a research-oriented component aimed at either the development tools used (hardware facilities, programmming languages, programming environments), or at learning or instruction theories. Experimental programs can be developed so that new input and output facilities (e.g., "mouse", touch-screen, speech input and output) are integrated; and extensive use can be made of graphic and window facilities, or animations; and intelligence can be added to programs. Such development efforts are made in universities or specialized institutes.

b. Level 2 Development

This is the level of development which demands the most attention. Until now most developments have taken place at this particular level - refer to Section 1. This occurred in either a strictly individual context, or in a more team-directed context. In most cases, attempts were made to market the product after it had been developed. However, this generally led to various additional difficulties with regard to conversion, and to extra cost. Thus, it is not attractive to commercial vendors.

Recently, it was thought that the development of administrative software could be used as a model for the development of educational software. For administrative software, the product can be completely specified by the requirements of the user. This situation does not (yet) apply in education. It is not generally realized that the use of computers in education is still evolving. It is for this reason that it is difficult for the ultimate users to indicate initially exactly what is required. There is also the fact that available equipment continually changes in such a way that many new didactic approaches are possible. All users of computers in education find themselves in a continual learning process which leads to new views and demands.

The consequences of this are that educational software must be developed in an iterative fashion. During the development activities the possibilities for interaction between developers and representatives of the target group are of essential importance. It becomes quite obvious that this does not adapt well to the industrial approach. The first step toward a solution is, therefore, the separation of the development in two levels. The first level (i.e., level 2 development) must provide a tested prototype which is well documented and accompanied by detailed specifications.

Level 2 development has a number of significant constituents:

- the establishment of a pedagogical design;

- the establishment of a system design and the programming of the prototype;

- the evaluation of the prototype (by teachers and students) by means of pilot projects.

From an organizational point of view, emphasis should be placed on:

- the fact that the pedagogical designers should be well aware of the requirements of those in the field of education and of the capabilities of the available technology;

- the interaction between the pedagogical designers and the programmers of the prototype;

- the technical aids which the programmers must have at their disposal; this must be equipment on which advanced development tools are available.

The most significant problem is the smooth organization of this kind of cooperative activity. The development of educational software at level 2 is primarily an organizational problem.

c. Level 3 Development

After the final specifications of the desired product have been established, the production of the software should be initiated in an economically effective manner. The interaction with the target group has already been completed in the previous stage and is no longer of significance at this stage. Because the entire specifications are available, one now can concentrate on the search for the most efficient development tools. Also, from the beginning of the level 3 development, the various target machines to be utilized can be taken into account. One is able to make a sensible choice between development on advanced equipment, and the conversion to target machines on completion, or to choose the direct development on various target machines. Combinations of these procedures also may be considered.

The "level 3 development" preferably takes place in an industrial environment. In an industrial environment, the correct atmosphere and experience is present. This is required in order to think and act in strictly economic terms. At the same time, a direct contact can be made with those firms which will introduce the end product to the market.

2.3. Broad Methodological Approach

The production of experimental programs by specialized institutions is not considered in this illustration. The procedure followed will differ from institution to institution, depending on the nature of the research and the selected aids, i.e., equipment and software. The experimental program, however, also has a service function, in particular as a library of ideas for use by others. It appears that, as soon as one knows which new and advanced possibilities are at one's disposal, there is a fanatic pursuit to make those capabilities available to a much wider circle of potential users. Illustrations of this can be found in the developments with relation to window software, the use of icons, the use of the so-called "mouse", and the large-scale implementation of comparable possibilities on such equipment as the Macintosh and Atari 5020ST.

Developers of experimental programs must keep abreast of newly developed products. For this reason, it is useful for those institutions active in the design of experimental programs to be involved in the wide national initiation of the development of educational software. With regard to the methodology used, however, each of these organizations follows its own individual procedures.

The broad methodological approach in the level 2 and 3 developments has been illustrated in figure 2. Here, a distinction must be made between the development of a prototype, and the production and distribution of the final product. The development of a prototype entails planning, design and the coding with ongoing review, evaluation and revision. This process must lead to a well documented, and fully

Development levels

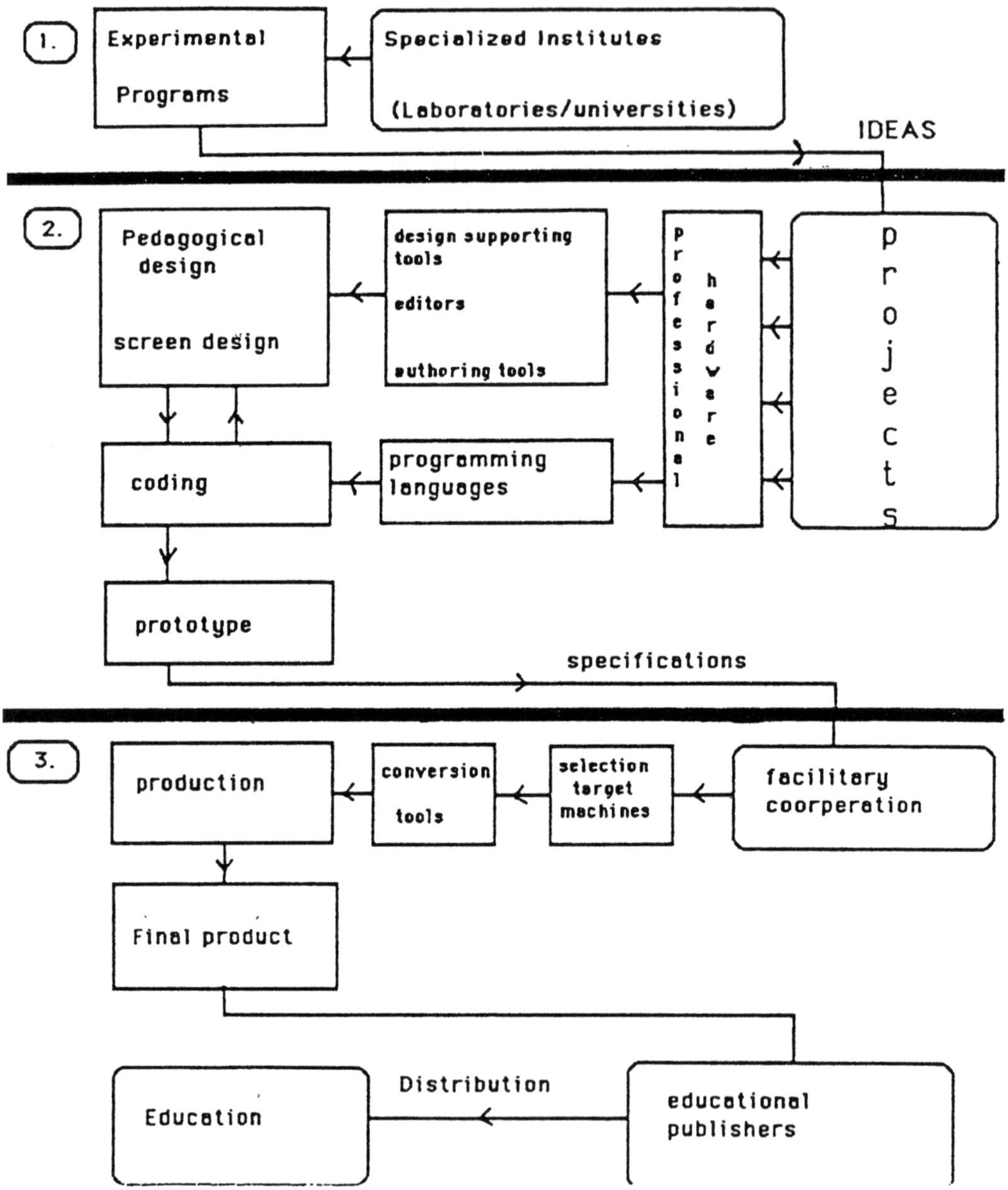

Figure 2

specified prototype. The development of this prototype should be carried out on equipment which is more advanced than the equipment used by the target group to whom it is made available. The evaluation also should be carried out on advanced equipment. Here, one might involve a specially selected target group within the potential group at which it is aimed. The use of more advanced equipment also means that more advanced programming tools can be applied. This is of great significance in the efficient organization of the iterative process which is indispensable at this stage of the development.

It has already been mentioned that the development process entails special development techniques. Because program interaction is essential to produce a quality product, an iterative process to allow for modifications must be built into the specification stage. Therefore, during the initial stages of the pedagogical design, one should carefully consider making available a number of user-friendly editors to the specialists involved in this design. In this context, one should have editors for text, graphics, animation, simulation, speech, creation of characters, and answer recognition and analysis. Various authoring systems already provide these facilities. Additionally, one should consider the use of authoring tools in which specific forms of computer-aided learning have been introduced: tutorials, drill-and-practice exercises, quizzes, etc. The so-called Author Application Models published by CDC in the PLATO-Courseware Development (PCDI) Program are product-line examples of this particular approach. Included in PCDI is a Certification Testing Model, a Graphics Simulation Model, an Advanced Tutorial Model and a Drill-and-Practice Model.

The use of these aids does not necessarily result in a ready to use program. The aids must enable the designer, in a simple fashion, to transfer ideas to the screen. If desired, a programmer could be used. The significance of this approach lies in the fact that the design team can pay constant attention to technical content, while newly created ideas can be rapidly assessed through screen presentation. This process is fruitful in contributing to the quality of the final product. Moreover, a computer program could enable the output of a well documented printout of activities after each design activity has taken place. This process must lead to a functional design. Characteristic of this process is the speed at which it can be produced.

The result is a product which is technically incomplete and only temporary. Subsequently, the functional design must be further developed and polished by the programmer. The programmer uses those programming tools which are most efficient and which offer the greatest possible flexibility, for example, a powerful programming language supplemented with an extensive collection of useful procedures. In order to stimulate exchange with other development groups, possibly in other countries, one should employ a language common to a wide variety of operating systems.

The approach chosen involves a prototype which is evaluated after use by first one student and subsequently by a group of students. This inevitably leads to program revision which must be carried out in an efficient manner. Eventually, this process will produce a definitive final version, fully documented. On the basis of this final version, the various products are programmed for specific computers. Consultation between designers and users is then no longer necessary.

3. Conclusion

At the end of the 1970's, there was over ten years of experience with computer-based learning, but a definite breakthrough in education had not yet been achieved. One can say that computer-based learning was saved from extinction at that time by the introduction of the micro-computer. A new wave of enthusiasm arose, and the whole process of considering the use of computers in learning situations started again.

Now, five or six years later, one is confronted with the same problem: Will there be a real breakthrough for computer-based learning? The situation is again critical. Some think that one needs additional technology (such as the videodisk or networking) to make it really happen. This is debatable.

A breakthrough will be reached only when it can be shown that computer-based learning results in an increase in productivity. That increase can be achieved in two ways: achieving the same educational goal as before, but in less time, and/or achieving additional educational objectives within the same period of time. Indications are that computer-based learning can achieve this objective. However, the efficient use of computers in education will depend entirely on the availability of good educational software. Until recently, one was quite satisfied with the partial availability of such software. Now, qualitatively good software must be made generally available on a much larger scale and at reasonable prices.

This means that the currently established mechanisms for the development of educational software require careful revision. The end product must be produced in an efficient, industrially-oriented fashion. This implies that detailed, well defined specifications be known before one commences with the actual programming. The establishment of these specifications must be preceded by a process-oriented, iterative approach. Both teachers, students and developers must be able to contribute to this process. Each specific part of the development activity should be planned as a separate entity. The organization of the entire development program - from experimental programs to prototype to final product - needs to be coordinated, whereby each of the participants can influence activities at the right time and in an efficient manner.

Although it is important to produce educational software in a professional manner, it is even more important to integrate the use of that software in education. This is a long process which will take years to complete, and which will have an important impact on the organization of education as a whole. This means that planning should extend over a number of years, so as to investigate the implications of such modifications on the totality of the structures of education.

References

Adcis, Journal of Computer-Based Instruction, Special Issue on Authoring Tools, volume 11, number 3, summer 1984.

Fox, Jean; Rushby, Nick; Guidelines for Developing Educational Computer Programs. Computers and Education, volume 3, 1979, 35-41.

Gordon, Randi-Lyn; Guidelines for the Design of Computer-Based Instructional Materials. Atlanta, Georgia: Academic Information Systems, 1985.

Kearsley, Greg; Microcomputer Software: Design and Development Principles. Journal of Educational Computer Research, volume 1 (2), 1985, 209-220.

Kontos, George; Instructional Computing: In search of better methods for the production of CAI lessons. Journal of Educational Technology Systems, volume 13, number 1, 1984-5, 3-14.

Le Corre, Yves; Schwartz, Jacob; Software and courseware for a multimedia educational environment. Organisation for economic co-operation and development, Centre for Educational Research and Innovation, CERI/NT/84.05, Paris, 1984.

Maget, Kenneth; Software Engineering Principles for Courseware Development. AEDS Journal, volume 13, number 2, winter 1980, 144-155.

Merrill, David M.; Computer Aided Instructional Design, Dean Lecture, presented at the 26th ADCIS Conference, March 25-28, 1985, Philadelphia.

Moonen, Jef; The Dutch Informatics Stimulation Plan: Activities of the Centre for Education and Information Technology. Educational Technology, vol. xxx, No. 11, November 1985.

Roblyer, M.D.; Instructional Design versus Authoring of Courseware: some crucial differences. AEDS Journal, volume 14, summer 1981, 173-181.

Peters, Harold J.; Johnson, James W.; Author's Guide, Design Development, Style, Packaging, Review. The University of Iowa: CONDUIT, 1978.

Walker, Decker F.; Hess, Robert D.; Instructional Software, Principles and Perspectives for Design and Use. Belmont, California: Wadsworth Publishing Company, 1984.

Watson, Deryn M.; A model for the production of CAL material. Computers and Education, volume 7, number 3, 1983, 167-176.

Weingarten, Nancy; The 1985 Guide to Computer-Based Training Systems and Courseware. Boston: Weingarten Publications, 1985.

THE COMPUTER IN THE EVALUATION OF LEARNING

Giorgio Olimpo
Istituto per le Tecnologie Didattiche, CNR, Genova
Via All'Opera Pia, 11 - 16145 GENOVA

SUMMARY

This paper deals with the use of computers in the evaluation of learning with a special concern for diagnostic evaluation carried out with a formative aim.

The described methodological framework for diagnostic evaluation is both oriented to produce highly individualized tests providing a detailed measure of students' achievements and to minimize the workload imposed by the test. The methodology relies on a hierarchical model of the subject matter but can apply to more general representations too. In fact, some network models can be converted to hierarchies if considered from a specific point of view.

The methodology is supported by Delfi, a computer system which assists authors in designing and implementing computer delivered diagnostic tests. It is a form of computer-aided design of educational material in which some phases are carried out by authors assisted by Delfi and other ones are fully automated. Some simple, yet significant examples are provided.

1. INTRODUCTION

The term "evaluation" refers to any possible kind of procedure capable of providing a description of students' achievement in connection with a specific learning process. The evaluation of a student (and of a course too) may be oriented to different goals. It is possible to have a selective evaluation, i.e., that kind of evaluation aimed at detecting (1) the students

NATO ASI Series, Vol. F 23
Designing Computer-Based Learning Materials
Edited by A. Bork and H. Weinstock

giving the best performance or (2) the most effective courses; it is possible to have summative evaluation aimed at presenting a global evaluation of a student, for instance a score which provides information as to whether (1) a student has reached a satisfactory level of performance or (2) a course is good enough to meet stated objectives.

Finally, we have formative evalutation oriented to providing precise and detailed feedback (1) to students to detect gaps in their knowledge or (2) on courses to detecting their less effective elements. Formative evaluation is often referred to as diagnostic evaluation because it acts as a diagnostic process detecting not only the flaws in students' knowledge, but also the possible causes of those flaws.

This paper deals mostly with diagnostic evaluation since it represents one of the most interesting fields for the use of computers in teaching/learning processes. It is a key element in the realization of individualized teaching processes based upon technological media, since it provides a precise map of the student's knowledge and of the gaps in that knowledge.
Good courseware based on the computer and even on the video disk can supply a number of different educational paths, or ways of presenting the same topic and remedial sequences. But the correct and effective use of these media requires appropriate administration, i.e., selection of the various instructional sequences on the basis of the needs and skills of each individual student. Hence, one sees the importance of evaluation, particularly of formative evaluation which aims at "forming" the student's knowledge.

Some of the major categories of computer use in this field are:

a) Computer Managed Testing (CMT)
The computer is mainly used for the automatic correction of a test, for statistical analysis of results, and for the survey of the characteristics of each test item (providing a discrimination and difficulty index);

b) Computer Assisted Testing (CAT)
The computer carries out a real dialogue with the student to evaluate the student's knowledge of given subject matter;

c) Computer Assisted Test Construction (CATC)
The computer supports the author in designing achievement tests, e.g., through the identification of items with given characteristics in a data base.

Generally, the applications belonging to one or more of the above categories are oriented to meet different requirements:

- to improve the quality of the evaluation by relating it to an actual measure of learning, providing a reliable and detailed description of the student's achievement;
- to improve the modalities of evaluation through the construction and administration of individualized tests in which the sequence and the content of the items are not predetermined and vary according to the answers given by the student;
- to reduce and partly automate the routine work required for test production, its delivery and correction, and for the analysis of results.

As mentioned above, another important possibility for diagnostic evaluation is to provide formative feedback on implemented courses. Individualization implies teaching a student what he or she does not know starting from what he or she does know. To validate and revise a course one must know its less successful parts in terms of achievement. Both of these require a detailed map of student achievement to be used to orient the teaching process in the former case; and to be used to evaluate average performances in the latter.

So far, diagnostic testing is not widely used because:

- diagnostic test design is hard work, requiring a high level of integration with the design of tutorial and remedial material;

- test delivery may become a heavy burden both for students and teachers because of the need to assess the usually large set of knowledge and skills in the content domain to be tested.

In this paper a methodology for the design and delivery of diagnostic tests is described which attempts to answer these problems in several ways:

- by providing a methodological framework to test design;
- by supporting test authors in their work by a computer assisted test design;
- by using the computer for test delivery and by adopting a delivery strategy which minimizes the load imposed on students by the test.

2. DESCRIPTION OF THE METHODOLOGY

2.1 Basic hypothesis

The following approach to evaluation is based on a few basic hypotheses.

<u>The diagnostic test and the related tutorial process must derive from the same content structure</u>.

This hypothesis gives a precise meaning to the test which can be defined as a procedure to detect which parts of the structure have or have not been achieved by the student as a result of a specific tutorial process; or to detect which parts of the structure correspond to a low average achievement to have corrective feedback on the related parts of the tutorial process.

All the different pedagogical phases involved in an instructional process (tutorial, drill, evaluation, remedy, etc.) should rely on the same content structure. This factor ensures coherence to the components of a course. From this point of view the definition of the content structure should be one of the first phases of instructional design, immediately following the analysis of the educational needs and of the target population, and providing a common basis to the following phases of design.

<u>The content representation must be of a hierarchical type, with each node of the hierarchy corresponding to a well defined student skill</u>.

This means that the approach lends itself very well to subjects of a procedural nature, possibly involving some heuristics; while for subjects of a higher taxonomic level the approach may become arbitrary or difficult to use. However, in many cases the hierarchical model is less restrictive than it seems, since more general representations of the subject matter based upon network models (such as entailment meshes or Petri nets) can always produce hierarchical representations if considered from a specific point of view.

A diagnostic test should assess the skills and knowledge of a student corresponding to all the nodes of the hierarchy.

2.2 The representation of the subject matter

In our model the subject matter consists of a hierarchy of nodes, each of which describes a specific element of knowledge and skill (that is, a topic and a class of tasks associated with it). In this representation, if a node B depends hierarchically on node A, it means that the "achievement" of B is necessary to achieve A or "A has B as a prerequisite;" or that "the accomplishment of a task associated with A involves the accomplishment of a task associated with B."

We should notice that usually a hierarchical link has no absolute value. In other words, the condition "learning B is a prerequisite to learning A" reflects the specific point of view of the author. For example, the skill "recognize the hypotenuse of a right-angled triangle" can be decomposed in different ways as represented in Fig. 1.

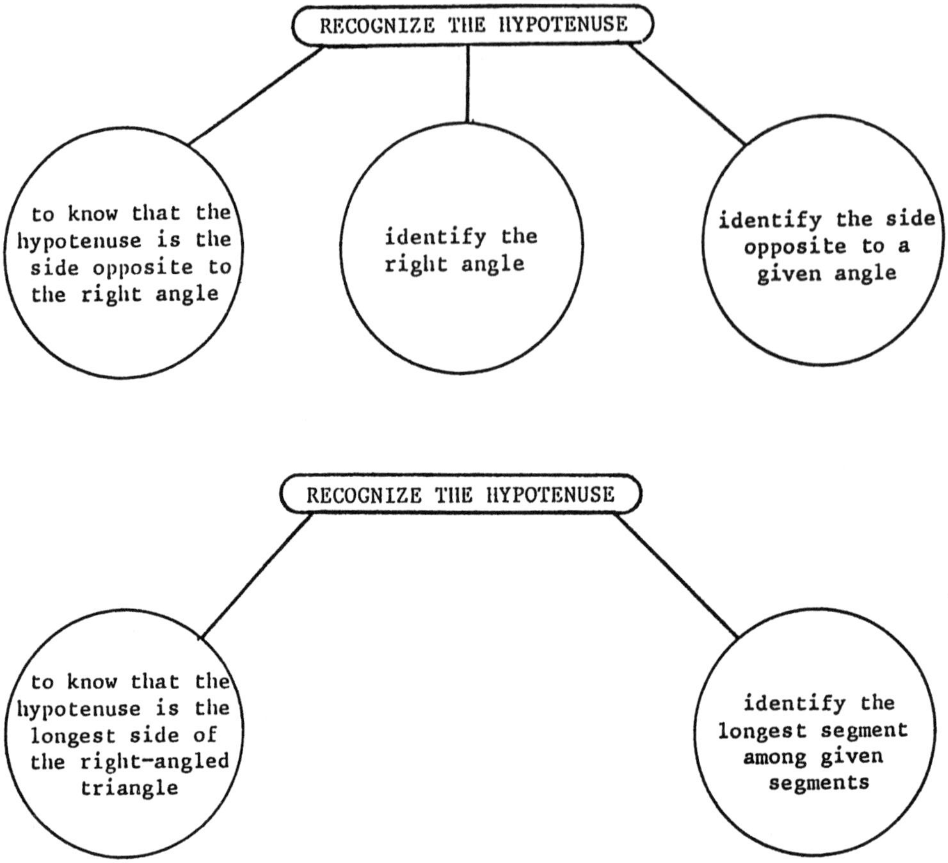

Fig. 1. Different hierarchical representations for the same skill.

Different approaches are therefore possible to attain a given result. A hierarchy can refer only to one of them, and as a result the property "to be prerequisite of" has only a relative value. To develop a hierarchical representation of the subject matter, we can start from the description of the most complex knowledge or skill and derive the subordinate nodes operating in a recursive manner as suggested by Gagné: "What would the learner have to know how to do already in order to complete this task?"

This is a top-down process which keeps on producing new nodes until the identified behaviour corresponds to one of the prerequisite skills which should be already possessed by the student - obviously such an assumption should already have been verified. For example, if our final objective is "to be able to calculate the 3rd side of a right-angled triangle using the Pythagorean theorem," one of its possible hierarchical decompositions is the one shown in Fig 2.

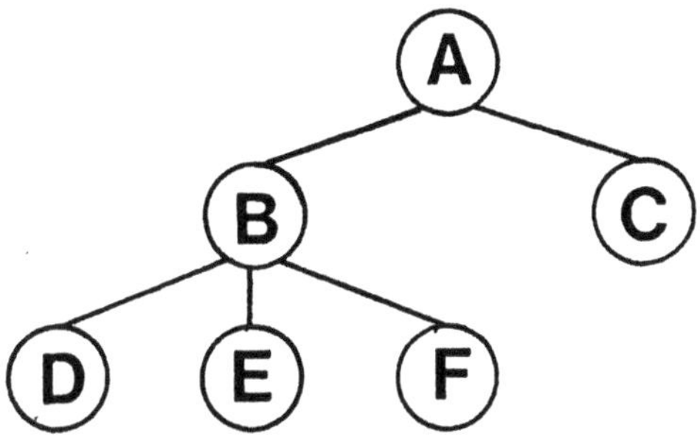

A: To calculate the 3rd side of a right-angled triangle using Pythagorean theorem
   B: To select the right formula to obtain the 3rd side
      D: To recognize the type of the unknown side
      E: To know the right formula to obtain a cathetus
      F: To know the right formula to obtain the hypotenuse

Fig. 2. A hierarchical decomposition for the skill "calculate the third side of a right-angled triangle."

This hierarchical link imposed on a given content domain is the basis for a top-down testing strategy. Students may be tested starting from the root of the hierarchy. If they answer correctly, the test may end, since the hierarchical link ensures that all the skills corresponding to the underlying nodes have been achieved. If the student fails, the test checks the nodes immediately depending on the root, and the procedure goes on recursively until either an acheived node or a leaf of the hierarchy is reached. Figure 3 displays as an example a possible testing procedure corresponding to the hierarchy of Fig. 2 (For the sake of clarity, the testing algorithm has not been written in recursive form).

The testing strategy depends on the assumption that if a student answers the questions associated with a node N of a hierarchy correctly, he has to use all the subordinate skills, i.e., he is tested not only on N, but also indirectly, on all its subordinate nodes. It has been shown, in principle, how the test can be based upon the content structure. However, to analyze in more detail the design of diagnostic tests, we must further refine our content representation.

From the point of view of testing, each node of the hierarchy may be interpreted as a class of tasks and the student must be able to accomplish any task of the class successfully if he or she has achieved the corresponding skill. This interpretation provides the basis for an operational definition of "achieving" a node: "A student has achieved a node N of the hierarchy if he or she can accomplish any task of the set associated with N."

This definition, though clear and understandable, must be further elaborated to provide a useful criterion to verify the student's achievement. In most cases it is impractical or even impossible to check whether a student can accomplish all the possible tasks associated with a node. Therefore, we need a criterion to select a (possibly) minimum set of tasks for each node in such a way that we can be reasonably sure that a student performing well on those tasks will also perform well on any task associated to the node.

A possible criterion is "topological covering" already in use in the field of software testing. This criterion consists in running a program with different input data so as to activate all the different paths of the program. In the field of educational testing this criterion means to associate a (possibly minimum) set of tasks (and of related test items) to each node in such a way that all the underlying nodes are activated at least once by those tasks.

To implement this criterion we need to specify the nature of the link existing between a node and its sons, i.e., the nodes immediately depending on it.

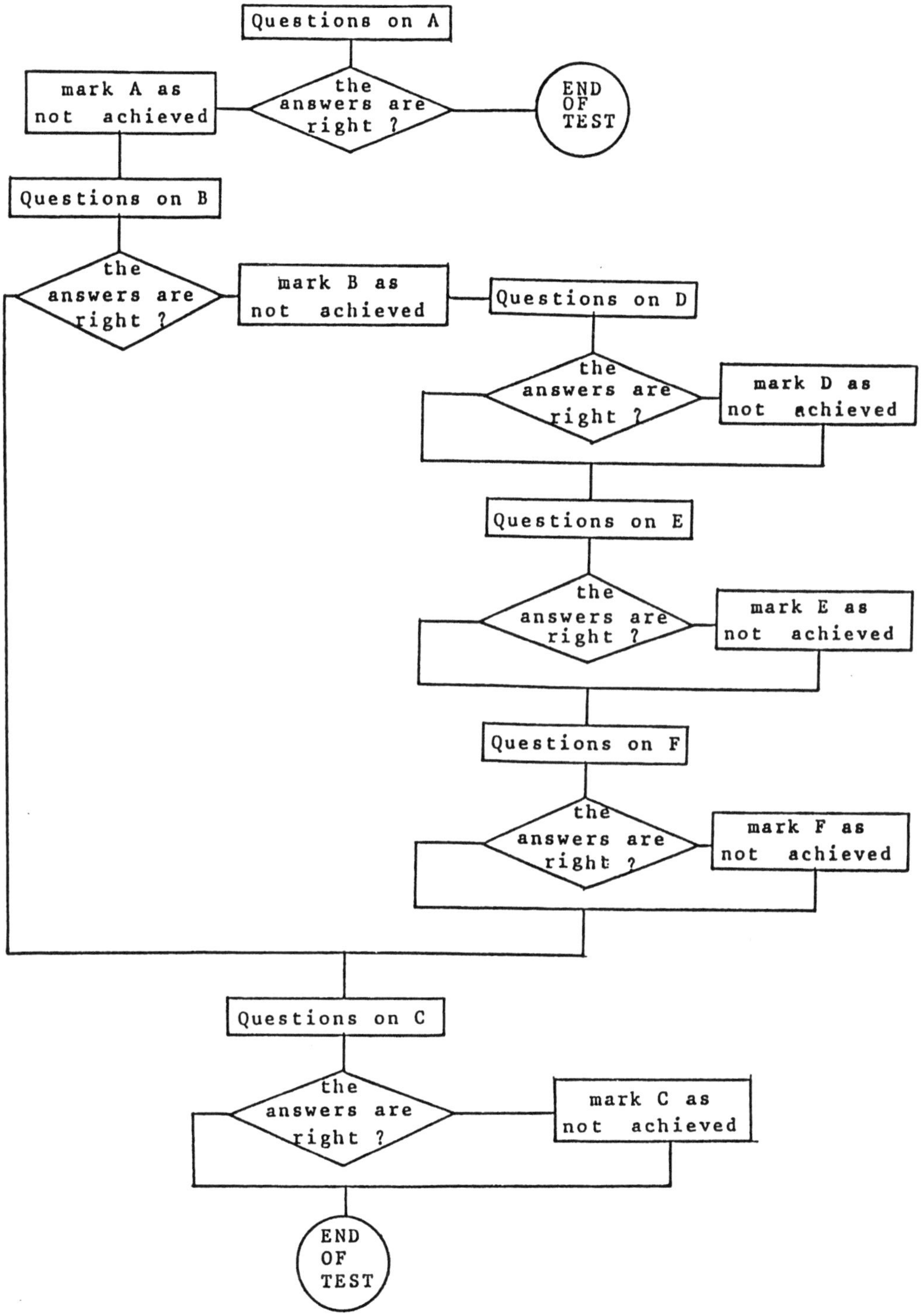

Fig. 3. A testing procedure for the hierarchy of Fig. 2.

Let us consider the simple hierarchy represented in Fig. 4a.

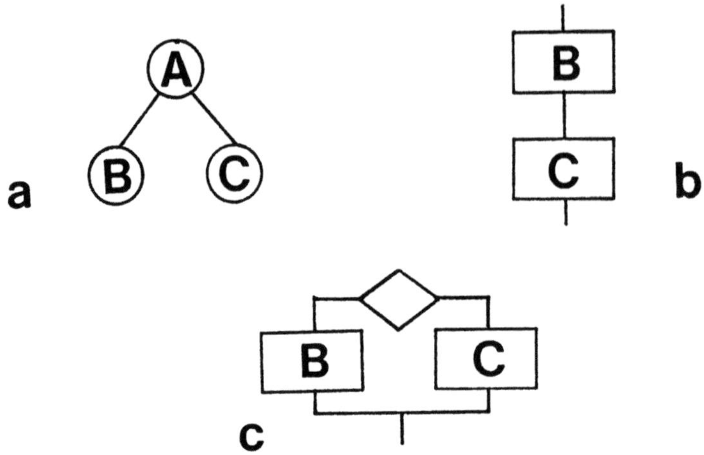

Fig. 4. An interpretation for *and* and *or* links in a hierarchy.

Let t_A, t_B, t_C be specific tasks associated with nodes A, B, and C.
The hierarchy of Fig. 4a may correspond to different situations:

a. the accomplishment of t_A involves the accomplishment of t_B *and* t_C;
b. the accomplishment of t_A involves the accomplishment of t_B *or* t_C.

Considering the task set A equivalent to a procedure, the situation A corresponds for instance to a sequential flow (Fig. 4b), while the situation B corresponds to an alternative (Fig. 4c).
The type of the link (*and*, *or*) has a direct influence on the test. In the case of *and* links, one item is enough to cover all the hierarchy (i.e., to activate B and C); while with *or* links one needs two distinct items associated with A to activate B and C.

It is also common to have links of a mixed type, i.e., the accomplishment of a task t_A may imply, for instance, the accomplishment of (t_B and t_C) or t_D. This means that, generally, the link between a node and its sons is described by a complex logical expression.

Summing up, our representation of the content to be taught and tested consists of a hierarchy plus the logical links between each node and its sons. This second aspect is required to define the (minimum) number and the structure of the test items which must be associated with each node to satisfy the topological covering criterion.

In some cases this criterion, which we have selected, because it is very simple and straightforward, may have some flaws. For instance the same hierarchy in Fig. 4a may correspond to the two different flowcharts shown in Fig. 5.

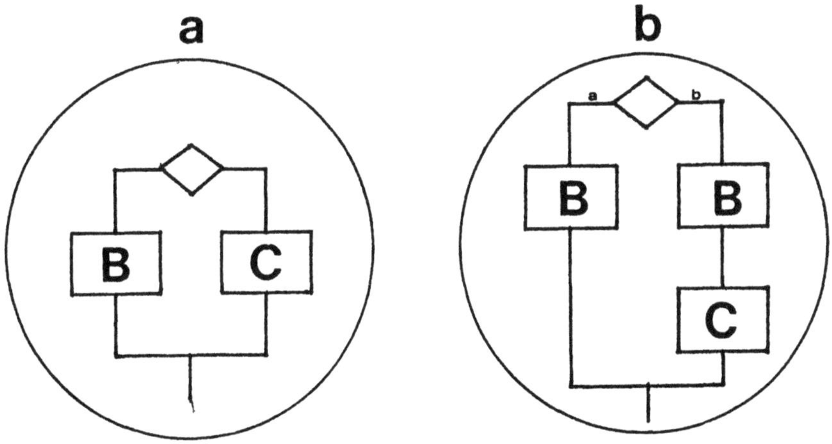

Fig. 5. Different procedural interpretation of the same hierarchy.

While in the case of Fig. 5a the topological covering criterion may ensure a satisfactory test, things are quite different for the flowchart of Fig. 5b. In this case a task activating the branch b of the flowchart meets our criterion, but may be a poor form of test since it does not activate the decision corresponding to branch a. In such cases we need more sophisticated criteria, for instance, to activate all the branches of the procedure.

3. FURTHER REMARKS ON THE DESIGN OF SUBJECT MATTER REPRESENTATION

The definition of the hierarchy is a critical point in the overall process of instructional design. As will be made clearer later, a consistent hierarchy is the very basis for test reliability and for the effectiveness of an instructional process. On the other hand, to develop a consistent hierarchy, a deep analysis and several professional skills are necessary. Among these are good knowledge of the subject matter, teaching experience and strong methodological know-how.

In this task of designing the content structure, we have found that considerable help may be derived from analyzing the structure of the tasks involved by means of Petri nets. The term Petri net refers to an intellectual tool originally devised to model the behaviour of computer systems. Subsequent developments have shown that Petri nets lend themselves very well to the representation of procedural knowledge. A Petri net is an oriented graph containing two different types of nodes: transitions representing activities and places representing resources produced or consumed by those activities - see Fig. 6.

When a transition fires, it consumes the resources in its input places and deposits a resource in each of the output places.
Any system or any complex procedure may be represented by a suitable Petri net. Petri nets may be profitably used in instructional design to represent learning processes or problem-solving procedures. In the first case, a transition corresponds to a learning (or teaching) activity. Its input resources are the prerequisites to learning, and the output resources are the knowledge and skills produced by learning. In the second case, the transition is a step in solving a problem, and the resources are input data or intermediate results in the problem-solving process.

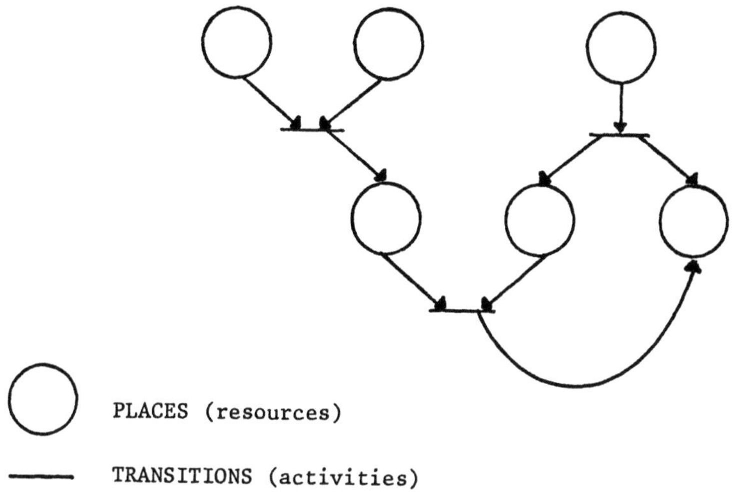

Fig. 6. An example of a Petri net.

To use Petri nets to represent procedural knowledge, i.e., a problem-solving skill, is of considerable help in producing suitable hierarchies and in making the logical expressions linking each node with its sons explicit.

Let us to consider again the case of applying the Pythagorean theorem to calculate an unknown side in a right-angled triangle. Figure 7 shows a possible structure for the problem-solving procedure represented by a top-down refinement of Petri nets.

We can verify that the hierachy can be immediately derived from it, as well as from the logical expressions. In the execution of the transition A, both transitions B and C are always activated. Therefore, we have for node A

$$E\ (t_A) \rightarrow E\ (t_B) \wedge E\ (t_C),$$

and for node B,

$$E\ (t_B) \rightarrow E\ (t_D) \wedge (E(t_E) \vee E(t_F)),$$

where the predicate $E(t_i)$ has value TRUE when the task t_i is executed.

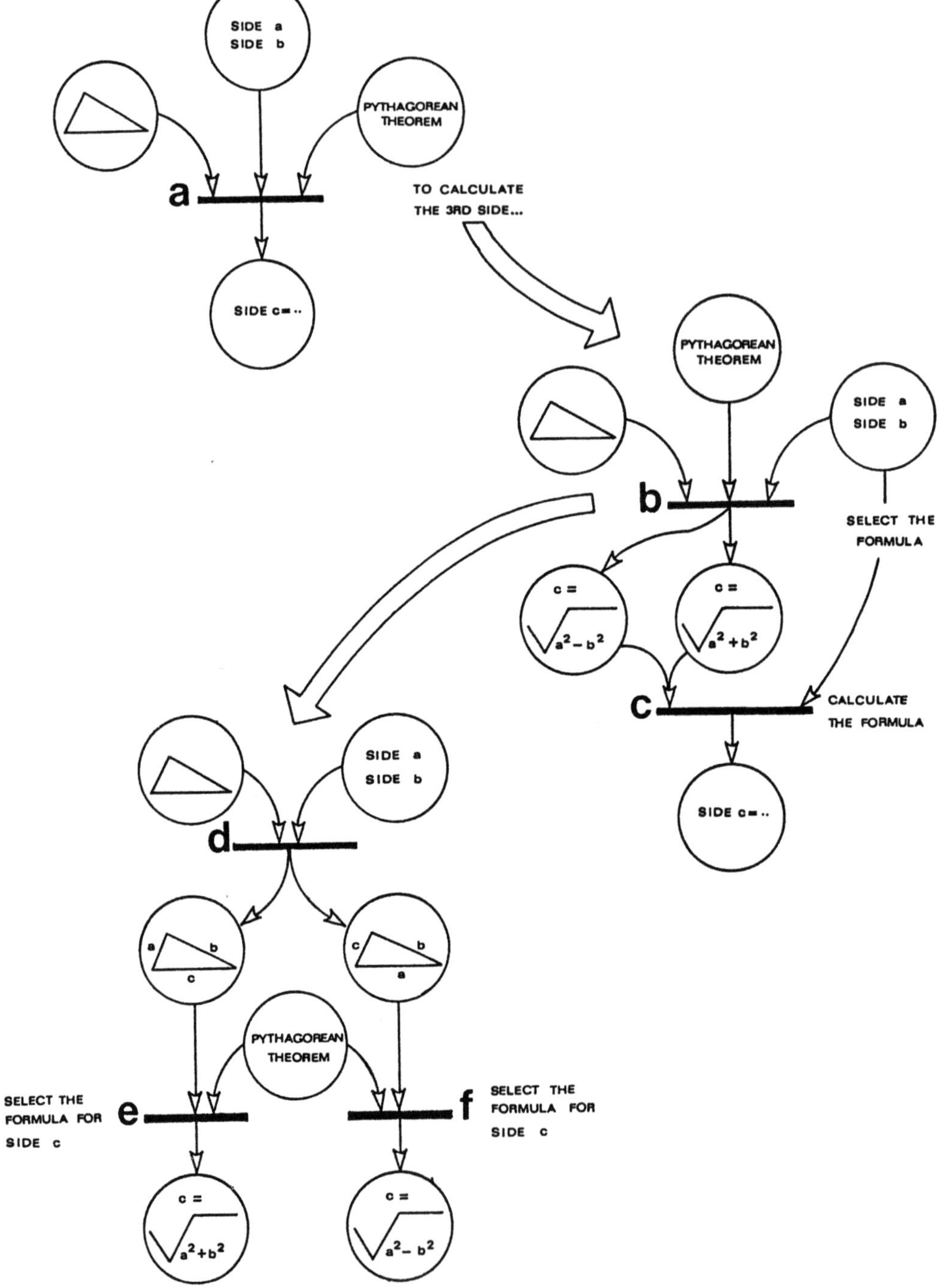

Fig. 7. A top-down refinement of Petri nets representing the application of the Pythagorean theorem.

4. TEST ITEMS DEFINITION

This phase aims at defining the test items required for testing each node in a hierarchically represented content domain, and it consists of two basic steps.

The first step involves the construction of an item table which, for each node, provides a number of items and the features of each item, i.e., the specifications of the nodes (skills) which are involved in the mental process of answering the corresponding question. Figure 8 shows the item table for a hierarchy concerning the Pythagorean theorem. For instance, node A, the highest in the hierarchy, has two distinct items associated to it, A1 and A2. A1 should involve the subnodes A, B, C, D, E; while A2 should involve A, B, C, D, F.

```
TEST ITEM TABLE FOR  PYTHAG

A 1 :    A B C D E

A 2 :    A B C D F

B 1 :    B D E

B 2 :    B D F

PRIMITIVES :  C, D, E, F
```

Fig. 8. The item table for the hierarchy related to the Pythagorean theorem.

The second step refers to the actual formulation of the items. In this step the author, under the guidance of the item table, must build a suitable set of questions for each node of the hierarchy. To formulate questions, we analyze the structure of each item, evaluating the type of cognitive activity involved, i.e., to remember, to discriminate, to apply, to detect, to calculate, and then choosing the more suitable type of item.

The clearer the formulation of objectives and tasks in the hierarchy, the easier and safer is the item formulation phase. If the nodes of the hierarchy are already described as task classes, writing the questions becomes much easier.

A question should satisfy also the two following requisites: it must be valid, i.e., comply with the objective, and reliable, i.e., allow for an unequivocal evaluation. In this methodology an item is valid if answering it involves all the skills listed in the item table for that item. For instance, the following question: "How do you calculate the hypotenuse given the two catheti?" is not a valid example for A1 because it does not activate the skills associated with nodes B, C, D, E, F as specified in the item table. An adequate formulation for item A1 is shown in Fig. 9.

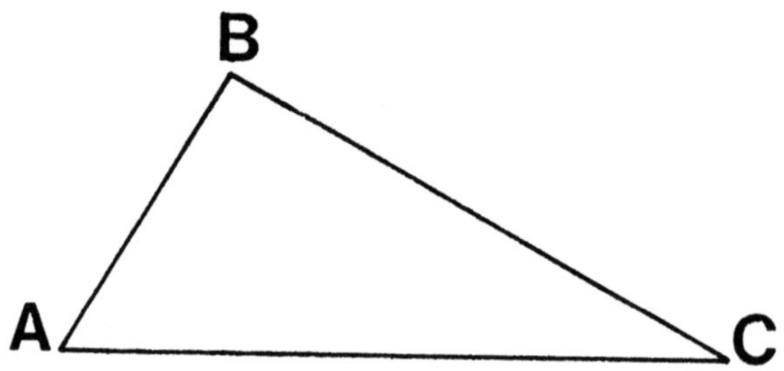

ABC is a right-angled triangle.
The length of ABC is 12 and the length of BC is 3.
WHAT IS THE LENGTH OF AC?

Fig. 9. An item in the test on the Pythagorean theorem.

When formulating a question it is necessary to discriminate those situations in which a multiple choice item is appropriate from those in which it is not. For example, by asking the student the following question:
"Which verb among the following is in the past tense?
a) I eat; b) I shall drink; c) I ate; d) I should steal"
is a good way to verify ability to recognize a verb tense, but it does not give any information on the ability of the student to use the verbal form suitable for a given situation.

A general criterion is that of associating with each item at least 3 or 4 possible choices, avoiding those choices obviously unreasonable. Moreover, it is possible to present a multiple-choice question in a concealed way, i.e., by requesting that the student answers TRUE OR FALSE to each of the possibilities. This decreases the probability of random choice of the correct answer.

No matter what is the type of the selected item, in this phase it is advisable to ignore the fact that the test will be implemented on a computer. When formulating a question, considerations or problems concerning its automatic delivery should not be taken into account, while a great deal of attention should be devoted to its validity. Here is a final hint on the "reliability" of items: no problems exist for multiple-choice items; as for open items, it is necessary to state the tolerated error in the case of numerical answers, or the acceptable alternative when a word or a sentence is required.

5. THE ITEMS DELIVERY SEQUENCE

We have already dealt with the top-down delivery strategy. In the previous section we considered the design of each test item without any consideration of the sequence in which the items should be delivered. In this section we shall consider the delivery control flow of the test. This flow is typically fairly complex, due both to the choice of the top-down delivery strategy and to the presence of the <u>or</u> links which may significantly increase the number of test items, and consequently, the number of different paths.

Starting from the item table and from the hierarchy, it is conceptually simple to define the delivery strategy of the test, i.e., the sequence in which the items will be administered on the basis of the student's answers. Figure 10 shows the delivery control flow for our very simple example on the Pythagorean theorem. The flow corresponding to correct answers is represented by straight lines (———), while the one corresponding to wrong answers, by dashed lines (-----). In this way it is possible to follow all paths and detect clearly the various inputs and outputs of each item, thus providing a basis for the coding process.

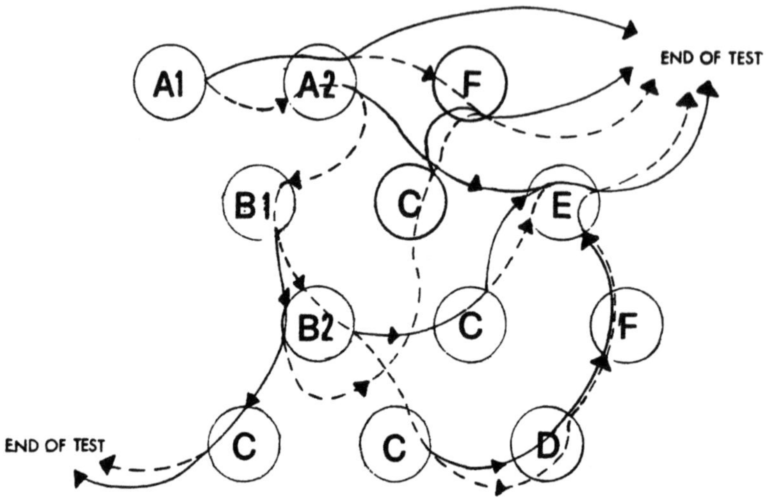

Fig. 10. A representation of the delivery-control flow for the test on the Pythagorean theorem.

6. ASSISTING THE AUTHOR IN TEST DESIGN: THE DELFI SYSTEM

The test methodology which has been described implies various activities of a different nature for test authors. Some of them, such as hierarchy definition or test item formulation, always require heavy human intervention, while others, such as the production of the control code for test delivery, can be automated.

The DELFI system has been designed and implemented to ease the work of authors and can be referred to as an actual system for computer-assisted test design. It gives assistance and support to the author in performing the most conceptual phases of design and fully automates the production of the code for test delivery, freeing the author from a complex task devoid of conceptual content and which can lead to numerous errors.

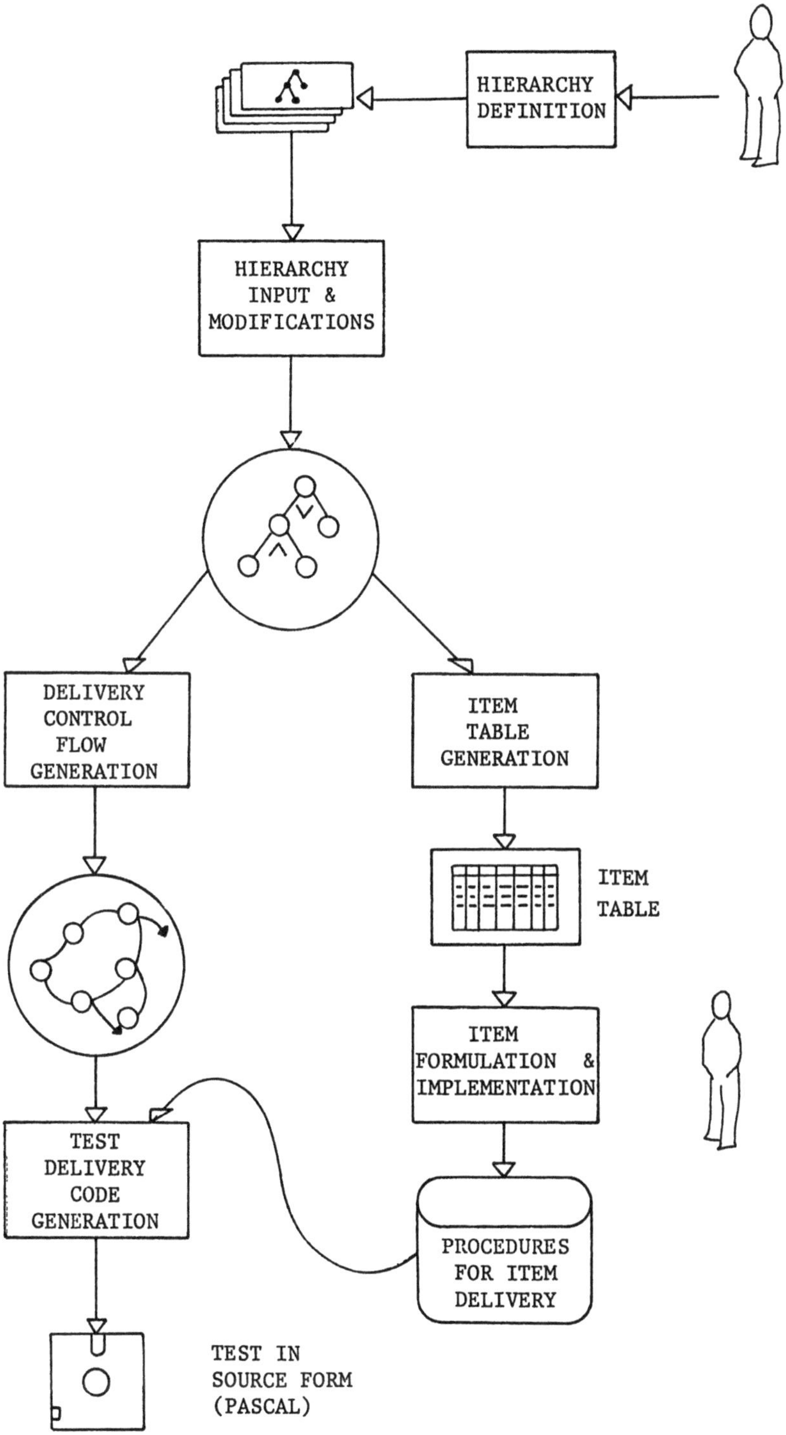

Fig. 11. The structure of DELFI.

Figure 11 shows the main functions of the system. The input of the system is the hierarchy representing the content domain, and is interactively supplied by the author, who also can modify it any number of times. On the basis of the hierarchy and of its associated logical expressions, the system automatically generates the item table. It is worth noting that item formulation and implementation are the only activities, together with hierarchy definition, which cannot be automated and require the following of the author:

- the selection of a suitable item type and the formulation of the item on the basis of the involved skills;

- the implementation of procedures to handle each item with regard to question presentation, answer acquisition, answer analysis and data collection.

It is the responsability of the author to build a file containing a procedure for each test item plus other possible auxiliary procedures. The control code defining the run-time flow of the test is automatically produced by DELFI. This process takes place in two steps. In the first one, a logical representation of the control flow, a guide for coding the test in any programming language, is generated.
The second step is oriented to the use of Pascal and refers to the automatic production of the actual testing code (control + item delivery). Though conceptually uninteresting, this facility is extremely helpful to the author, especially for the case of very large hierarchies. The code produced by DELFI is also instrumented for collecting and filing data on test results.
In this second step the procedures for item delivery written by the author are automatically included in the generated code, which can be compiled and executed as a normal Pascal program.
Figure 12 represents the test delivery stage and the use of the test results. The testing program generated by DELFI interacts with the student and stores the test results in a suitable file, which can be accessed at any time by the DELFI results-analysis facility.

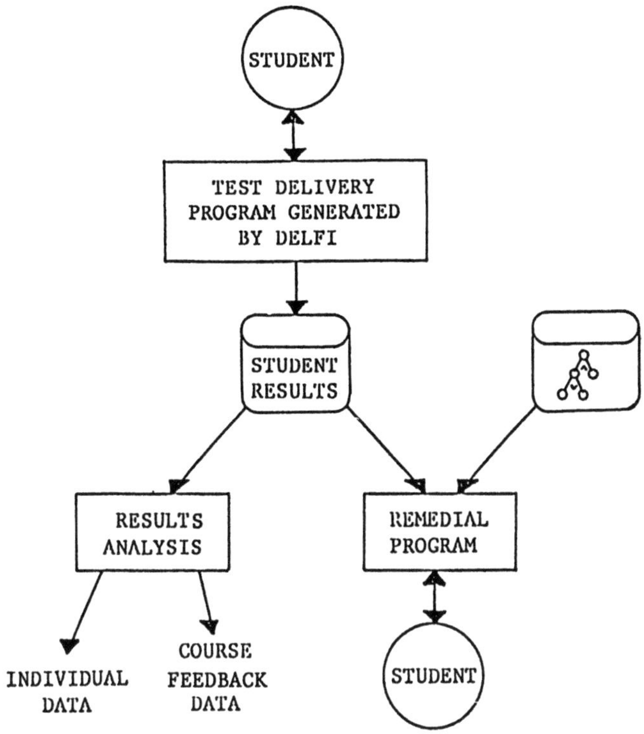

Fig. 12. The test delivery phase and the use of test results.

This can provide both individual performance data (oriented to individual feedback) and average performance data (oriented to courseware feedback).

One should mention also the possibility of building tutorial programs which provide individualized remedial sequences administered on the basis of test results. After a test has been completed by a student, each node of the hierarchy is marked as achieved or not achieved. A remedial program can therefore be built in such a way so as to teach only the not-achieved nodes according to a suitable strategy - top-down, bottom-up or mixed, according to the nature of the subject matter or to the student's learning style.

7. USE OF DELFI: AN EXAMPLE

In this section an example of the construction of a diagnostic test with the use of DELFI is provided for which the subject is the skill of performing the four arithmetic operations on complex numbers, both in binomial and exponential notation. This subject, which is considered fairly critical from the instructional point of view, does not produce a very large or complex hierarchy. However, it provides a real-world case which can be effective in illustrating the use of DELFI.

For brevity, we disregard all the troublesome processes necessary in building the hierarchy, and we present it in its final form in Fig. 13.

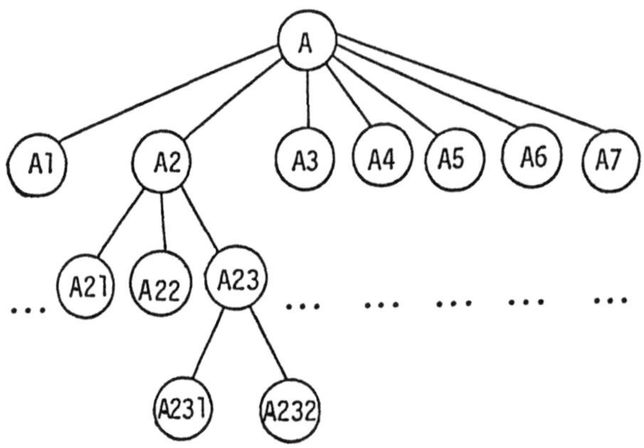

A: to perform the four arithmetic operations on complex numbers both in binomial and exponential form.
A1: to perform the sum upon numbers in binomial form.
A2: to perform the division upon numbers in binomial form.
A3: to perform the multiplication upon numbers in binomial form.
A4: to perform the division upon numbers in exponential form.
A5: to convert from exponential to binomial form.
A6: to convert from binomial to exponential form.
A7: to detect the need to convert from exponential to binomial form (when summing complex numbers in exponential form).
A21: to find the conjugate of a complex number.
A22: to detect the need to multiply both numerator and denominator for the conjugate of the denominators (when dividing complex numbers).
A23: to perform the product of complex numbers in binomial form.
A231: to calculate the product of two binomials.
A232: to know that J**2 = -1.
....

Fig. 13. A possible hierarchy for the skill of "performing the four arithmetic operations on complex numbers."

In the figure only a fragment of the hierarchy is displayed - its complete version includes 26 nodes. However, this should be enough for the purposes of our example. It should be noted that there are some aspects of the hierarchy which may seem unnatural. These arise from a process of analysis which is iterative in nature and which may lead to quite a different structure of the hierarchy from that initially devised. For instance, the skill "perform the product of complex numbers in binomial form" (A23), is not directly subordinate to the root as might seem natural. That is because this skill is also subordinate to "perform the division upon numbers in binomial form" (A2), and therefore, it appears at a lower level.

Considering this hierarchy, the meaning of the logical links (<u>and</u>, <u>or</u>) may become clearer. We could associate an item like "compute the sum of two complex numbers in exponential notation and express the result in the same form" to the node A1. This item involves A1, A5, A6, A7, but does not require the use of A2, A3 and A4. It is therefore easy to see that the link among the sons of A is (A1 <u>and</u> A5 <u>and</u> A6 <u>and</u> A7) <u>or</u> A2 <u>or</u> A3 <u>or</u> A4. When the hierarchy is in a satisfactory form, it can be interactively supplied to DELFI. Figure 14 shows how the input hierarchy is displayed on the screen by DELFI.

```
A = (A1 & A5 & A6 & A7) + A2 + A3 + A5
     A1
     A2 = A21 & A22 & A23
          A21
          A22
          A23 = A231 & A232
                A231
                A232
     A3
     A4
     A5
     A6
     A7
```

Fig. 14. The hierarchy referring to the operations on complex numbers as displayed on the screen by Delfi.

After the input of the hierarchy, DELFI allows the automatic generation of the item table which, for our example, is displayed in Fig. 15.

TEST ITEM TABLE FOR "COMPNUM"

A 1	: A A1 A5 A6 A7 A11 A12 A51 A52 A61 A62
A 2	: A A2 A21 A22 A23 A231 A232
A 3	: A A3 A31 A32 A33 A34 A35 A36
A 4	: A A4 A41
A1 1	: A1 A11 A12
A2 1	: A2 A21 A22 A23 A231 A232
A3 1	: A3 A31 A32 A33 A34 A35 A36
A4 1	: A4 A41
A5 1	: A5 A51 A52
A6 1	: A6 A61 A62
A23 1	: A23 A231 A232
A11	: PRIMITIVE
A12	: PRIMITIVE
A21	: PRIMITIVE
A22	: PRIMITIVE
A231	: PRIMITIVE
A232	: PRIMITIVE
A31	: PRIMITIVE
A32	: PRIMITIVE
A33	: PRIMITIVE
A34	: PRIMITIVE
A35	: PRIMITIVE
A36	: PRIMITIVE
A41	: PRIMITIVE
A51	: PRIMITIVE
A61	: PRIMITIVE
A62	: PRIMITIVE
A7	: PRIMITIVE

Fig. 15. The item table for the example on complex numbers.

One sees from this table, for instance, that the node A requires four items to be thoroughly tested, i.e., A1, A2, A3, A4. For each of them, the item table provides the subordinate nodes to be involved in the corresponding question.

As an example of item formulation, consider the entry A1 of the item table. We obtain from it the information that the question should involve:

- arithmetic operations upon complex numbers (A)
- the sum in binomial form (A5)
- the conversion from binomial to exponential form (A6)
- the decision to convert from exponential to binomial form (A7)

From this information the author can build a suitable question, which could be the one of Fig. 16.

COMPUTE THE FOLLOWING SUM AND EXPRESS THE RESULT IN EXPONENTIAL NOTATION

$$\frac{5}{3} e^{J \Pi \frac{1}{3}} + \frac{1}{3} e^{J \Pi \frac{2}{4}}$$

Fig. 16. An example of an item for the test on complex numbers.

Figure 17 displays a representation of the possible test-delivery control flaws automatically produced by DELFI for our hierarchy.

Since supplying a global picture of the flowchart would produce in most cases a very complex diagram, DELFI output deals with one node at a time, providing for each possible outcome (achieved, not achieved) of the item associated with that node, the next possible nodes to test. The test starts from node A and if the answers to A1, A2, A3, A4 are correct, it ends immediately. If, for instance, only A1 and A2 are achieved, the process must go on, testing node A3 or node A4, etc. No example of the control code automatically produced by Delfi is reported because this code is fairly long and complex, and may be of interest only for those wishing to edit it.

It should be noted that the automatic coding facility also produces a code for collecting data on student performance.

A 1	A 2	A 3	A 4	
F	F	F	F	---> A1 A5 A6 A2 A3 A4 A7
F	F	F	T	---> A1 A5 A6 A2 A3 A7
F	F	T	F	---> A1 A5 A6 A2 A3 A7
F	F	T	T	---> A1 A5 A6 A2 A7
F	T	F	F	---> A1 A5 A6 A3 A4 A7
F	T	F	T	---> A1 A5 A6 A3 A7
F	T	T	F	---> A1 A5 A6 A4 A7
F	T	T	T	---> A1 A5 A6 A7
T	F	F	F	---> A2 A3 A4
T	F	F	T	---> A2 A3
T	F	T	F	---> A2 A4
T	F	T	T	---> A2
T	T	F	F	---> A3 A4
T	T	F	T	---> A3
T	T	T	F	---> A4
T	T	T	T	---> EXIT

```
--------
| A1    |
--------
|     F | ---> A11  A12
|_____T_| ---> EXIT
```

```
--------
| A5  1 |
--------
|     F | ---> A51  A52
|_____T_| ---> EXIT
```

```
--------
| A6  1 |
--------
|     F | ---> A61  A62
|_____T_| ---> EXIT
```

Fig. 17. A fragment of the possible test delivery control flows on complex numbers.

```
TEST  RESULTS

YOU DO NOT KNOW HOW TO PERFORM THE FOUR
ARITHMETIC OPERATIONS ON COMPLEX NUMBERS
BOTH IN BINOMIAL AND EXPONENTIAL FORM
BECAUSE YOU DO NOT KNOW:

- HOW TO PERFORM THE SUM UPON NUMBERS
  IN EXPONENTIAL FORM
- HOW TO DETECT THE NEED TO CONVERT
  FROM EXPONENTIAL TO BINOMIAL FORM,
  (WHEN SUMMING COMPLEX NUMBERS IN
  EXPONENTIAL FORM)
```

Fig. 18. An example of presentation of test results for the test on complex numbers.

This can be subsequently analysed by the Delfi results analysis facility, which presents the test results in a friendly form very close to natural communication.
In Fig. 18 an example of test results output is presented corresponding to the case:

A1	failed
A2, A3, A4	achieved
A7	failed

9. CONCLUSIONS AND PERSPECTIVES

The use of Delfi for design, implementation and delivery of diagnostic tests has made apparent the advantages and the limitation both of the methodology and of the system. The methodology is particularly effective for rather small hierarchies dealing with algorithmic topics. It allows considerable time to be saved when assessing a test and provides a precise description of the student's knowledge.

Some problems may arise with large hierarchies involving many nodes with complex links. The items corresponding to the highest nodes may become difficult to formulate, complex and scarcely understandable. It is suggested that the main hierarchy be split into a small number of sub-hierarchies chosen in an appropriate way, so that each hierarchy may be tested independently, following a bottom-up approach (starting from the sub-hierarchies at the lowest level).

An important side effect of the methodology is that of bringing into evidence possible inconsistencies within the hierarchy. This suggests, as a methodological guideline for instructional design, that designing the test can be a very useful form of feedback to the content structure before one begins the actual design of the tutorial sections.

The use of Delfi represents an example of Computer Aided Design in the field of education. Our application is limited to the production of tests, but we believe that as a result of the growing diffusion of learning processes based on interactive media, the use of the computer as a supporting tool in instructional design is bound to increase in the next few years. Other aspects of instructional design may be assisted or fully automated, leading to the development of the concept of a "courseware factory," intended as a set of integrated tools and methodologies aimed at reducing the time involved in developing, and at improving, the quality of courseware.

An analogous process has already occurred in the field of software development. This trend means that the field of educational design is becoming quite similar to a branch of engineering, but one should not fear that education risks becoming concerned only with technical problems. Actually the methodologies are merely guidelines, and the software tools are the instruments used to apply the methodologies. They help to simplify the complexity of educational design, but not at the expense of creativity. On the contrary, they tend to free the authors from many ancillary tasks and let them concentrate more directly on their creative efforts, with a concomitant reduction in development costs and an improvement in courseware quality.

10. REFERENCES

(1) Brian, R., Laganà, S., Flowcharting: a Procedure for Development of Learning Hierarchies, PLET. 14 (1977) 305-314.

(2) Ferraris, M., Midoro, V., Olimpo, G., Petri Nets as a Modelling Tool in the Development of CAL Courseware, Comput. Educ. 8 (1984) 41-49.

(3) Ferraris, M., Midoro, V., Olimpo, G., Diagnostic Testing and the Development of CAL Remedial Sequences, Comput. Educ. 8 (1984) 407-414.

(4) Gagné, R., The Conditions of Learning. (Reinhart and Winston, N.Y., 1965).

(5) Jantzen, M., Structural Representation of Knowledge by Petri Nets as an Aid for Teaching and Research, in: Net Theory and Applications. (Springer Verlag, Berlin 1980).

(6) Landa, L., Algorithmization in Learning and Instruction, (Prentice-Hall, Englewood Cliffs, N.J. 1974).

(7) Morrison, W., Cunningham, R., Diagnostic Assessment-a teacher's view, PLET. 20, 1 (1978).

(8) Okey, J.R., Developing and Validating Learning Hierarchies. AVCR. 21 (1973) 87-108.

(9) Pask, G., Conversation Theory Applications in Education and Epistemology. (Elsevier, Amsterdam, 1976).

(10) Thorndike, R.L., Educational Measurements, American Council on Education, Washington (1971).

INTEGRATING PHYSICS AND COMPUTER EDUCATION IN A SINGLE PROCESS

Elena Sassi
Dipartimento di Fisica, Università di Napoli
Mostra d'Oltremare, Pad. 20, I 80125 NAPOLI

1. WHY INTEGRATE PHYSICS AND COMPUTER EDUCATION

Computer science learning and use of computers in education are activities which differ in nature and tradition. Informatics involves learning informatics concepts, methodologies and the use of computers, while the use of computers in education consists of exploiting the computer at its best as an educational agent to improve the teaching-learning process in any discipline.

In the great majority of activities grouped under "Computer Assisted Learning" (CAL), the user interacts with educational software designed and implemented by others. The software is used to study a specific topic of a discipline; it aims at concentrating the attention and effort of the user on learning a topic, with facilities which try to make this process pleasant, stimulating and personalized. The structure of the program very often is not known to the user and the software is used as a "black box"; the functions it can perform are manifest while the way they are implemented is unknown. Usually this type of educational software, which is the most common, does not require any prerequisite in informatics and does not include education in basic informatics in its aims.

These two realities - computer science education and use of the computer as a learning agent, merge in some situations, and it is difficult to keep them apart. This happens, for instance, in the Italian schools. Perhaps the situation is temporary and is due to the rapid expansion and pervasiveness of informatics in many fields of activity. Problems related to

NATO ASI Series, Vol. F 23
Designing Computer-Based Learning Materials
Edited by A. Bork and H. Weinstock

these situations are discussed in this paper.

In the classroom the distinction between the computer as an educational agent and the learning of elements of computer science tends to disappear. It is practically impossible to use the computer as a learning tool in schools while keeping a veil of mystery on basic notions of informatics. The student may ask "How does a computer work? What is its potential? How can I apply it to help solve other problems?" The distinction between informatics and the computer as an educational medium is questionable from both an educational and cultural point of view and very likely would not be accepted by students.

The need for informatics education which does not require the study of a specific programming language is increasingly evident. Computer literacy is likely to become a job requirement and to be of importance in many activities. It is the opinion of many that some kind of introduction to informatics is strongly needed in basic education. Great educational value is attributed to informatics, and it is seen both as a specialized technical discipline and a type of methodology to be used in a wide range of subjects and activities. Different points of view are under discussion as to the educational value of informatics, and how it should be integrated into school programs.

The model of informatics education which provides the framework for the experiment referred to in this paper has been proposed by G. Olimpo (1) and is illustrated in Fig. 1.

As shown in Fig.1(a) the model integrates the component of informatics learning with the use of appropriate software and has as the third essential component, integration with disciplines other than informatics. This model is aimed at informatics which finds its motivations and references in other disciplines rather than informatics in a self-contained universe.

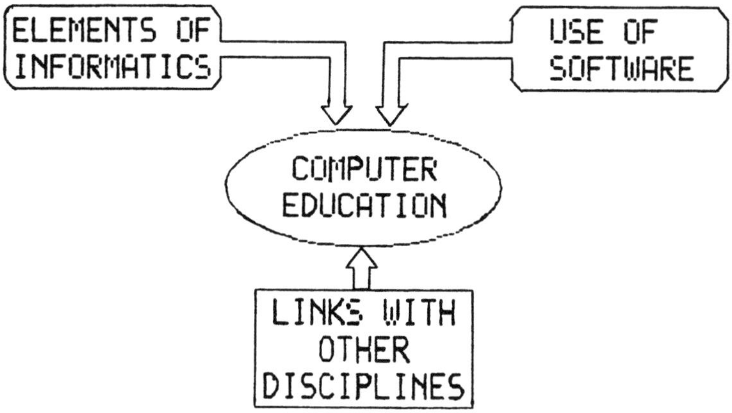

a)

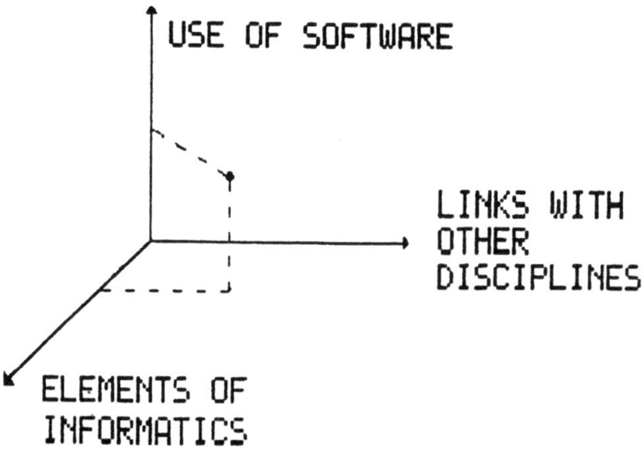

b)

Figure 1. a) a three component model for basic computer education; b) a geometrical representation of the model.

The elements of informatics referred to by the model are mostly concepts and methods of a high formative value, aimed at developing general purpose intellectual skills such as problem solving, mastering complexity, and information handling and communications. Two informatics methods often quoted as general tools are top-down decomposition and functional abstraction. The attitude proposed here is to educate broadly in informatics, rather than to train programmers or computer experts.

The component labelled "use of software" and which relates to the computer as a tool, involves at least two issues:

a) the use of the computer to access and manipulate information. Nowadays it is becoming a necessity to use utility software such as a word processor, a data base, and a spread sheet.

b) the need for independent learning via the computer and other technological media. Very likely, future educational activities, including in-service training, will rely heavily on information technology.

The third component, i.e., "links with other disciplines," deals with the need to illuminate abstract concepts with more concrete applications to problems in other sciences or the humanities. A fundamental goal of computer education is to develop the skills to apply information methodologies and tools to many disciplines and to real-life problems. The same consideration may be applied to the use of utility software for solving problems.
Another issue to support the integration of informatics with other disciplines involves the lack of solid tradition in teaching informatics.

In Fig.1(b) a formative intervention is symbolized as a point in a three-dimensional space whose coordinates are the components of the model shown in Fig.1(a). Each "component" depends on the particular educational context one is dealing with. For clarity we discuss the extreme cases when one coordinate is missing and the spatial representation collapses into a plane.

When the use of the computer is missing, one is on the plane of "paper and pencil informatics," so it is more difficult to integrate informatics with other disciplines and to make informatics concepts more concrete. For example, think about the roles played by computing power and graphic display in the applications of informatics to many subjects.

If the link with other disciplines is missing, one moves on

the plane of "informatics as an autonomous discipline." The educational interventions of this kind better suit technical education. If the integration with other disciplines is not attempted, there is the risk that informatics will become too abstract.

Finally, when the coordinate "elements of informatics" is missing, one moves on the plane of "mysterious informatics." Here it is difficult to use informatics tools knowingly without having some basic informatics concepts. In many contexts it is difficult to work with computers if one must treat them as black boxes.

The above considerations motivated the design and testing of a teaching unit for high school students; its aim is to integrate physics and informatics in a single learning process. This work has been developed and put into practice by Progetto DAE - Didattica Assistita da Elaboratore (Computer Assisted Education) of Naples University, which for many years has been performing educational research in computer-assisted learning (CAL) in the sciences both at the college and high school levels (2, 3).
The Progetto DAE has developed many prototypes of educational software for science topics (4, 5, 6). Its experience in developing and experimenting with different CAL strategies on a large number of students was a strong factor in support of the proposal for a two-fold teaching unit for the age range 15-18 years.

2. GENERAL FEATURES OF THE EXPERIMENT

2.1 Context

Unlike, for example, the United Kingdom and France, there existed until now no national plan for generalized introduction of informatics into school curricula in Italy. Very recently the Minister of Education announced a specific project for stimulating and guiding a gradual process of introduction of informatics into school curricula, starting with the high schools. Over the past few years (in Italy) there have been several initiatives involving informatics instruction by cultural groups, teachers' association, single schools, and groups of teachers.

The experiment described here took place in the context of the IRIS project, coordinated by CEDE (Centro Europeo dell'Educazione - European Centre for Education), an independent agency of the Italian Ministry of Education. The IRIS project (Iniziative e Ricerche per l'Informatica nella Scuola - Initiatives and Research for Informatics at School) (7) is aimed at producing models and materials for computer education in schools at all levels.

The IRIS project supports different approaches for introducing basic informatics, the main feature being that informatics is not introduced as a specific discipline, but is integrated in the traditional curriculum. Both the learning of basic informatics and the training in the use of informatics technology aim to improve the quality of the teaching-learning process in disciplinary contexts which include sciences and humanities.

The educational approach followed in our experiment for secondary school students consists of two steps: first, the students are introduced to informatics with a unit called "Corso di introduzione all'informatica" (8); then, at a second stage, computer education is embedded in physics. Physics has been chosen as the link to informatics not only because of its intrinsic interest, but also because of its presence in all curricula of Italian secondary schools.

2.2 Methodology

The basis for the integration of physics and computer education is provided by the use of a CAL package. A CAL package is an information system aimed at educating in some specific field of learning, but its use may also provide several stimuli of an informatics nature which may be exploited to start a process of computer education which can be developed within the context of the more traditional process of disciplinary education. In this section there is a discussion of some possible paths which can be followed to develop a process of computer education starting from the use of a CAL package.

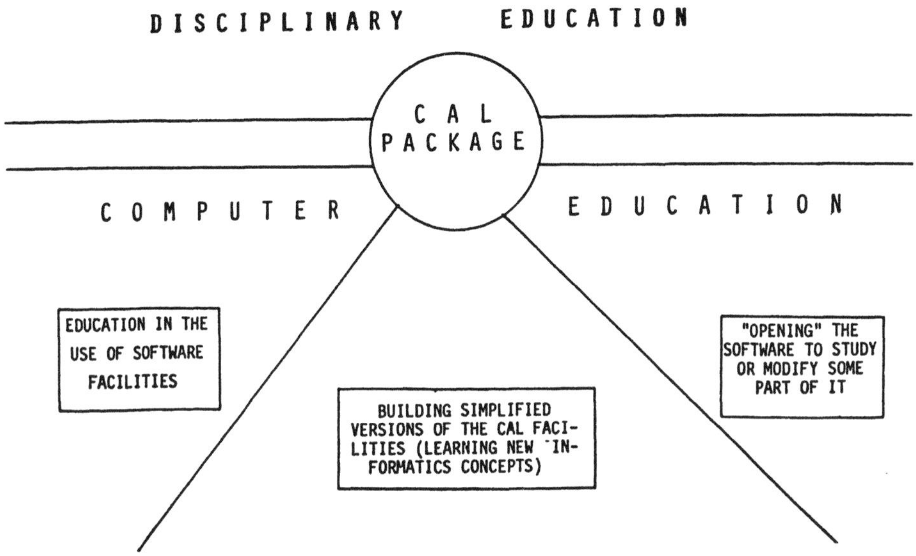

Figure 2. A representation of the educational aspects involved in the use of a CAL package

Figure 2 provides a rough schema of some educational aspects which may be involved in the use of a CAL package. The representation indicates that a CAL package may integrate aspects of disciplinary education and of computer education (even if the separation between the two is not as well defined as the figure may suggest).

The first partition of our "halfplane" of computer education suggests that the use of any program oriented to a specific goal is a powerful means to produce computer education. The student using the system becomes familiar with its behaviour, realizes what can be done and what cannot, and sees a function performed by a computer program as a transformation which maps a given input into a given output.

The second partition is the possibility of "opening the software," and using it as an object of study to understand the structure of some part or of some specific algorithms, or to implement on it small modifications to obtain a behaviour different from the original one.

The third partition refers to the implementation (in a simplified way) of the functions provided by the CAL package. The student treats the existing package as a model and tries to build a simplified version of some of its facilities. The student must understand the structure of the program and the problems to be solved to implement its functionalities. Thus, the student is given motivation for learning new informatics concepts and models.

Such an approach does not lend itself to a first introduction to informatics, but is more suited to second-level courses in which students are already familiar with algorithms and with a programming language. The students with a background in informatics can concentrate on more "advanced" topics, and especially on the link between informatics and physics. They may find how informatics can help in solving physics problems or may find in physics problems a motivating factor for learning new informatics concepts.

This approach exhibits also good flexibility as to the level and the depth of computer education to be achieved. Even where computer education does not fit into the class schedule or is outside course objectives, it still is possible to integrate education in basic physics with a little computer education provided by the use of the CAL package. The computer education process briefly described here imposes requirements on the structure of the software for the package.

A CAL package not explicitly designed for "informatics opening" can seldom be used in such a process. The logical and physical structure of the program must reflect the nature of the problem and the operations on physical entities; the code must have a high degree of readability achieved by the use of structured coding and by modular design. Modules should have high coherence, small dimensions and loose coupling. Software modifications performed by students should be minor and should be envisioned in advance. The overall structure should include suitable interfaces which allow for easy module identification and possible module replacement.

2.3 Students' previous exposure to informatics

The teaching unit to be described is offered to students who have been exposed to an introduction to informatics, the "Corso di introduzione all'informatica". This unit is presented in the first two years of high school and uses as a captivating software instrument, the robot Martino, a modified version of "Karel the robot" by R. Pattis.
Martino is fully described in reference 9. A brief description can explain how students are introduced through the use of Martino to two concepts: a) structured construction of algorithms and programs, and b) handling information with preprogrammed modules. Students use the Pascal language, the UCSD operating system and the robot Martino, an arrow capable of moving step by step on a two-dimensional grid. At the crosspoints there may be objects which Martino may pick up or put down; there may be "walls" which Martino cannot pass through. The student writes a program in Pascal to get Martino to perform a task.

Robot control primitives have been embedded in the Pascal language. Instructions are given to allow Martino to perform operations (e.g., forward, right, left, pick up, put down), and information is provided on the world around Martino by means of suitable predicates (object-present, free-right, free-ahead, facing-south, facing-north...).

Students program Martino to perform increasingly difficult tasks. The world is created by the user with a software facility for setting walls and objects. The student sees on the screen the robot moving on the grid and performing operations according to the program he or she has built. An important feature is that of seeing on the screen the instruction being executed and its visual effect on Martino's world. This visual check helps students discover bugs in their programs and in finding the correct solution to their problems. Figures 3 a, b, c, and d show some possible tasks for Martino.

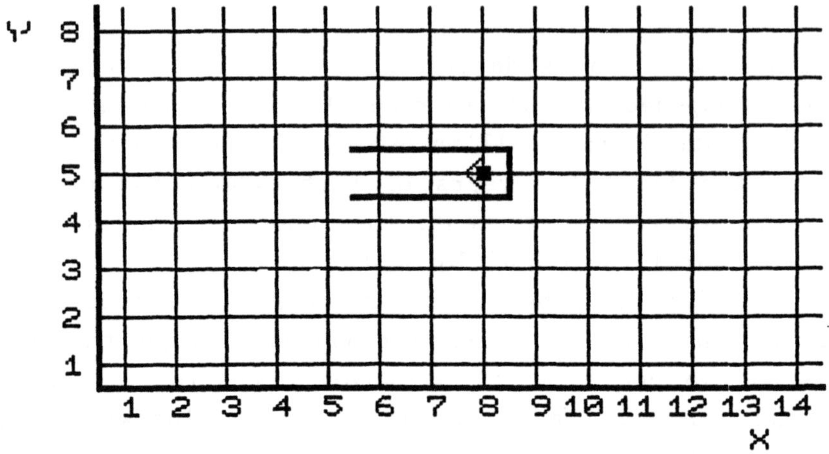

a)

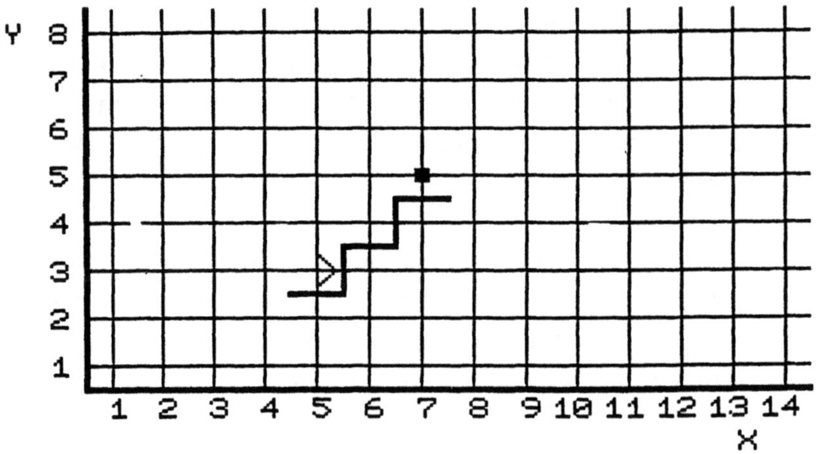

b)

Figure 3 a, b Examples of worlds where Martino the robot manipulates objects according to Pascal programs written by students.

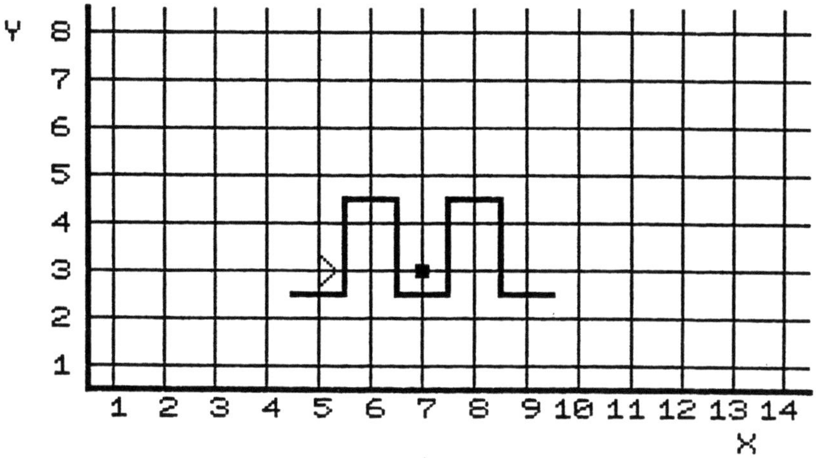

c)

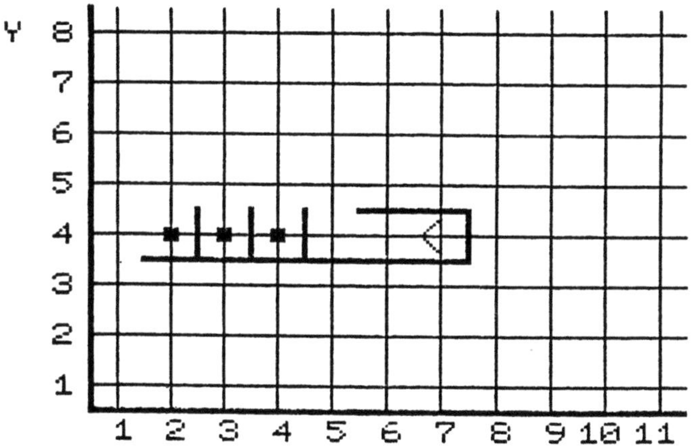

d)

Figure 3 c, d Examples of worlds where Martino the robot manipulates objects according to Pascal programs written by students.

Other basic concepts of informatics are introduced later, with reference first to Martino and later on by means of real-world examples.

3. THE TEACHING UNIT "GRAVITA'"

In this section the criteria for the teaching unit GRAVITA' (10, 11) are sketched:

- Choose a fundamental topic in basic physics whose study

needs the use of analytic tools such as graphic representation of data, elements of data analysis, etc....

- Develop a CAL package to study the physics topic according to the criteria for easy "opening" already described.
- Propose, together with the use of the CAL package, to study the physics topic, and to study informatics topics. The motivation for learning comes from experiencing how useful and powerful the informatics tools are.

The proposed pedagogical strategy can be summarized as follows:

- A stage of basic physics education with a CAL package. This experience allows the students to become familiar with, and educated in using the computer as an educational agent.
- A stage of basic computer education in which advanced topics are studied. The aim is to introduce the students to facilities whose usefulness they have already experienced in using the CAL package.

The advantages of this approach are:

- The support of the disciplinary content for informatics education. Concrete problems which students have experienced in the study of the discipline are linked to informatics.
- The teacher is encouraged to enter into the structure of the software of the teaching unit. This allows the teacher to become aware of both didactic and informatics problems connected with the making of complex educational software;
- Even in the case where informatics education is not possible, there is still the possibility of using the CAL package only for physics education. In addition, one would still have some education in informatics tools.

This structure of the teaching unit allows two sequences in

the study of physics and informatics topics. The first sequence is one in which the first stage is the study of basic physics, and the second is the study of informatics topics based on the analysis of the tools used in the preceding stage. In the second sequence the study of informatics proceeds parallel to the study of physics. The choice between these sequences depends on conditions at the school and on the teacher.

3.1 Physics education content

The physics content in GRAVITA' concerns the discovery of the laws which describe the fall of bodies under different conditions. This topic has been selected because of its underlying relevance in mechanics. It is part of all physics courses and can be correlated to a familiar phenomenology. The students analyze data, couples of "h" and "t" values, where h is the height from which the body falls and t is the time of fall.

We make available to the users various sets of data, instead of requesting them to collect data, for several reasons:

- To collect these data is not trivial. We need time accuracy of about 10^{-2} sec.
- The unit becomes somewhat longer if the laboratory work is included.

If the students or the teacher want to use data different from those stored in GRAVITA', this can easily be done. The first activity is to create the data file. This choice has been made also because of the value of providing experience in data analysis. The utility of this topic goes beyond the study of falling bodies.

This first phenomenology brought to the students' attention involves data on the fall of small heavy bodies. The proposed activities are:

- to build the data file;
- to sort the values according increasing time values;

- to plot height vs. time;
- to try to fit data with a linear function;
- to try to fit data with a quadratic function.

During these activities students use files and operate upon graphic representations of data.

Figures 4a, b, c, and d show typical hard copies of the screen. The straight line for fitting the free fall data can be obtained by inputting the parameters a and b for $y = ax + b$, or by pointing to two points on the line. When graphic input is used, the student is given the equation of the line.

The possibility of using two input options, alphanumeric and graphic, helps students having problems with the equation for a straight line and with the meaning of the angular coefficient and intercept. The students see how data deviate from the assumed linearity by studying linear and quadratic deviation as visualized on the plot. The sum of quadratic deviations is drawn in the left upper corner of the plot as a visual measure of the fit. The fit is repeated until the student discovers that a straight line is not adequate to represent the data. Students can compare the least-squares straight line with their best fit. The visual appearance of these fits on the plot provides an intuitive approach to the study of the least-squares criterion.

The second step is to fit the data with a parabolic function. Again the students can input the quadratic equation i.e., the coefficients a, b, c in the usual form $y = ax^2 + bx + c$, or they can select three points on the plot. These two facilities allow students to become familiar with parabolas and the meaning of the coefficients in the equations. The process is repeated until a reasonable fit is reached; again students compare their best fit with the least-squares parabola. The data presented are for the case of free fall, where friction is negligible, and for which there is no initial velocity.

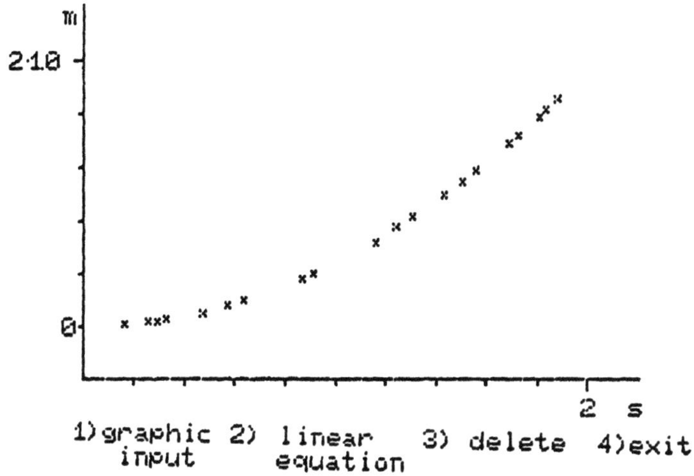

a)

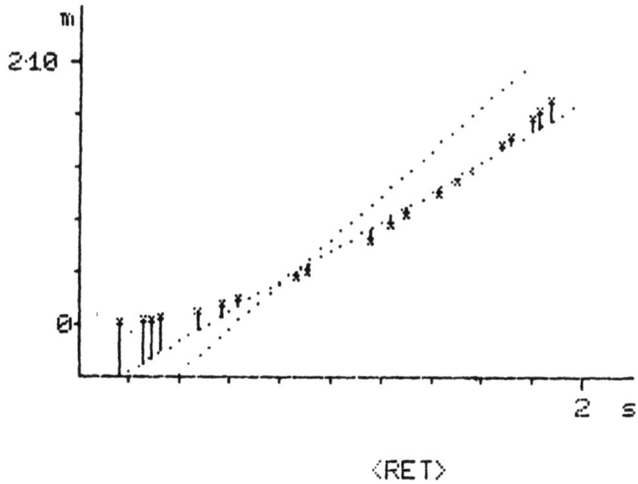

b)

Figure 4. Some stages of data analysis for "free fall".
a) Students can use graphic input or give the equation to identify data fitting a straight line.
b) Linear deviations are shown to help in optimizing the linear fit.

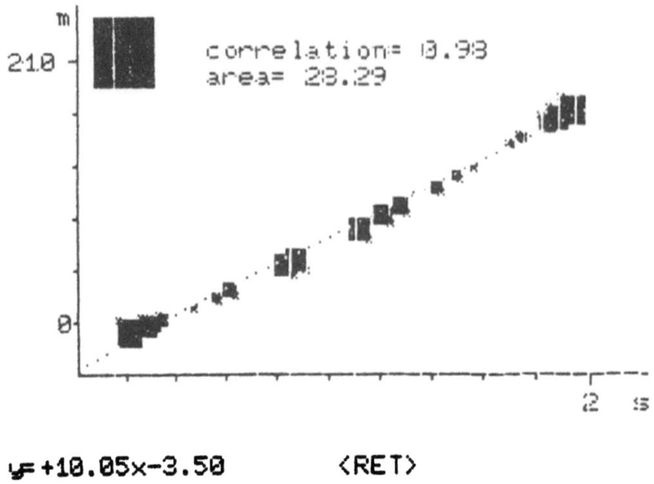

c)

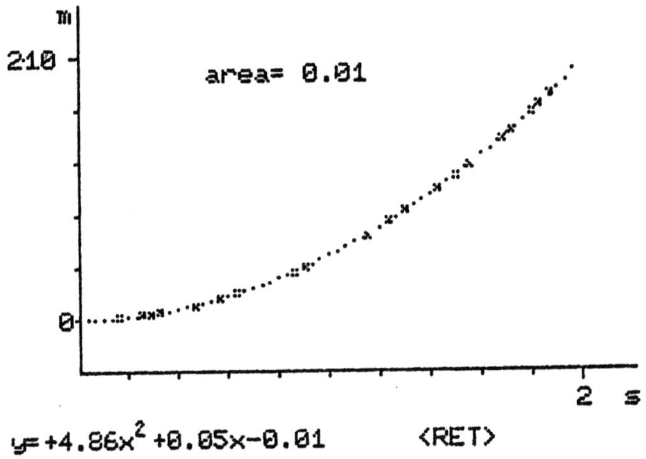

d)

Figure 4. Some stages of data analysis for "free fall".
- c) Quadratic deviations and their sum are shown to introduce a least-squares best fit.
- d) The least-squares parabola for the given data is shown.

Once students are convinced that a parabolic curve gives the best fit, they are given other sets of data to analyze. This activity is aimed at having them discover that the second-order coefficient of the parabola is the same for all sets of data, i.e., that gravitational acceleration is constant. Using data files for graphical representation of data allows students to visualize linear and quadratic deviations following a "trial and error" procedure to discover the relation between height and time.

After analysis of free-fall data, new data refer to situations where friction is not negligible, and where the final velocity tends to become constant. The students are guided to recognize that two trends appear in the data: the free-fall parabola is a good fit for data with small time values; and is a bad fit for data with large time values, which show a linear trend.
The proposed activities are:

- to find the subset of data which can be reasonally well described by the free fall parabola;
- to find the subset of data characterized by a final constant velocity, and to find the value of this velocity;
- to identify the transition region between these two trends.

Students can select a rectangular window on the plot and zoom any plot region to improve the analysis. Using different data files students find that the value of asymptotic velocity depends on the situation analyzed.
Figures 5a, b, c, and d show typical screens.

The last situation to be considered is the falling of very light (feather like) bodies, where no simple relation between height and time can be found. This last stage of development is now in progress. Other activities are suggested, such as the study of the plot of h versus the square of time or the plot of average velocity versus time.

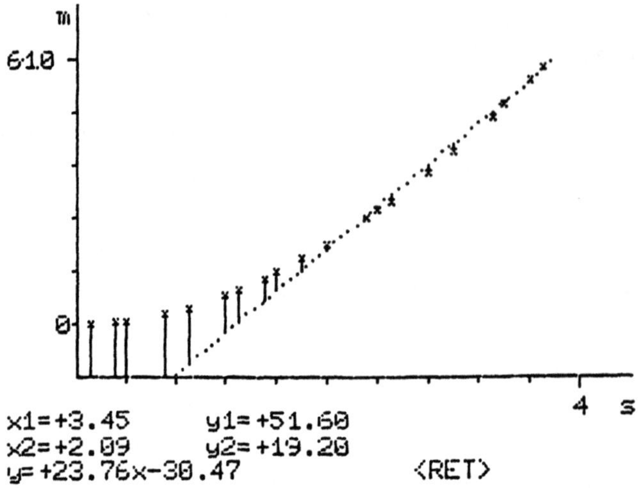

a)

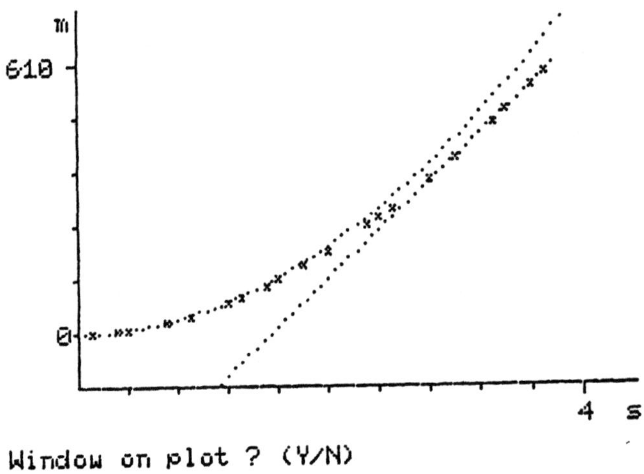

b)

Figure 5. Some stages of data analysis when friction is not negligible.
a) Linear fit of data with large t.
b) The "free fall" parabola and the constant velocity fit.

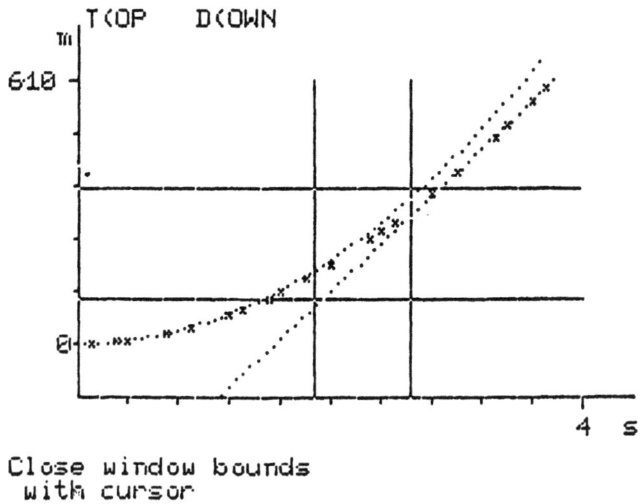

c)

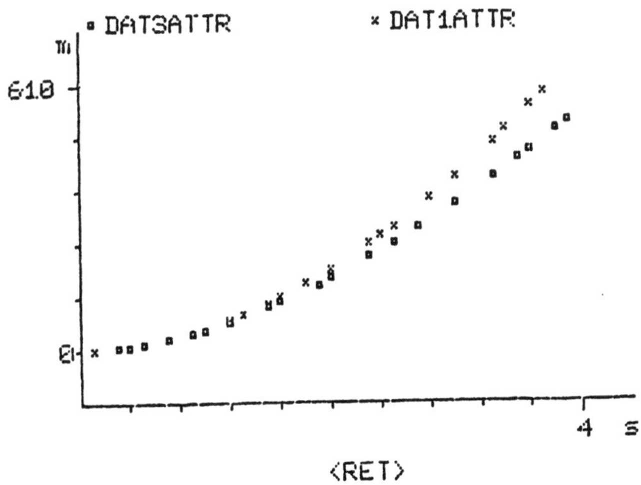

d)

Figure 5. Some stages of data analysis when friction is not negligible.
c) Exploring data in more detail by zooming.
d) Different data sets are shown to verify the influence of the particular falling body.

3.2 Computer education content

So far we have discussed GRAVITA'. In this section, aspects concerning computer education are considered in reference to the general criteria discussed in section 2.2. As far as instruction to the use of software facilities is concerned, i.e., the left segment of Fig. 2, the software of GRAVITA' is organized as a set of modules performing the following functions:

INPUT	to create the data file
ARCHIVIO	to manipulate the data file
ORDINA	to sort the data according to increasing time value
CADLIB	to analyze the "free fall" data
ATTRITO	to analyze data referring to situations where friction is not negligible

The students choose the modules appropriate to their stage. In this activity they refer to the workbook. They reinforce the knowledge of the operating system, a subject of the introductory course on informatics, and become aware of the different roles of the modules. They build an intellectual model of computer facilities quite close to that of functions mapping input into output.

The right segment of Fig. 2, i.e., the "opening" of the software to be studied or the modification of some part of it, applying new informatics concepts is discussed for the case of the module entitled INPUT. First, students analyze the INPUT function, the first program they use in the unit. This module reads couples of t-h data from the keyboard, and transfers them to a file on a floppy disk. The features the student should appreciate are:

- the program handles non-integer numbers - at this point, the only numeric type known to the student is INTEGER;
- the program writes onto the disk.

Non-integer numbers allow the teacher to introduce the real data type (while INTEGER and CHAR were sufficient in previous applications). As an immediate extension of the concept of data type, structured data are introduced.

Next, disk I/O is discussed. The students have learned the importance of having their data on disk so that they can be read and used in subsequent programs. Therefore, they are ready to understand the technical aspects of this operation. The type FILE is then introduced, defined as an indefinite sequence of data of some type. Since a file resides on a peripheral device and is permanent, the necessity of opening and closing the file can be explained. In particular, the student will be guided to become familiar with the instructions needed for: a) opening the file, b) writing data to the file, c) closing the file.

In the final phase, students are encouraged to apply the elements of Pascal they have learned in their own simple programs. For instance, the activities proposed for the REAL data type are to make calculations involving non-integer operands, and/or results, to evaluate expressions with integer operands, yelding non-integer values, and to compare the results obtained for INTEGER or REAL variables.

Similarly, students may extend the notion of the RECORD data type they have learned while analyzing the module INPUT; in fact, they can apply it to problems involving more complex data types consisting of several related values, possibly belonging to different elementary types.
The ARRAY data type can be introduced in the opening of the module INPUT in connection with the use of files. Experimental data (for instance t, h couples) can either be stored in a file and processed by accessing them a couple at a time or stored in an ARRAY resident in the main memory. The student can learn how to use an array and can be guided to understand mutual advantages and disadvantages of files vs. arrays through different problems.

The middle (and final) segment of computer education represented in Fig. 2 is achieved by guiding students in building simplified versions of the facilities they used when studying physics. Implementing utilities similar to the ones in the CAL package - a "living" model to be understood and approximated - has several educational implications:

- students make an active effort to understand the utilities existing in the package;
- students must understand the program architecture needed to implement those utilities as well as the simplifying hypothesis adopted to keep the implementation simple.

Some of the experimental studies done in connection with GRAVITA' utilize the module ORDINA, which sorts input data into ascending time, and the plotting facilities for the (t, h) couples. This is rather significant from standpoint of computer education since it provides motivation for the advantages and disadvantages of different sorting strategies, and it exposes students to simple graphics, giving a concrete example of automatic scaling.

3.3 The structure of the teaching unit

GRAVITA' is a teaching unit of the IRIS project; it has been developed in conformity with standards for the entire project. The unit material consists of a teacher's manual, a student's manual and two floppy disks containing the software. GRAVITA' is divided into stages articulated in activities to be done in the classroom, at home and in the laboratory, where the computer is located. Both the student's and teacher's manuals are structured according to this subdivision of GRAVITA'. The teacher's guide presents the aims of the teaching unit, its content, a plan for use of the material, and instructions for carrying out the different stages.

4. PRELIMINARY TESTING

The first testing of GRAVITA' was carried out in 1984-85 in different types of high schools. The students were attending the second and third year, and their average age was 15. The official curricula for these classes did not include informatics. These students had worked the previous year with the preliminary teaching unit which introduced Martino. The teachers involved in the experiment were volunteers and were familiar with the students through normal curricular activities. The teachers attended a short refresher course using as teaching material the unit they would subsequently use in their own classroom.

For the control of the progress of the students' achievement, a rating test was used at the end of each stage, together with a final test where the basic contents of the teaching unit were checked. Because of the small numbers, no data are presented for this preliminary test; students showed good comprehension level for both physics and informatics content.

5. CONCLUSIONS AND PERSPECTIVES

The first experimental test of the teaching unit GRAVITA' has yielded useful suggestions and criticism, now being incorporated in preparing the revised version of the unit, to be tested in the 1985-86 school year on a wider scale. GRAVITA' has been well accepted, both by students and teachers. The students and teachers involved in this experiment had already experienced the previous unit "Corso di introduzione all'informatica," which met with considerable success. This previous experience probably acted as a motivating factor and generated a positive attitude toward GRAVITA'. The teachers involved were enthusiastic about the proposed integrated approach and found no major difficulties in managing the entire process.

The scheme of integration between physics and informatics discussed in this paper is only one of many examples that can be considered. Other topics can be chosen in physics, and the integration process with informatics can occur for informatics concepts at other levels or in other disciplinary contexts. In particular, a process of integration is possible for non-scientific disciplines. As simple examples let us consider history and geography, where the use of data can support a proposal for discovery-based learning or linguistics, and where the theme of natural language versus artificial languages can be introduced via grammar, syntax and semantics.

The preliminary results which have been obtained with the first version of GRAVITA' suggest that the three-component model proposed for computer education is reasonably well grounded and promising. This process of integration between traditional disciplines, in our case physics and informatics, is just evolving; both creativity and experimentation are needed to find the best method for doing this. Despite the difficulties encountered with the integration of informatics with other disciplines, it is important to pursue such an integrated approach in order to counter the tendency toward excessive specialization within the educational process, particularly so in the case of informatics.

6. REFERENCES

1. Olimpo, G., "Computer education and learning via computer" (in Italian), Proceedings of the ANTEM Symposium on "Informatica e Nuove Tecnologie per l'Educazione e la Formazione", Bologna 1985 (in press)
2. Avitabile, G., Formisano, M.R., Russo, E., Sassi, E., Spadaccini, G., "CAL: experiences and perspectives of project D.A.E. at Naples" (in Italian), Proceedings of the XX National Congress of AICA (Associazione Italiana per il Calcolo Automatico e l'Informatica), Pavia 1981, pp. 1173-1181
3. Avitabile, G., Russo, E., Sassi, E., Spadaccini, G., "DAE project: experiences in using a main frame in teaching sciences at university level", Proceedings of the Symposium on "L'Università e l'evoluzione delle tecnologie informatiche", Milano 1983, pp. 1.1-1.4
4. Avitabile, G., Chioccariello, A., Mosca, P., Russo, E., Sassi, E., Spadaccini, G., "Computer Assisted Learning: a graphic dialogue on Schroedinger equation", ACM-SIGCUE Bull., 15, 14-24, 1981

5. Avitabile, G., Lepore, U., Sassi, E., "DINAMPOP: a CAL package to simulate the behaviour of systems of two interacting populations" (in Italian), Proceedings of the XXII National Congress of AICA (Associazione Italiana per il Calcolo Automatico e l'Informatica), Napoli 1983, pp. 237-244
6. Chioccariello, A., Sassi, E., Spadaccini, G., Olimpo, G., "Production of CAL packages. A set of criteria and an example in the electric circuit field", Proceedings of the IV Canadian Symposium on Instructional Technology, Winnipeg, 1983, pp. 488-493
7. "IRIS Project (Initiatives and Research for Informatics in Schools)" (in Italian), Ricerca Educativa, n. Ø, 1984, pp. 61-70
8. Various Authors, "Introduzione all'Informatica", teaching unit developed by Istituto Tecnologie Didattiche and Istituto Matematica Applicata, CNR, Genova, 1984
9. Olimpo, G., Persico, D., Sarti, L., Tavella, M., "An experiment in introducing the basic concepts of informatics", Proceedings of WCCE '85, Fourth World Conference on Computers in Education, Elsevier Science Publishers/ North Holland, 1985, part 1, pg. 31-37
10. Various Authors, GRAVITA', teaching unit developed by DAE project, Naples University, 1984
11. Avitabile, G., Balzano, E., Lepore, U., Milano, M., Sassi, E., Velotti, F., "CAL in basic physics education and basic computer education: an experiment in secondary school" (in italian), Proceedings of the ANTEM Symposium on "Informatica e Nuove Tecnologie per l'Educazione e la Formazione", Bologna 1985 (in press)

INTEGRATING COMPUTERS AND TUTORS INTO COST-EFFECTIVE PHYSICS AND MATHEMATICS INSTRUCTION

Harold Weinstock
Office of Technological and Continuing Education
and Department of Physics
Illinois Institute of Technology
Chicago, Illinois

1. INTRODUCTION

I must state at the very beginning that the subject of this paper does not compare in elegance or imagination with many of the other computer-based instructional methods described in this volume. Nevertheless, I hope the reader will find that what follows represents a relatively quick and cost-effective means for improving the quality of science and mathematics instruction in the interim period (of perhaps several years) before a higher level of computer-based instructional methodology becomes commonplace. In order to understand the rationale for adopting a computer- and tutor-based instructional program, the reader first must be acquainted with the context into which it was introduced and how the program helped solve two apparently unrelated problems.

The first problem related to the financial and institutional support for the Educational Technology Center (ETC) at the Illinois Institute of Technology (IIT) [Weinstock (1983)]. ETC was established in late 1979 with the aid of a $250,000 three-year grant from the National Science Foundation (NSF) and matching funds from IIT. It "opened for business" to IIT students in October 1980, serving as a form of electronic library, featuring a variety of personal computers, audio-visual media and student tutors to service those enrolled in the introductory physics, mathematics and chemistry courses primarily. We, four participating faculty members and

NATO ASI Series, Vol. F 23
Designing Computer-Based Learning Materials
Edited by A. Bork and H. Weinstock

numerous student programmers, worked rather diligently that first year to identify and adapt existing educational courseware, and to create our own instructional dialogs and drill-and-practice routines. I should mention that we were well aware that most commercially available (and free) courseware was mediocre at best. Furthermore, we were under no illusions about the task required to improve upon this situation with our own resources while keeping attuned to the progress of others in a similar situation. Our goal then (as it is now) was to continue to work at producing courseware we felt would be of value to our students. Meanwhile, the undergraduate student tutors proved to be a popular feature of ETC.

During the 1979-1982 period of the NSF grant, in which the funding decreased each succeeding year, we did obtain additional grants from local foundations and a modest amount of funding from the academic budget of IIT. Everyone seemed to declare ETC a success as a source for educational enrichment and remediation. Despite the accolades for a Center I had created and for which I had obtained substantial initial funding, I was growing concerned in early 1982 about the chances for ETC's long-term survival.

There was a history at IIT - and I suspect at many other institutions - of abandoning experimental educational programs once "seed money" from external sources had been exhausted, and the burden for financial support fell solely upon an internal budget. There was nothing diabolical in this; it was often a matter of having to support an optional educational program with not enough student participation to make the operation financially viable. In 1982 student enrollment at IIT was declining, with an attendant decrease in the budget for academic support services. ETC was an expensive entity to maintain as an adjunct to the "real" library, and it would be years before we were sufficiently endowed with quality courseware to be able to convince our faculty colleagues to integrate interactive computer dialogs into their course delivery. This being the case, I had to find some other means for bringing ETC into the mainstream of the educational program.

This means presented itself when I addressed a problem which had existed for some time for my colleagues in physics, as well as for the faculty in chemistry and mathemetics. Typically, in the introductory courses for science and engineering majors there are three 50-minute lectures presented each week in a large hall seating on the order of 200 students. There is little opportunity for interaction with this format, so it usually is implemented by a 50-minute recitation period once each week with about 20 to 25 per class under the supervision of either a faculty member or a graduate teaching assistant. At one time (at IIT) these recitation sessions had been optional for the students, and many of those who needed help the most failed to attend. This was remedied some years ago by requiring students to come, or more precisely, requiring them to take a 10-minute quiz (of typically one problem) at the conclusion of the period. In the time preceding the quiz, the students were expected to request assistance on homework problems or on concepts covered during lectures. Most questions came from the weakest students, with the answers of little interest to the others in the class. Occasionally, questions came from the very best students, with the answers again of little interest to the majority of the class. Still other times, no questions came at all. Then the instructor could choose a variety of approaches, including giving the quiz early and dismissing the class before the end of the hour. The semester quiz average, plus an average homework grade were used to determine a recitation grade which counted only 14 to 17% toward the computation of the final grade.

With the exception of the quiz itself, the recitation represents a mostly passive experience for the student, and over the years, it generally has pleased neither student nor instructor. Most of my colleagues in the Physics Department were indifferent (at best) to ETC, but in the matter of recitations they were unanimous in declaring that they were of little value and an unpleasant chore. On the other hand, the recitations could not be eliminated without causing serious administrative and educational problems: I HAD FOUND MY OPPORTUNITY TO INTEGRATE ETC INTO THE FABRIC OF THE IIT SCIENCE CURRICULUM.

2. THE PLAN

The missing ingredients in a conventional recitation included: a method for identifying student comprehension of the material covered; the ability to help students individually once specific weaknesses were uncovered; and a mechanism for providing the study discipline that some immature students require. We had at our disposal computers which could generate the test questions to interrogate the students, to grade their responses instantly, and to keep records for the benefit of the faculty; and we had a corps of trained undergraduate tutors to whom students would come (until then) only on a voluntary basis. I should say also that my ETC faculty colleagues and our student programmers were supportive of and helped refine the plan I shall now describe.

Figure 1 shows the "flow chart" for a student to progress through each week's assigned work in lieu of the standard recitation described above. It represents only a small deviation from my initial scheme and was modified to this form as the result of extensive discussions with my colleagues, Earl Zwicker (Physics) and Jerry Frank (Mathematics). Amazingly, we have carried out this scheme exactly as planned and have found no reason

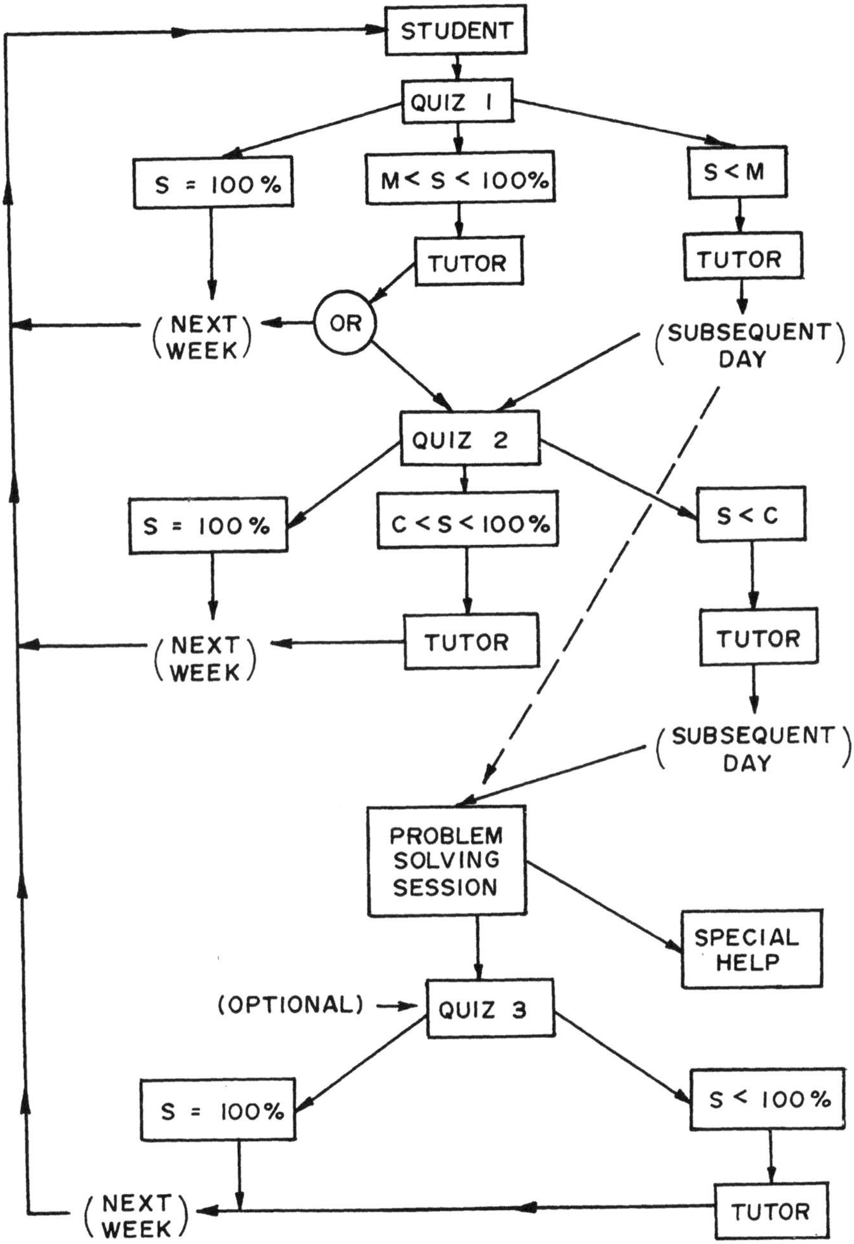

Figure 1. Flow chart for student progress during one week.

to make any significant changes after more than two years of extensive use.

Instead of attending an assigned 50-minute recitation each week, a student must come to ETC at almost any time during either Monday or Tuesday to take a computer-generated, four-problem quiz which has been printed off-line. He or she obtains this quiz from a (student) monitor in a room added to ETC specifically to support this testing. In obtaining the quiz, the student must surrender his or her college identification (ID) card containing his or her photograph. The monitor enters into the computer the student's name and the unique three-digit number of the quiz given out. The monitor's display screen then shows the name and the time remaining for the student to complete the quiz - a total of 30 minutes is alloted. The student goes to a vacant carrel, works on the solution to each of the problems, doing all written work on the paper provided, and then enters the four one-letter answers at a terminal, having first entered his or her ID number. The terminal then responds immediately with the student's score and instructions on the next step in the process.

If the student has answered all problems correctly, we assume that mastery has been achieved for that week's required material, and there seems little need to require any other activity. Thus, the computer congratulates the student and tells him or her to return the written quiz to the monitor. Upon surrendering the quiz, the ID card is returned to the student, and there is no need to show up again until the following week. If the student has answered all but one of the four problems correctly, we treat this in much the same way, but with one major exception. No student who has answered one or more problems incorrectly may leave ETC without discovering how to solve those problems correctly with the assistance of a tutor. Only then may the student retrieve his or her ID card and leave ETC. We consider only one incorrect problem to be indicative of "mastery" and do not require the student to return that week. In order to help minimize student procrastination, we offer a 10% bonus to those who can achieve 75% - 3 out of 4 - or 100% - 4 out of 4 - correct on Monday.

The plot thickens for those who do less well on their first quiz of the week (which must be taken either on Monday or Tuesday). If mastery, at least 3 out of 4 correct, is not achieved, the student must return a subsequent day to take another quiz on the same material, although we sometimes have given the option of having the student attend the 50-minute, problem-solving session if he or she chooses to bypass the second quiz. On the other hand, by taking the second quiz, the student is assumed to have achieved mastery if his or her combined score for the two quizzes is 62.5% or 75% - 5 or 6 out of 8. Again, I reiterate that no student can leave ETC without having all incorrect problems discussed with a tutor.

For those students who do not achieve mastery after two attempts, there is a requirement to attend a Thursday problem-solving session presided over by a faculty member and/or (on rare occasions) a graduate teaching assistant. Although this session may occupy the same time period as the originally scheduled recitation, it differs from the recitation in that it requires active student participation and, as indicated above, it actually is called a problem-solving session. The students are given a list of problems they must solve at their seats. The chosen problems are taken mostly from a required book of problems, although they can include textbook problems or ones supplied by the instructor. It is important to note that the essential difference between the standard recitation and these sessions is that here a student must be occupied for the entire 50 minutes by solving problems while an instructor circulates about the room offering assistance when requested, and often when not requested, i.e., he may wish to provide hints to those who don't realize they are having trouble. Typically, between 1/3 to 2/3 of the students enrolled in the course come to these sessions in a given week, somewhat dependent on whether it is the first or second semester of the course and on the specific material covered in a given week. I should note also that those students not required to attend these sessions are free to do so.

It is perhaps worth elaborating on the requirement for some students to attend the problem-solving sessions. If a required student fails to attend, he receives a zero recitation grade for the week; if he misses a required session on the following week, he not only receives another zero, but he is prevented from taking any quizzes on the following week until he has had an interview with the course instructor. Specifically, this means that after the second consecutive zero grade has been entered into the computer, the computer will inform the system monitor that the student in question may not be issued a quiz until a note is received from the instructor to inform the system that the prohibition has been removed.

Upon completion of the (Thursday) problem-solving session, a student has the option of taking yet another quiz by the end of the week, with the average of all quizzes taken that week as the student's weekly recitation grade. As mentioned earlier, the recitation grade makes a relatively insignificant contribution to the computation of the student's course grade. The major goal of the recitation has always been to improve problem-solving skills, and the assignment of a recitation grade was meant to provide an incentive only.

Under the new ETC-based recitation, the student would be forced, when needed, into paying greater attention to problem solving in the hope that this would bring rewards in the form of not only a higher recitation grade, but in a higher course grade. The recitation grade itself never counts for more than about 15% of the course grade, and typically 1/3 of that value is attributable to the homework problems submitted on a weekly basis. Furthermore, to account for variations in the grading standards of the various recitation instructors and the various teaching assistants who grade the homework, a normalization procedure is applied to the recitation grades. The recitation grade then is added to the raw scores of three one-hour exams and one two-hour final exam, these exams in totality accounting for 80 to 85% of the final grade - the difference being due to whether or not there is a laboratory component to that semester's segment of the course.

3. IMPLEMENTATION

Although the plan described above was devised in the spring of 1982 with the hope of implementing it in the fall of 1982, inevitable delays in the software development and in the assembly of a quiz-problem data base caused us to delay a pilot study of the new system until the spring 1983 semester. It should be noted that the hardware for this operation consisted of nothing more than a small network of Apple II personal computers tied together by a 20-megabyte Corvus hard-disk drive. Although this network contained several Apples, a large number of students could be handled quite easily with a minimum of two, with a corresponding cost for all hardware being about $5,000.

The data base was obtained by generalizing problems taken from old multiple-choice examinations. The answers, both correct and incorrect, had to be specified in symbolic form. Numerical limits and increments were placed on each of the variables. Groupings were made of equivalent problems, i.e., those testing the same material and of the same level of complexity.

The software was designed so that equivalent problems are chosen randomly for each of the four quiz problems. Within the range of variables, random numbers are selected, and the position (A, B, C or D) of the correct answer also is selected randomly. Although initially we did not print diagrams on the problem sheets, this is now done routinely.

Part of the motivation for adopting this new system of recitations was to make the instructor's job easier, specifically by relieving him or her of the work associated with test generation, grading and record keeping. Table I illustrates a printout given to an instructor on a Wednesday afternoon so that he or she knows, by noting the asterisks at the left, which students are required to attend the Thursday problem-solving session. The printout provides, as well, a record of each student's quiz performance, indicating the score and day for each try, and the average (up to that point) for the week. On Friday afternoon of each week the instructor is presented an updated version of this printout, plus a summary of the weekly final average of each student for the entire term thus far.

Programming also has been done to record the use of the system as a function of time each school day. This does not have any immediate benefit to the instructor, but is quite useful in helping to schedule or reschedule available tutors. Table II illustrates a typical printout of system use. This shows the usage for a specific week, although one can obtain the integrated usage over several consecutive weeks as well.

RECITATION P103-9 - STUDENT SCORES - WEEK #2

	NAME	SSN	TRY 1	TRY 2	TRY 3	AVG
1.	*Ab...., Z	349-72-3415	25 M	75 W		50
2.	Ai...., D	399-68-6074	85 M			85
3.	*Br...., J	327-60-4494	25 T	50 W		37.5
4.	*Ca...., S	332-52-9303	50 T	25 W		37.5
5.	Ca...., A	322-64-2753	85 M			85
6.	*Cl...., J	270-60-9380	50 M			50
7.	Co...., R	340-66-5407	85 M			85
8.	Ga...., R	341-62-5295	75 T			75
9.	*Gr...., M	417-11-0606	50 M	50 T		50
0.	Hi...., J	352-64-2669	75 T			75
1.	*Hi...., J	322-70-3444	50 T	50 W		50
2.	*Hu...., S	353-68-0136	50 T	25 W		37.5
3.	Jo...., G	177-54-8242	50 M	75 T		62.5
4.	*Kl...., V	358-68-0323	25 M			25
5.	Li...., S	340-70-0649	75 T			75
6.	McG..., J	336-66-2133	75 T			75
7.	*Mi...., B	353-46-6137	50 M			50
8.	*Mi...., G	349-56-0298	25 T	0 W		12.5
9.	Ng...., T	332-70-3586	110 M			110
0.	*Ol...., D	350-68-1669	50 T	50 W		50
1.	Pa...., H	357-52-3652	50 M	100 T		75
.						
.						
.						
.						
.						
.						
.						
4.	Us...., R	344-56-4851	50 M	75 T		62.5
5.	Wa...., J	283-64-8342	100 T			100

LASS AVERAGE FOR QUIZZES TAKEN 55.5% 51.92% 57.17%

Table I

TOTAL QUIZZES TAKEN DURING WEEKS 4 THROUGH 4

TIME	MON	TUES	WED	THURS	FRI	TOTAL
9:00 AM	0	0	0	0	0	0
10:00 AM	0	11	0	6	0	17
11:00 AM	2	16	3	8	2	31
12:00 PM	4	7	2	2	3	18
1:00 PM	0	5	0	2	1	8
2:00 PM	16	11	10	2	4	43
3:00 PM	10	16	9	7	3	45
4:00 PM	12	8	7	1	0	28
5:00 PM	5	8	3	1	0	17
6:00 PM	0	0	0	0	0	0
TOTALS	49	80	34	29	13	205

Table II

A discussion of implementation must deal also with the key human element of the new form of recitation, namely the undergraduate student tutors. At the conclusion of each semester, I request a list of the "A" (i.e., top grade) students from those faculty members in charge of the physics and calculus courses which complete the introductory sequences - typically such students are in the midst of their second year of university studies. I then write a personal letter congratulating each student and pointing out both the intellectual and financial advantages of becoming a tutor. If the student is interested in pursuring the matter, I suggest that he or she come for an interview. This interview is essential because we must have tutors that can converse easily with no language impediment and who have a reasonable personality. The interview also gives me (or whoever is in charge that year) an opportunity to provide guidance on good tutoring habits, e.g., keep calm and don't be afraid to admit you don't know the answer to a particular question. Our best tutors often continue in this role until their graduation.

Each Friday afternoon all tutors meet to be briefed on the subject matter in physics and calculus that will be covered during the following week. They are addressed by a graduate student who supervises their activity and provides guidance on topics expected to be of unusual difficulty.

4. RESULTS AND ANALYSIS

The pilot study for the first semester of introductory physics in the spring of 1983 (alluded to earlier) was carried out with slightly over 20 students within a total course enrollment of about 200. While it was only with considerable effort that each week's problems were entered into the data base in time, the operation functioned without any major difficulty. The two faculty members involved were positive in their preliminary evaluation, and more importantly, the students seemed enthusiastic about the experience. Table III presents a summary of the response to a questionnaire of 12 of the students who completed the course.

Although the opinions of such a small number of students can not be accorded much weight, and being ever mindful of the infamous Hawthorne effect, we were encouraged by the response, sufficiently so to expand our efforts to produce a more meaningful trial of the new system. It seemed clear that the students believed they not only were encouraged to work harder, but that it paid off in a higher level of understanding. They were enthusiastic about the instant grading of quizzes and indicated a willingness to enroll again in a computerized recitation section if one were available.

In the fall 1983 semester, with the next segment of the introductory physics sequence, we established a test and control group, encompassing all 166 students who eventually completed the course. We were fortunate in convincing all four Thursday recitation instructors - I and Earl Zwicker, the course lecturer, were two of them - to supervise ETC-based recitations. Furthermore, two of the Thursday recitation instructors also conducted Tuesday recitations, which were to be conducted in the standard manner, thus presenting an even greater opportunity for an unbiased comparison of the old and new recitation formats. Due to technical problems, computer-generated quizzes were not available until the semester was about 25% completed, or somewhat relevantly, not until after the first hourly exam. This gave us an additional control, since we then could monitor the change in relative standing between the two groups in subsequent exams. Note that prior to that first exam, there was no difference in the format of the weekly recitations. Due to scheduling

QUESTIONNAIRE RESULTS

May 1983

Scale: 1 = Strongly disagree with the statement.

5 = Strongly agree with the statement.

QUESTION	RESPONSE
1. The computerized system encouraged me to work harder.	4.00
2. I believe I learned more/better as a result of the computerized quizzes.	4.41
3. I believe that my grade will be better as a result of the computerized quizzes.	3.91
4. I like the flexibility in time scheduling that is possible with this system.	3.75
5. I got more out of the recitation period because it was separate from the quiz.	2.83
6. The testing center was open for an adequate time each week.	3.41
7. It is really helpful to have instant grading of the quiz.	4.66
8. I would enroll in a computerized recitation section again if available.	4.25

Number of responses: 12

Table III

problems, there also were no ETC-based recitations in two of the last three weeks of the semester. For instance, the week following a one-hour exam is reserved for a discussion of the exam problem solutions by the recitation instructors.

The results of testing of the two groups are presented in Table IV. The numbers at the top of each column represent the maximum possible score for each test (which equals the number of multiple choice questions) except in the case of the course grade. In that case, an A is assigned 4.0; a B, 3.0; a C, 2.0; a D, 1.0; and an E (a failing grade), 0.0. In addition to the comparison of the entire group of students, I show also the comparison for the classes of the two faculty members (Professors Y and Z) who each handled both a standard recitation and an ETC-based recitation. The third row of each section shows the percentage change in the relative performance of each group as compared to the relative performance in the first one-hour exam (which was preceded by standard recitations for all students).

It may be of interest to note that Professor Z was also the course lecturer, an experienced, dedicated, caring teacher who has won national teaching awards and who is much admired by colleagues and students alike; Professor Y was a junior faculty member who seemed most concerned with furthering his own research career and who expended the absolute minimum effort in handling his teaching responsibilities. Despite this disparity in teaching experience and dedication, the relative improvement of the ETC-based students was about the same for each recitation instructor.

While the data comparisons in Table IV are encouraging, we wanted to understand more clearly the type of student

ETC vs. Standard Recitations

Physics 104 - Fall 1983

		No. of Students*	T1 (15)	T2 (15)	T3 (15)	F (25)	Course Grade (4)
	I Std. Recs.	98	7.92 ± 2.41	8.88 ± 2.56	7.89 ± 2.57	12.21 ± 3.97	2.05 ± 0.91
	II ETC Recs.	66	7.65 ± 2.54	8.97 ± 1.89	8.80 ± 2.29	13.47 ± 3.43	2.21 ± 0.93
	% change from T1 (II-I)		-	2.4%	7.9%	2.5%	6.5%
PROF Y	I Std. Recs.	19	7.89 ± 2.02	9.26 ± 2.88	7.94 ± 2.01	13.63 ± 2.33	2.11 ± 0.85
	II ETC Recs.	20	8.00 ± 2.26	9.40 ± 1.53	9.40 ± 1.88	14.40 ± 3.10	2.45 ± 1.16
	% change from T1 (II-I)		-	+0.2%	+9.0%	+2.2%	+7.8%
PROF Z	I Std. Recs.	31	7.55 ± 2.58	9.52 ± 2.26	7.80 ± 2.74	12.12 ± 4.42	1.97 ± 1.03
	II ETC Recs.	18	7.49 ± 2.60	8.88 ± 1.96	8.71 ± 2.38	13.47 ± 3.43	2.21 ± 0.93
	% change from T1 (II-I)		-	-3.9%	+6.5%	+5.8%	+6.4%

* Only students who took all tests are included. Originally 101 and 70 students were enrolled in standard and ETC-based sections respectively.

Table IV

we were helping the most. Roughly speaking, we were doing little more, if anything, for the superior student than was done in a standard recitation. Basically, that is a student who exhibits good comprehension and study habits; she or he needs little help in any form of weekly recitation. On the other hand, a student with poor comprehension and/or poor study habits, should benefit significantly from an ETC-based recitation because it forces such students to engage in far more drill-and-practice activity and to obtain face-to-face assistance on solving problems from both student tutors and faculty instructors.

To test the hypothesis that we were aiding significantly the weaker students, I identified those students whose test scores were in the lower third of the class for the first one-hour exam, i.e., those with six or less correct answers from among fifteen questions. Following the progress of those students, gave rise to Table V, which is identical in form to Table IV. Here, the difference in performance of the test and control groups is more obvious. In fact, statistical analysis shows that the (lower third) ETC-based group was superior with a confidence level of 93%. Although Physics 104 is the second semester course in the introductory physics sequence, it is a fact that three of the students in the standard recitation sections failed the course, while no student failed in the ETC-based sections.

During the spring 1983 semester, the same process was repeated, this time with a completely different set of students who were enrolled in the first course (Physics 103) in the sequence. The ETC-based recitations were not delayed as in the previous semester, but in an attempt to measure the relative ability of the two groups initially, a 20-minute quiz (worth 15 points) was given to all students after one week of lectures. This admittedly is a

ETC-Based vs. Standard Recitation

Lower Third of Class*

Physics 104 - Fall 1983

		No. of Students	T1 (15)	T2 (15)	T3 (15)	F (25)	Course Grade (4)
	I Std. Recs.	29 of 98	4.93 ± 1.20	7.86 ± 2.32	6.83 ± 2.57	10.62 ± 3.61	1.31 ± 0.70
	II ETC Recs.	22 of 66	4.73 ± 1.01	7.05 ± 1.80	7.55 ± 2.23	11.59 ± 2.55	1.64 ± 0.57
	% change from T1 (II-I)		-	1.9%	6.1%	5.2%	9.6%
PROF Y	I Std. Recs.	4 of 19	5.25 ± 0.83	9.25 ± 2.59	7.00 ± 1.58	11.50 ± 4.39	1.25 ± 0.43
	II ETC Recs.	8 of 20	4.50 ± 1.12	8.25 ± 0.97	8.50 ± 2.24	11.75 ± 2.22	1.75 ± 0.66
	% change from T1 (II-I)		-	-1.7%	+15.0%	+6.0%	+17.5%
PROF Z	I Std. Recs.	13 of 31	4.92 ± 1.07	8.08 ± 2.23	7.15 ± 2.77	11.08 ± 3.45	1.38 ± 0.74
	II ETC Recs.	9 of 18	4.78 ± 1.03	7.78 ± 1.99	7.00 ± 2.16	11.78 ± 2.20	1.67 ± 0.47
	% change from T1 (II-I)		-	-1.1%	-0.1%	+3.8%	+8.2%

* All students who reeeive 6 or less on T1, for which 7.7 was the class average.

Table V

somewhat dubious basis for establishing relative ability. However, if one looks at Table VI, one sees progressive relative improvement in the scores of the ETC-based students through the three one-hour exams.

Included on Table VI are the results for the students in the standard and ETC-based recitations of Professor X, who actually was given a double-sized ETC-based recitation and who was assigned a graduate teaching assistant to aid in handling it. Professor X is yet another of my colleagues who considers his teaching duties as an intrusion upon his scientific research (although his academic year salary is derived solely as a result of student tuition). Even in the problem-solving sessions he was rather inactive in circulating through the class. Despite his attitude and performance, it appears that those of his students in the ETC-based program fared far better in the course grade achieved. As with the students in the earlier comparison study, we see (from further analysis not shown here) that the weakest students are helped the most using the new form of instruction. This comparative improvement is remarkable in that the weak ETC-based students had a higher average score in the initial quiz, and both groups had a number of sub-standard students who ultimately failed the course.

A pilot program using ETC-based recitations for the first semester of the introductory calculus sequence was begun in the spring 1985 semester. Although the number of students involved was small, the instructors were impressed with student performance, and during the current fall 1985 semester, all of about 150 students are assigned to ETC-based recitations for the first calculus course.

5. CONCLUSIONS

It would appear obvious from the analysis of the

ETC vs. Standard Recitations

Physics 103 - Spring 1984

		No. of Students	Q (15)	T1 (15)	T2 (15)	T3 (15)	F (25)	Course Grade (4)
	I Std. Recs.	66	9.55 ± 2.90	10.17 ± 2.35	8.14 ± 2.11	7.26 ± 2.29	11.61 ± 2.91	2.11 ± 1.00
	II ETC Recs	92	8.88 ± 2.71	10.43 ± 2.32	8.57 ± 2.42	7.86 ± 2.53	12.49 ± 2.92	2.34 ± 0.94
	% change from Q (II-I)		-	+6.2%	+7.4%	+8.5%	+7.6%	+10.3%
PROF X	I Std. Recs.	22	7.82 ± 3.27	8.59 ± 2.46	7.55 ± 2.39	6.09 ± 2.37	10.32 ± 2.55	1.59 ± 0.89
PROF X	II ETC Recs	46	8.70 ± 3.01	10.00 ± 2.28	8.37 ± 2.43	7.45 ± 2.47	12.22 ± 2.52	2.26 ± 0.90
PROF X	% change from Q (II-I)		-	+2.8%	-0.4%	+3.9%	+1.7%	+10.9%

Table VI

data presented that those students - particularly the weaker ones - who were enrolled in the ETC-based recitations, received better test scores in subsequent examinations and ultimately higher course grades. Furthermore, this differential in scores seemed to evolve over the period of the semester from a starting point at which both groups of students seemed about equal in ability. One could conceivably argue that there is some underlying reason to cause students enrolled in Tuesday recitations to learn at a slower rate than those enrolled in the Thursday recitations. Based on observations made when there was no difference in the form of recitation presented, this hypothesis can be rejected.

Of far greater concern is whether the improved grades obtained via the ETC-based recitations really represent improved comprehension of the subject matter. About the only way this might be measured precisely would be to follow the students in the test and control groups as they take other physics, engineering and mathematics courses. While we may yet attempt to do this, it is not entirely clear whether, because of other factors, this would be entirely meaningful.

The case also could be made that students in the new form of recitation do better on hourly exams and on the final exam because we are giving them a multitude of multiple-choice problems which are similar in form and substance to the problems on these more important exams. This is an argument which can not be refuted by any purely objective test. On the other hand, I defer to the opinions of my colleagues in both physics and mathematics, who state unequivocally that students who experience the new computer- and tutor-based recitation leave the course in question with a better understanding of the course content.

I don't really see anything surprising in this assessment, because students who fail to master the material on their own are (1) tested far more thoroughly and have their specific weaknesses exposed; (2) receive personalized and timely assistance from well coached and competant student tutors; and where necessary, (3) personalized assistance in problem solving from faculty or graduate-assistant instructors. Of course, one could counter this argument by saying that given all the additional work required of an average or weak student, and all the additional help we offer, it is not surprising that such students show significant improvement. I have no disagreement with this sentiment. My response is to quote a colleague in the engineering faculty. One of his advisees did indeed complain that his ETC-based recitation was taking too much time. The faculty advisor replied: "But that's exactly what you need'" The point I'd like tomake is that we provide all this extra attention to students without spending any more money in the course delivery. In fact, once everything is in place, the cost can be less than under the old system of recitations.

I can summarize the benefits to students utilizing our new system as follows:

(1) Good students have no more work to do than previously, and they may actually save time. Some eventually become tutors, gaining additional insight and earning money.

(2) Weaker students are identified impersonally and obtain the personal help they need.

(3) Immature students are forced into a discipline which maximizes their productivity.

(4) All students receive instant feedback on quiz results and instant help on questions answered incorrectly.

The role of the faculty has been modified under the new system. They are relieved of quiz generation, grading and record keeping. They help students to solve problems on their own, i.e., the students take the lead in solving problems with assistance from the faculty. Finally, the faculty deals mainly with those students requiring the most assistance.

The process of revising the form of physics and mathematics recitations which has just been described was motivated (as indicated at the outset) by a desire to involve ETC in the mainstream of course delivery, and thus to ensure its continued existence. In this we have been successful. At this writing, during the beginning of the fall 1985 semester, there are about 350 students who participate in ETC-based recitations - approximately 200 in introductory physics and 150 in beginning calculus. With all those students coming to the Center and taking a combined total of over 500 quizzes weekly, we find that they are likely to utilize other ETC resources. In the previous semester, with only about 200 students being tested on a weekly basis, our Apple network of instructional dialogs and drill-and-practice exercises showed an average of 50 log-ins daily, and use of our stand-alone micros and audiovisual media was also substantial.

In order to handle the increased number of students currently being tested, ETC's space has just been expanded for a third time, the total area now about 330 m^2. Our computer- and tutor-based recitation procedure will be expanded to handle more students in still other large enrollment science, mathematics and engineering courses.

In summary, I return to my original comment that the use of the computer for test generation and record keeping is not very elegant. What I hope I have shown, however, is that this particular use has enabled us to restructure the learning process to produce a higher degree of understanding and more personalized instruction in courses with large enrollments. In principle, this restructuring could be made without the use of a computer, but in practice it would be too time consuming and too expensive. It is also useful to note that once the software and data base are in place, an instructor can utilize this computer-based resource in modes other than that adopted in the ETC operation, e.g., it could be accessed to create homework assignments and major exams, or it could be modified to manage self-paced instruction.

Although the software and data bases were developed originally with the goal of improving the educational process within the local environment, our success in this regard has encouraged us to plan on marketing these software/courseware products for use by other schools and universities. At the present time we are engaged in perfecting the data bases and making our software more user friendly. We fully expect to have marketable products by September 1986.

6. ACKNOWLEDGEMENTS

It is rather amazing that such a complex and ambitious program could have been brought to fruition in such a short time (by academic standards). My colleagues Professors Earl Zwicker and Jerry Frank have been of prime assistance in first helping to shape the process and then in building data bases in their respective fields of physics and mathematics. Professors John Kallend and Platon Deliyannis have assisted also in various ways.

Special thanks must go to Mr. David Gavelek, who starting as a part-time employee while being an undergraduate physics major, progressed to becoming full-time ETC manager and part-time graduate student. Over that period of time he worked on the generalization of problems for the physics data bases, coached tutors, supervised the entire operation on a daily basis, and generally kept the system running smoothly without any major shutdown over the entire life of this new form of recitation.

I am equally awed by the programming skill and dedication of several IIT students who responded so well to the software challenges of the new system. There are many who have contributed, but the work of Mr. George Brousalis, who was in charge of the software implementation during the 1982-1983 academic year and Mr. Michael Sheehan, who has been in charge ever since, merit special attention.

Finally, it is a pleasure to acknowledge the support of the Dr. Scholl Foundation and of IIT itself in making funds available for the purchase of equipment and the development of software and courseware. In particular, I wish to cite IIT President Thomas L. Martin, Jr., Vice President Edwin F. Stueben and Dean Robert Filler for their continued support and encouragement.

7. REFERENCE

Weinstock, Harold, Establishing and Maintaining a Multimedia Learning Center: A Case History. J. of Col. Sci. Teach. 12 (1983) 142-150.

THE COMPUTER AS AN INTEGRAL PART OF THE LABORATORY

John M. Pitre
Department of Physics
University of Toronto
Toronto, Ontario, Canada. M5S 1A7

Not many years ago the use of computers in any role in the undergraduate laboratory was thought to be innovative. Indeed, until recently it was standard for the computer to play some role, but its use was still regarded as important enough to be pointed out as an indication that the laboratory was 'up to date'. Today the computer should be pervasive in all areas of laboratory teaching, so much so that it should be considered commonplace by students.

I am not going to dwell at length on hardware. Technology is changing so rapidly that by the time that some particular hardware has been chosen, installed, tested and found to be pedegogically worthwhile, it is already obsolete. Furthermore, it is rare that one can choose hardware for reasons that are not severely restricted by financial constraints or the internal politics of one's institution. I could write extensively about the ideal situation, but so could any of you possessing some imagination. What I would like to discuss is the laboratory as it is run at the University of Toronto and how students react to it. I shall mention the philosophy behind our computer usage in the laboratory and what we hope to accomplish with the various tools provided. As you read this paper I hope that you will thinking of ways that you would improve and extend what we are trying to accomplish.

NATO ASI Series, Vol. F 23
Designing Computer-Based Learning Materials
Edited by A. Bork and H. Weinstock

I shall cover how we use the computer for data acquisition, general curve fitting and data analysis, courseware presentation, online testing, and as an information source or reference library. I shall describe a large-laboratory situation, since we have about 1500 students taking the first-year laboratory course, with about 160 students in the laboratory at any one time. However, most of what I shall say applies to the small-laboratory situation as well. In the laboratory every student should have access, to as much computing as the average student can handle. I would like to say unlimited access but I have a fifteen-year-old son, and I know what the combination of unlimited access and games means. In some laboratories there must be a sufficient number of microcomputers which may or may not be networked. For us it means that each student is given an account number and essentially unlimited computer time. To the student, the use of the computer should seem as common a tool as a book or oscilloscope.

Fig. 1: A typical laboratory

Figure 1 shows a room of the first-year laboratory and some typical apparatus. There are two things that should be noted in this picture.

The first is that there are several computers in the laboratory. These should be there independent of whether or not one uses microcomputers for on-line data acquisition. In our laboratory we stress that all work should be performed in the laboratory. We are trying to avoid giving the students the impression that the laboratory is the room where you take some readings to be understood later and that understanding will come as you survey the data at home. To stress this pedagogical point we do not even let the students take their books home. The laboratory books are for records and not for well-crafted essays with beautiful artwork produced at leisure while watching television. This means that not only must the laboratories be accessible at times when formal laboratories are not in progress, but also that students must be provided in the laboratory with computational aids, computer-assisted tutorial help and curve fitting and data analysis packages. In addition, courseware is an integral part of some experiments.

The second thing to note in Figure 1, which was taken at the start of the 1985 summer session, is the large number of hoops which are part of a physical pendulum apparatus. Students are free to choose from a large number of experiments; the only experiment that is required is the experiment on the pendulum, the first experiment that the student must perform. This initial experiment involving basic time and distance measurements is a vehicle for teaching about the meaning of measurements, about error analysis and about the propagation of errors. To ensure that students master the topic of error analysis, rather than just being exposed to it, a stand-alone computerized test on error analysis was created. The results of this test, taken as many times as the student wishes, determines a fraction of the laboratory grade. Because records are kept, it is easy to compute a most recent grade for the test from: test grade = (previous average + this result)/2. The test consists of a random selection of four of ten topics which range from calculating standard error of the mean to propagation of errors for multiplication and powers. Each of the topics makes reference to apparatus in the laboratory and each of the three versions has meaningful, but randomly generated numbers.

Figure 2 shows an example in which a student's knowledge of repeated measurements, precision and accuracy is tested. Figure 2 does not pretend to illustrate sophisticated testing. We are not interested in

YOU ARE MEASURING A VOLTAGE USING A PHILIPS PM2400/02 METER.
YOUR MEASUREMENTS WERE DONE USING THE 3 VOLT SCALE AND YOU HAVE REPEATED YOUR MEASUREMENTS 9 TIMES.
EACH TRIAL GIVES YOU AN IDENTICAL RESULT OF 1.842 V, AND YOU DECIDE THAT YOUR READING ERROR IS PLUS OR MINUS 0.009 V.
THE ACCURACY OF THE METER IS SPECIFIED AS PLUS OR MINUS 3 PER CENT OF THE SCALE BEING USED ON THE METER.
WHAT IS THE ERROR, IN VOLTS, IN YOUR AVERAGE VALUE OF THE VOLTAGE BEING MEASURED? (NO UNITS PLEASE)

Fig. 2: Error test sample

testing as much as we are in providing an incentive to encourage the mastery of the material. In that respect we have been completely successful. Students do learn the material, as subsequent performance in the laboratory showed. The instant feedback of their test grade, and the ability to improve it, are adequate inducements for them to acquire complete mastery of the topic. In fact, we were surprised at the extent to which students retook tests (after additional study) in order to improve their grades. This is probably due to messages in the test which indicate topics and questions causing difficulty.

The software for lesson preparation and record keeping is available not only in the laboratory, but is part of a larger CAI system for use in the undergraduate teaching program. This system is self contained and is user friendly, enough so that students can use it much as they would a library. Most of the lessons are concerned with topics important to first year students: graphs in kinematics, Newton's laws, circular motion and rotational kinematics, torque and angular momentum, gravitational and electrical potential, potential energy, wavemotion and relativity. Thus, courseware for lectures and laboratories is integrated.

Although this type of system could be implemented on networked micros, for historical reasons our learning materials were developed starting over ten years ago on the university's large mainframe. One year ago all our software was transferred to an HP9000, series 500 computer, which is dedicated to undergraduate use in the physics department. This machine, which runs under UNIX*, has two megabytes of main memory and twenty four ports. This information is not provided as an argument for larger systems as opposed to micros, but it does seem that if a coherent program is to be presented to our students, some form of integration is necessary. We see the next logical step to be the down loading of compiled programs to smaller micros, and if funding is forthcoming, we hope to start integrating micros with the undergraduate computer this year. Different circumstances dictate different hardware options. On one of our smaller satellite campuses where much of the first year undergraduate equipment is identical, but funding for computing is not so generous, microcomputers have been interfaced directly to the experiments. With the micros, software is written in assembly language and burned into ROM. Under this constraint, preparation of material takes considerably longer, but the performance of these small dedicated systems is quite remarkable.

Figure 3 shows the main menu of options available to the student in the laboratory. The courseware option, including the test on error analysis which I have described above, also is available. Traditionally our programs have been command driven. For experienced users I still think that this is the best approach. However, for first year students, menu driven programs have the advantage that the student need never remember commands which don't apply for other computer systems to which they will be exposed in other undergraduate studies. The menu is driven from the keyboard. This seems to be the best option since most of the applications in the laboratory require keyboard input. Most of our terminals have some device for pointing, such as a joystick or thumbwheel-driven cursors. We have reserved these devices for courseware where their use seems most appropriate, e.g., pointing to specific positions on a graph.

---

* Trademark of AT & T Bell Laboratories.

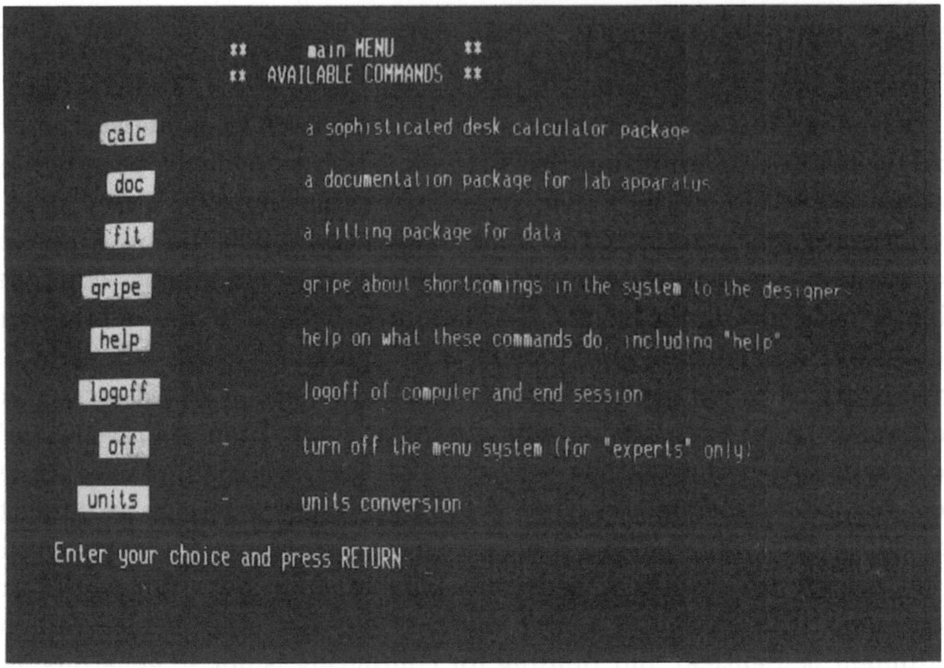

Fig. 3: Main menu

I noted earlier that the student should be given as much computing power as can be used usefully. The "off" option turns the menu off and gives the student access to our UNIX operating system. The student has access to FORTRAN, Pascal, C and APL, and our software is written in these languages. When the average student types "off", a restricted shell is entered. This is useful if one wishes to protect the student from getting lost and to protect the integrity of the system. Students wishing complete access to the system are routinely supplied with unrestricted accounts. This gives us some control over and knowledge of those who may consume a considerable amount of our resources. It also provides us with the currency with which we can 'buy' student programming, some of which is of very high calibre. One example is that of a pair of students who wished to write a simulation of model rocket flight which would predict the highest point of flight based on the type of engine and various aerodynamic properties of the rocket. A simple, but realistic, program was produced. The students, now enthusiastic, wished to refine the program by adding many other variables which they predicted would make the program more realistic. I agreed to let them do this on the condition that they build one or more rockets to test the predictions of their program. To my surprise, they not only built the rocket and were able to measure by triangulation its apogee with the help of friends using transits, but they built a movie camera into the rocket which took continuous pictures of scale objects on the ground. The apogee results based on scaling factors agreed well not only with the triangulation results but with the predictions of the computer program which they had written.

Although computing power is available to the student, we assume that the average student has neither the ability nor the desire to perform independent computer programming in the physics laboratory. However, a calculational facility should always be readily available, and this is the facility that the "calc" option in Figure 4 provides.

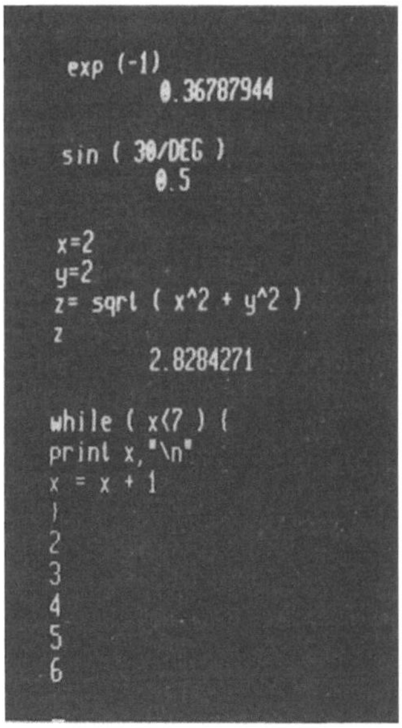

Fig. 4: The *calc* option

Figure 4 shows some examples, of the types of things that students can accomplish with "calc". In the first example DEG is the number of degrees in a radian, and in the second, the student has defined and used variables. In the third example some rudimentary programming is demonstrated in which continued use is made of a variable defined in the second example. The important thing to realize about the "calc" facility is that it is software that was not developed by us, but it is an adaptation of a facility called "hoc" developed by Kernihan and Pike. This package is readily available to UNIX users and can be transferred from one UNIX site to another using the standard uucp (UNIX-to-UNIX Communications Protocol). We should become more aware of and try to incorporate as much as possible, software developed at other sites. Many national and international user networks are accessible for this purpose, and AT & T is now offering a catalogue of software that may be purchased over the telephone provided that the user has a simple modem.

Figure 5 shows some examples from the "units" option and it is another instance of an adaptation of software written elsewhere, in this case at the University of California, Berkeley. This facility is included because we think that unit conversions should be instantaneous in the laboratory. The first three examples are somewhat facetious, but they do point out the wide range of conversions possible. The fourth example demonstrates the advantage of this facility because it can identify incompatabilities between units and assist the student in dimensional analysis.

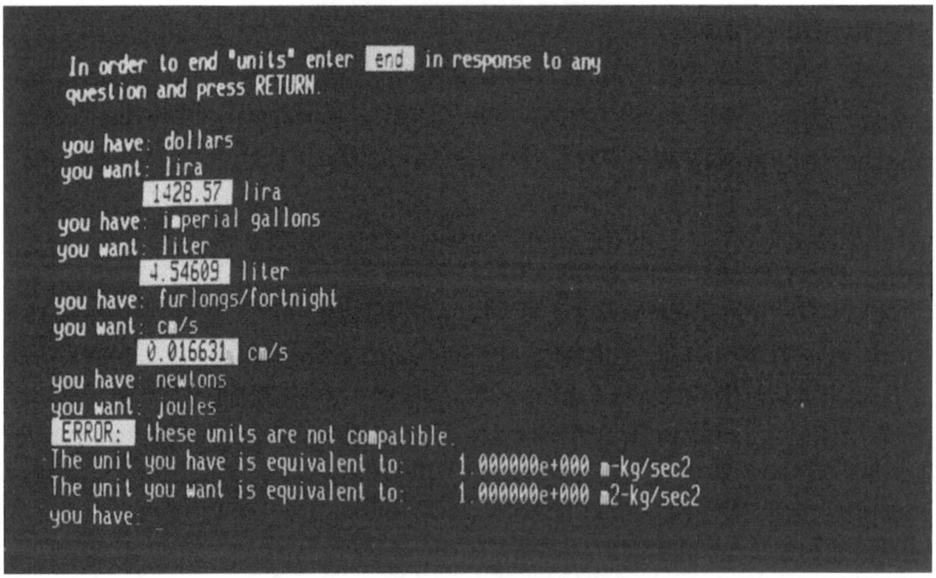

Fig. 5: The *units* option

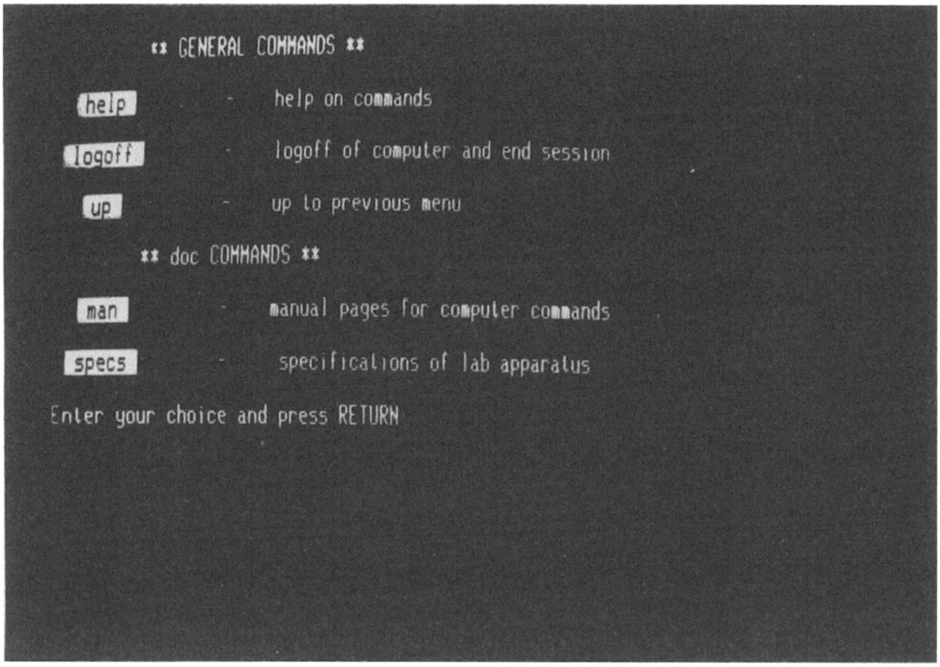

Fig. 6: *doc* option

Figure 6 is the result of the student choosing the "doc" option. The "man" and "specs" options simply allow the student to use the terminal next to an experiment as an on-line library. The "man" option follows the same philosophy and style as the "man" command in the UNIX operating system, which provides an extensive manual explaining all commands. The "specs" options is similar, except that it is a manual on the specifications of equipment available in the laboratory. Such a facility is necessary if one stresses, as we do, that the much of the meaningfullness of experimental results depends on a knowledge of the precision and accuracy of the equipment that one is using. Of course, manufacturers' manuals provide the same information, but an on-line system has two advantages. First, the advantage of having the information at one's fingertips is obvious; and second, the laboratory staff is able to distill the pertinent information from the manuals, thus saving much time for the average student. Manufacturers' manuals are needed only for very specific detailed information.

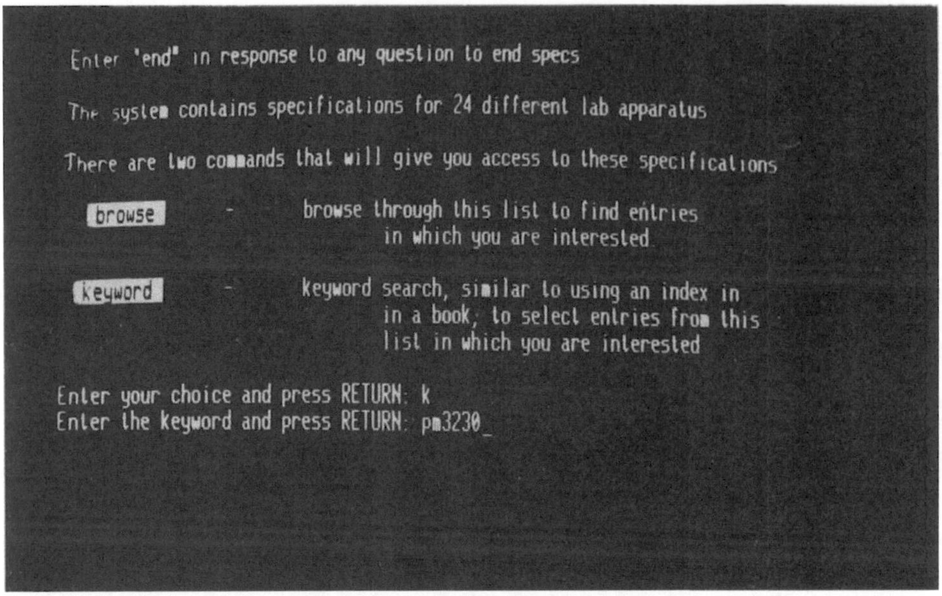

Fig. 7: The ***specs*** option

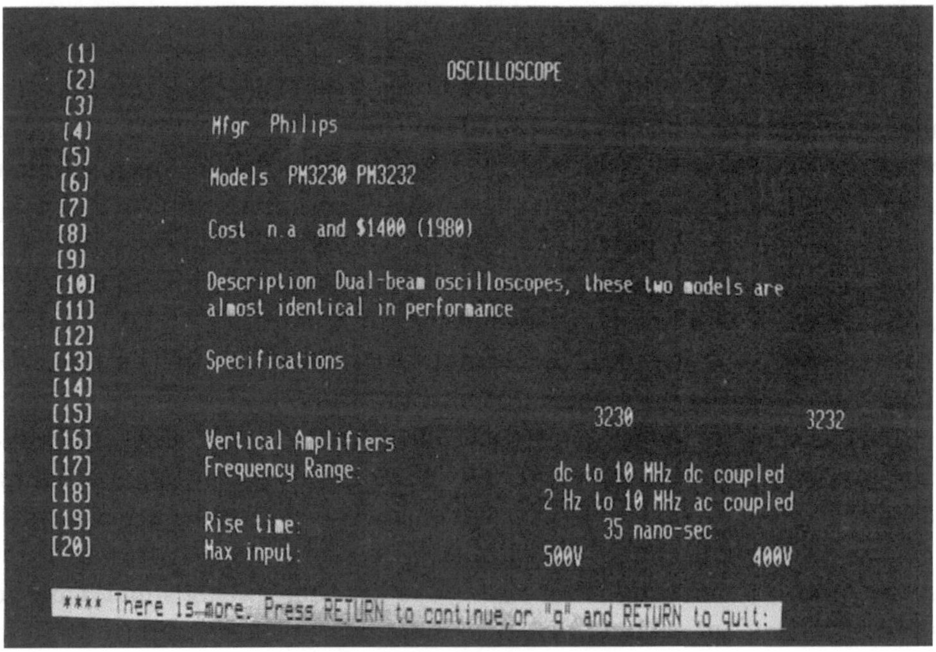

Fig. 8: ***Specs*** information

Figure 7 shows the student searching by keyword where the keyword is simply the model number of the equipment. Figure 8 shows an example of the kind of summary information presented to the student. Figure 9 is the continuation and conclusion of the specifications and is included

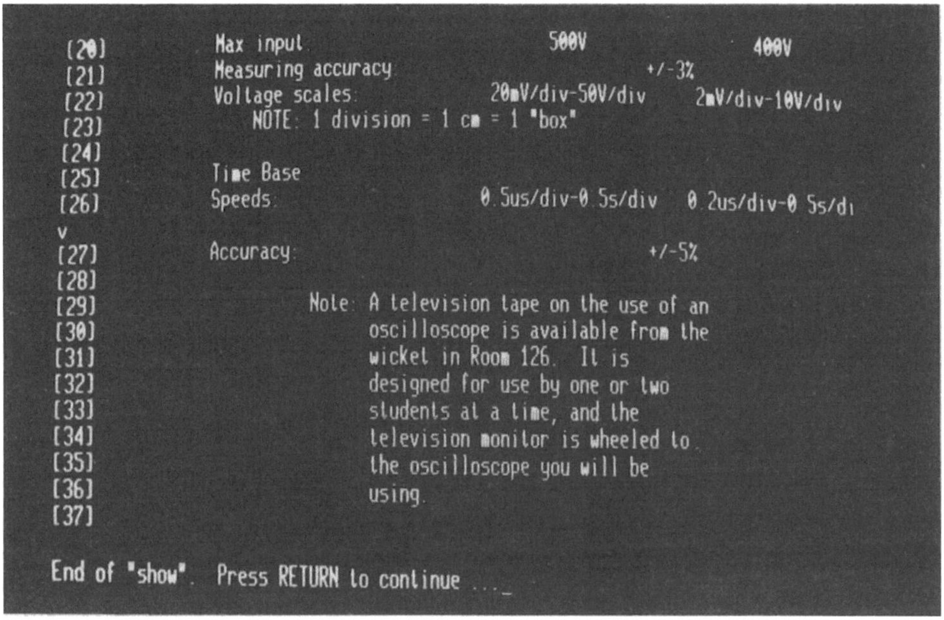

Fig. 9: More *specs* information

because of the reference to videotapes in the last paragraph. We have produced videotapes for the laboratory to aid in teaching the use of basic instrumentation such as oscilloscopes and micrometers. As with computer-based lesson material, only professional material will survive initial usage. When complaints are heard regarding the time required to produce a good computer-based lesson, it should be noted that to produce one fifteen minute instructional videotape program it took us a full week to write the dialogue and another full week for production in which the author, a director, a soundman and two cameramen were involved. In addition, three days for professional editing were required. The final product will be useful for several years, but subsequent editing is not practical. In principle, computer-controlled, random-access, videodisc-based systems are more versatile. However, the editing of video sections is just as impractical. With the high-resolution graphics now available, I think our next efforts might go in this direction. Although the visual representations would not be as realistic as those on tape or videodisc, they can be more easily updated as equipment changes or as laboratory personnel see the need to stress some educational aspects more than others. In any institution where there is a rotation or turnover of staff, the assumed need for the personnel to leave their imprint on the laboratory requires a built-in flexibility for all pedagogical tools.

Curve fitting and data analysis are an integral part of every laboratory. We should remember that curve fitting and data analysis are not the ends, but are only the means to physical insight. We must teach students how to use these tools, although knowing how to use them is only a necessary intermediate step. Our goal must be to provide our students with powerful, flexible and easy to use tools, immediately accessible when required. Learning how to use these tools must not get in the way of insight; it should stimulate the student and promote insight.

So far I have not mentioned what some consider to be the most important aspect of computers in the laboratory, the computer as interface or as data acquisition device. I am sure that many are familiar with talks with titles such as 'The Computer as an Inexpensive Multichannel Analyser' and 'The Computer as an Expensive Timer.' I don't look down on such presentations. I would suggest that these efforts have undoubtably resulted in better laboratories. One should not ignore the relation between one's motives and the Hawthorne Effect. Invariably, when one asks what motivated an instructor to introduce computer hardware into the laboratory, one finds that it was based on the personal curiosity of the instructor. The introduction of the hardware is almost always successful in stimulating student interest, and this is usually because the instructor is working closely with the students. When the apparatus is used by a larger number of students, or if the instructor is changed, then problems generally appear. In larger laboratories especially, the decision to introduce computer or any other hardware should be based upon advantages of the new equipment and not just upon the fact that it is new equipment. The versatility and the ease with which data can be acquired and analysed using computers should be obvious to us. That ease and versatility also must be obvious to the students, and this requires the preparation of

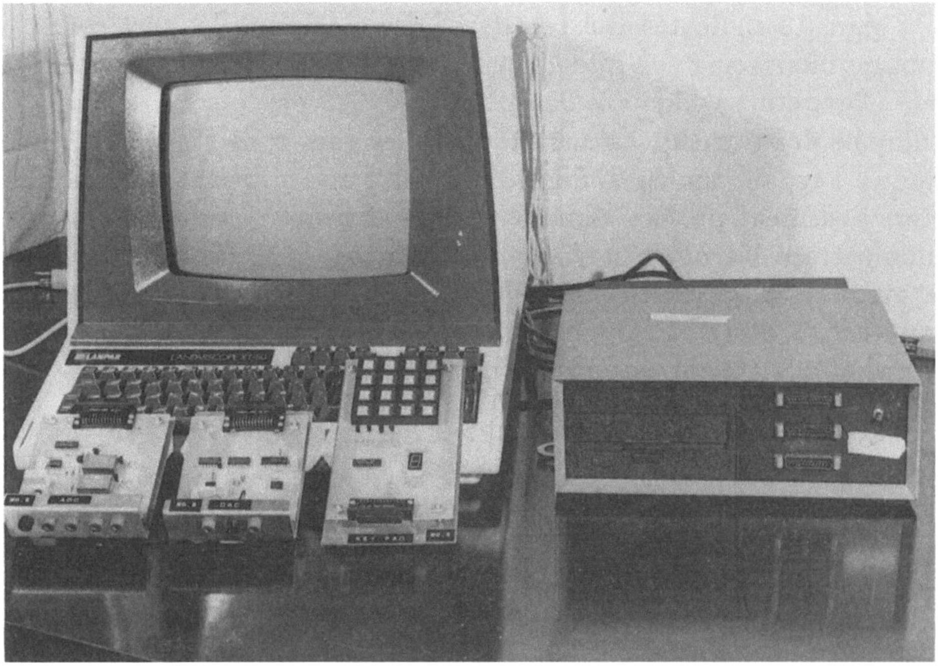

Fig. 10: Interfacing laboratory

user-friendly software on the part of the instructors. Many institutions now are taking this integrated approach, an approach which I believe shall lead to success.

Beware of those who say that some knowledge of assembly-language programming is valuable to students who will be using the computer interfaced to a multimeter or some other such device. In my first year as an undergraduate I calculated linear regressions with a pencil, paper and an electromechanical calculator because 'it was good for me'. I suppose one could use the same argument as my father that it must have been good for me 'because look at how you turned out'. Yes, assembly language and a detailed knowledge of the electronics are necessary for a few, but not for the vast majority of the students that we teach. The laboratory staff at the main campus of the University of Toronto met a couple of years ago, and after reviewing the limited financial and personnel resources, decided how these resources would be expended with regard to microcomputer interfacing in the laboratory.

Figure 10 indicates the results of this decision. A new course on computer interfacing was introduced for students at the junior and senior level. Computers which are based on the 6809 processor are assembled within the department, as are the modules shown in Figure 10. These include a keypad, analog-to-digital converter and a digital-to-analog converter; a student project completes the hardware. Students using this equipment are learning interfacing techniques, but I do not think that this material is appropriate for first-year students. When we interface computers to other experimental equipment, it should be clear beforehand what the advantages are and what we expect to teach.

The demands on students have never been greater than they are today. There is not only a larger body of factual knowledge to be accumulated, but also a greater need to see interrelationships between areas of knowledge. Laboratories, although necessary, are time consuming, and we must do all in our power to provide the student with all the aids required to make the best use of the available time. At the current time reductions in funding are causing laboratory tutorial groups to become ever larger. This trend can be changed since computers offer the possibility of providing each student with an individual tutor. The hardware is here. All we need to do is recognize the opportunities which it provides and then write the software. No small task indeed!

APPENDIX 1

THE COMPUTER - THE TEST BED FOR MODELS

Before the construction of any large scale project, a scale model is produced. Although these models are often used by public relations, the models of interest to mathematicians, physicists and engineers can be placed on test beds and subjected to stresses and strains that simulate the conditions the structure will experience. Often, a computer model will be developed simultaneously to help in analysis of data. The resulting data do not produce a direct test of the structure which one hopes to build. In fact, the computer model generally does not even provide a test of the mechanical model. Rather what is tested is the mathematical model of the mechanical model of the proposed structure.

In the laboratory, the data taken reflect physical reality, and the goal is to understand the underlying patterns. First-year university students exposed to a mathematical treatment of a topic being considered in the laboratory tend to think that the mathematical model describes what is really there and that 'correct' experimental results are those that agree with the model. This is the 'recourse to authority' approach, and it is this attitude which we must change if we wish students to be more critical in the collection and interpretation of data.

In a true discovery situation, the data come first, patterns are observed, a model is proposed and this model is then tested by further experimentation. Although some laboratory instructors might disagree, students seldom come to an experimental situation without preconceived notions. Much research also proceeds in this way. One is usually in the process of refining models. We should acknowledge this and emphasize the testing and refining of models in the laboratory. The computer is the ideal test bed of mathematical models. Students can use physical insights to extend these models even though they lack the mathematical sophistication to proceed with the calculations.

Two experiments where the computer is used to analyse data will be described. The specific examples are not important. What is important is the insight that the student will obtain into the models and the physical situation.

The first is the free-fall experiment to measure the acceleration due to gravity. The apparatus at the University of Toronto, in Figure 1 is perhaps more sophisticated than at most other institutions. It is also more sophisticated than necessary to demonstrate only the basic aspects of free fall.

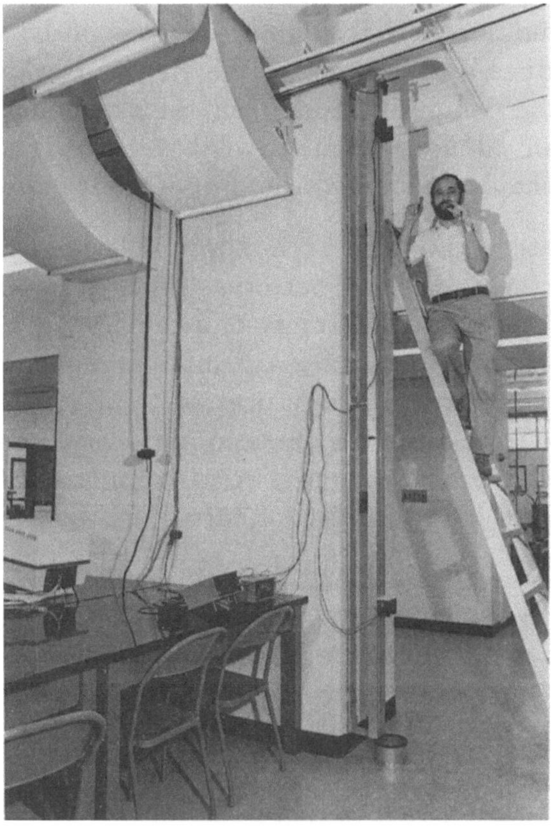

Fig. 1: Free-fall apparatus

A metal bob suspended from an electromagnet near the ceiling is released by throwing a switch. A timer is started and stopped when the bob passes through photogates. Since both photogates are moveable, the initial velocity (v_O) and the total distance travelled (d) are independently variable. The height of the ceiling - in our case 3.3 meters - limits the value of d . Cross hairs on the photogates allow values of d to be taken from a good steel tape with an accuracy of about one part in four thousand. The mathematical model with which students come equipped from their first year courses is

$$d = v_o t + \frac{1}{2} g t^2 \tag{1}$$

where d, v_o, t and g are distance travelled, initial velocity, elapsed time and acceleration due to gravity, respectively.

The first use of the computer is to perform a least squares polynomial fit, to obtain v_o and g. With a spherical metal bob students obtain values for g closer to 970 cm s^{-2} than to the accepted value of 980 cm s^{-2} for Toronto.

Students are encouraged to investigate their model more carefully. If a graphics display is available, plotting the fitted curve with the raw data reveals that data points for the large values of d are anomalous. Even without graphics terminals, since the student now knows that $g = 980 + \epsilon$ (where ϵ is small), the data can be manipulated so that ϵ can be calculated. However, a plot of

$$\{\frac{d}{t} - 490t\} = \frac{1}{2}\epsilon t + v_o \tag{2}$$

will not yield a straight line with slope ϵ if there are large values of d.

It is important to have computers in the laboratory so that manipulation and analysis of data can take place immediately. Software should be friendly, so that students are not tempted to take data and then go away until they have enough time to understand how to use the programs. Once data analysis is not so time consuming, students can edit their data or repeat the experiment with the maximum value of d being 1 meter. Values of g closer to 980 cm s^{-2} are obtained. Another approach which shows that their model neglects the effects of air resistance is to have the student repeat the experiment with a streamlined tear-shaped bob. Again values of g much closer 980 cm s^{-2} are obtained.

The advantage of the computer is evident when a student asks "What results would be obtained if the data were analysed in a different way?" This is equivalent to the question, "What if I used a modified model to represent the reality upon which I have just made measurements?" The benefits also are obvious if instant analysis of the data prompts the student to attempt the experiment again under slightly modified conditions. The computational delay between insight and conclusion must not be long enough to derail the train of thought.

The second example is the measurement of the frequency response of AC circuits. From a selection of resistors capacitors and inductors the student connects some in series or parallel. For example, the combination of a resistor, capacitor and inductor in series, as shown in Figure 2, may be chosen. The experiment measures the impedance and phase shift of the circuit over a wide range of frequencies. The values of R, L and C are then determined by selecting a mathematical model and adjusting the parameters until the results of the model agree with the data.

Fig. 2: AC circuits apparatus

Second-year students do have idealized models for resistors, capacitors and inductors and they have the mathematical skills to do simple circuit analysis. Problems arise when circuits become complicated, or if students do not realize that all real coils or inductors have resistance and stray capacitance, and that real capacitors have inductance as well.

Once the student has chosen components of unknown value and placed them in a certain configuration, data are taken. The selection and manipulation of the model proceeds with the aid of a menu-driven program. Figure 3, a photograph of a video screen, shows the main menu. The intersection of the large crosshairs is used to select items from the menu. After the data have been entered, edited, tabled or plotted, the modelling begins when a circuit is chosen from a selection such as that shown in Figure 4.

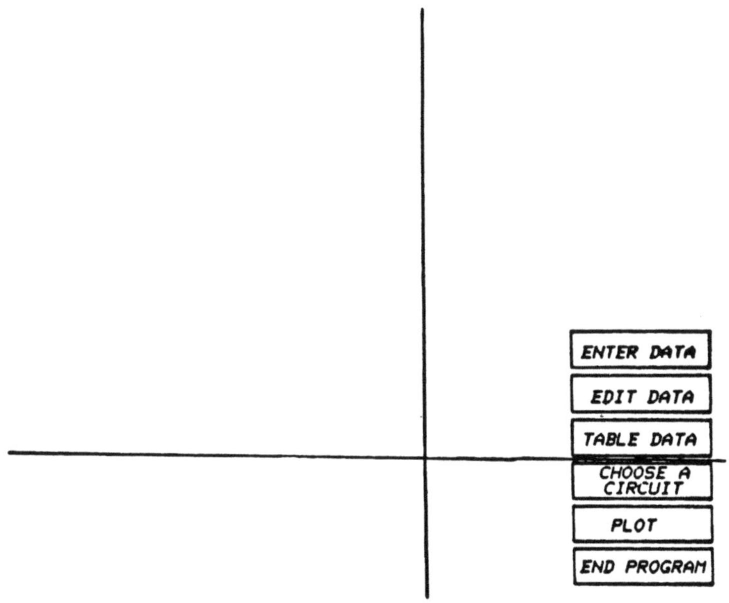

Fig. 3: AC circuits menu on a terminal screen

Once the choice of a circuit has been made, R, L and C labels appear, and the student is prompted for trial values which are printed next to the labels as shown in Figure 5. It appears that the student has insight into

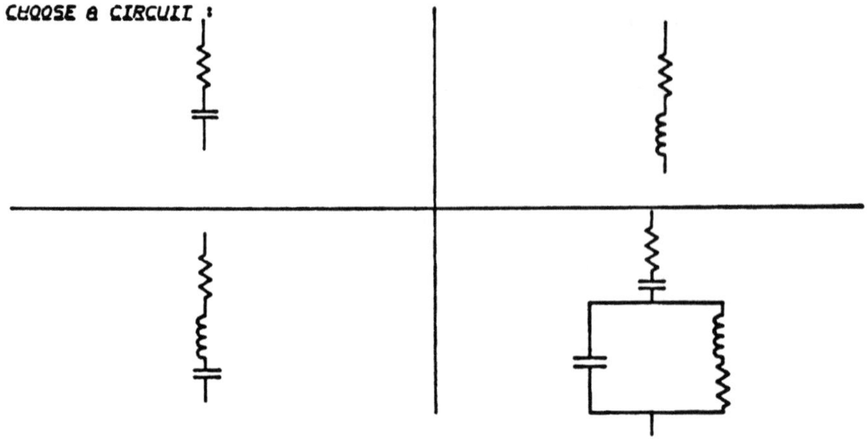

Fig. 4: Circuit models

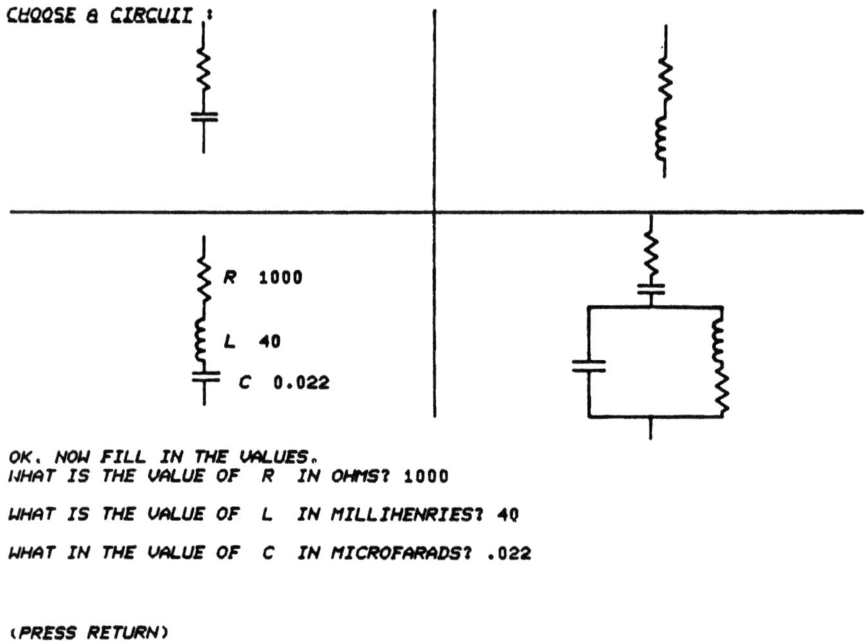

Fig. 5: Circuit model with values for R, L and C

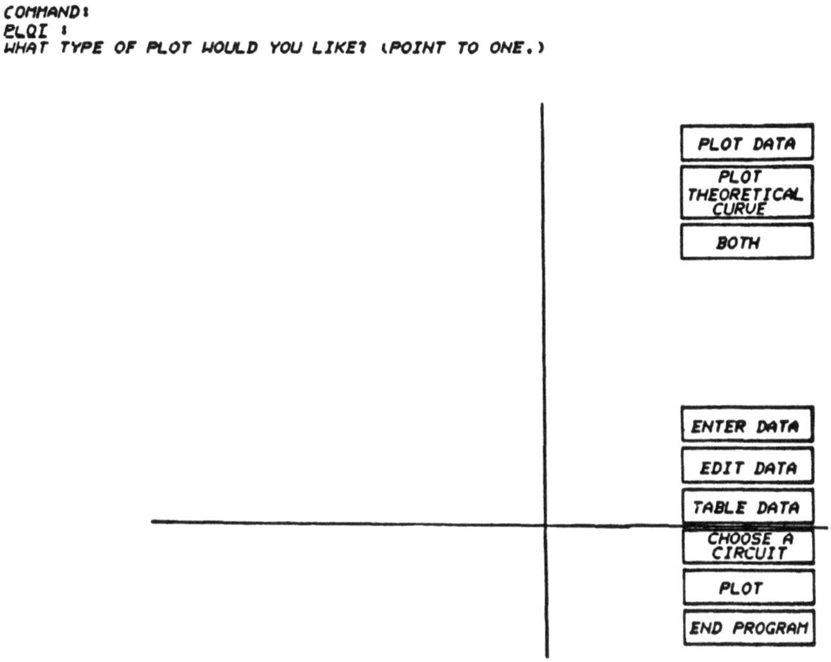

Fig. 6: Plotting choices

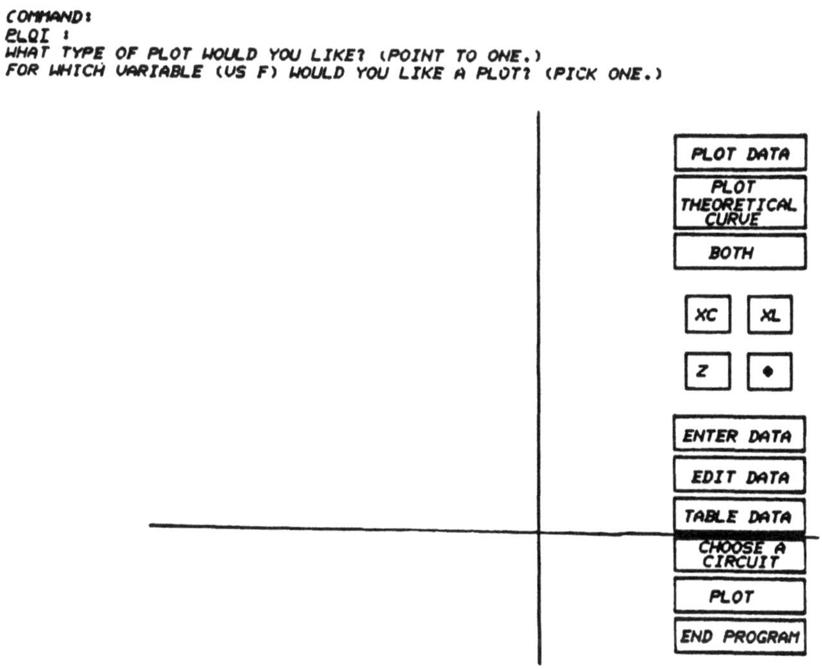

Fig. 7: Variable choices

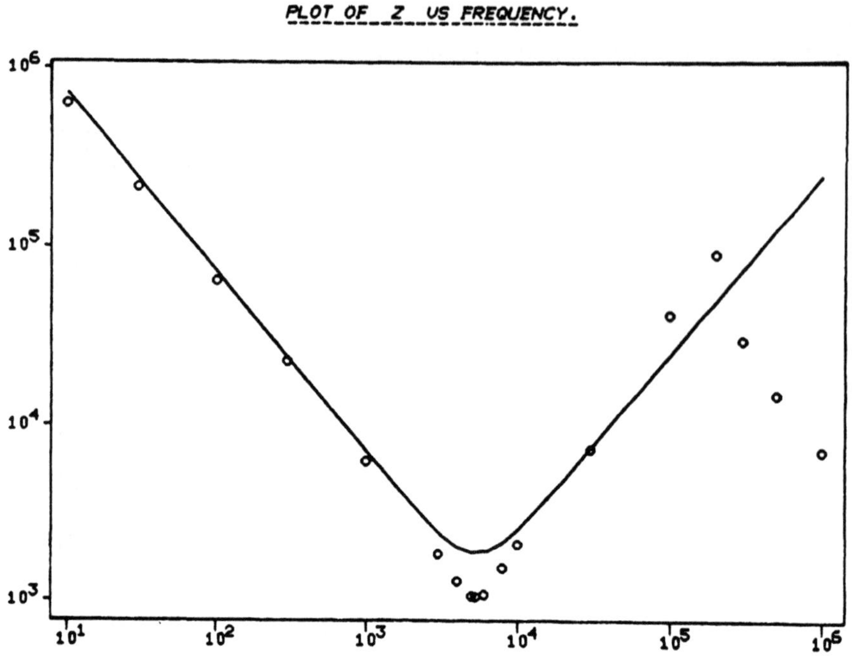

Fig. 8: Data and predictions

the model, either through classroom experience or through experience with the program. The smallest experimental value of the impedance is about 1000 ohms, and at resonance for a series circuit the impedance is simply the resistance R. The student now returns to the main menu. This is indicated in Figure 6. A choice is made to plot, and a submenu of plotting choices is provided. If, for example, a choice is made to plot both data and the computations based on the chosen model, then a further submenu of variable choices to be plotted is presented, as in Figure 7. If the choice is made to plot impedance as a function of frequency then Figure 8 shows the results, where the open circles are the experimental data, and the solid line is the prediction.

The student has started from unknown values for the physical components. The student should be aware that as frequency increases, the impedance of a capacitor decreases; that of an inductor increases; and that of a resistor is constant. The student also has been exposed to, but may be less aware of, resonance conditions for series and parallel circuits.

The adjustments of parameters that students make to obtain reasonable agreement with the data is highly dependant on understanding the underlying physics. It is hoped that the student will recognize patterns as the adjustments are made, if that understanding is not already present. The computer shortens the time between insight and the subsequent prediction and observation of the results.

One might think of several superior alternatives. Perhaps a touch-screen with increasing and decreasing keys for R, L and C could be manipulated, while the values were displayed and the model-generated curve dynamically changed shape. Keyboard input or the use of a mouse or of analog devices could be used to accomplish the same end. This does not, of course, change the basic thrust of the program, but the ease of use is generally critical in the acceptance of a program by the students.

The results plotted in Figure 8 are close to, but not exactly, the students choice that we saw in Figure 5 (in particular, $R \neq 1000$ ohms). This plot shows about the best agreement that can be obtained between predictions and data, provided one restricts oneself to the simple model of idealized components. Many students will be satisfied with this agreement even though the model predicts an impedance too high in the mid-frequency range, and there is definitely something unusual happening at higher frequencies. Good students will persist in improving the model. It is open to question as to what is pedagogically the best way to encourage this experimentation. This program adopts a strategy of limited choices, since our target is the average second-year student. A more successful strategy for brighter students is probably to give help only when requested.

Students with some insight see that the circuit in the lower right corner of Figure 9 will reduce to any of the others given the appropriate values for the components.

After experimentation with component values one can obtain good agreement between the model and the data, as in Figure 10. The addition of the stray capacitance C1 in parallel with the inductance L, gives rise to the resonance at about $10^5 Hz$. Confirmation that the model is reasonable is given in Figure 11. In the plot of phase angle as a function of frequency, the student will be reminded that the model chosen is a combination of

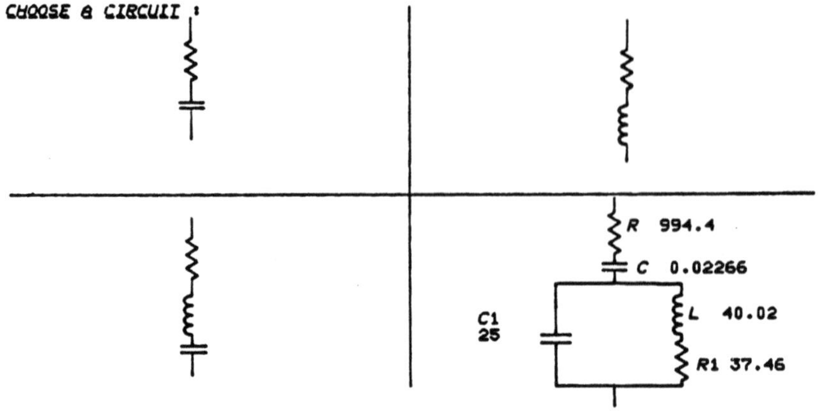

OK. NOW FILL IN THE VALUES.
WHAT IS THE VALUE OF R IN OHMS? 994.4

WHAT IS THE VALUE OF C IN MICROFARADS? .02266

WHAT IS THE VALUE OF L IN MILLIHENRIES? 40.02

WHAT IS THE VALUE OF C1 IN PICOFARADS? 25

WHAT IS THE VALUE OF R1 IN OHMS? 37.46

(PRESS RETURN)

Fig. 9: Example of a more complex model

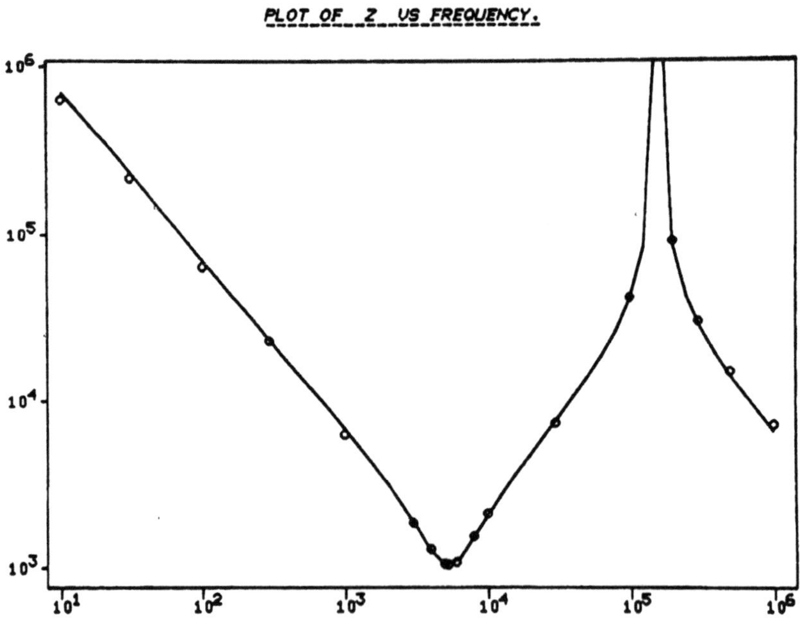

Fig. 10: New model predictions

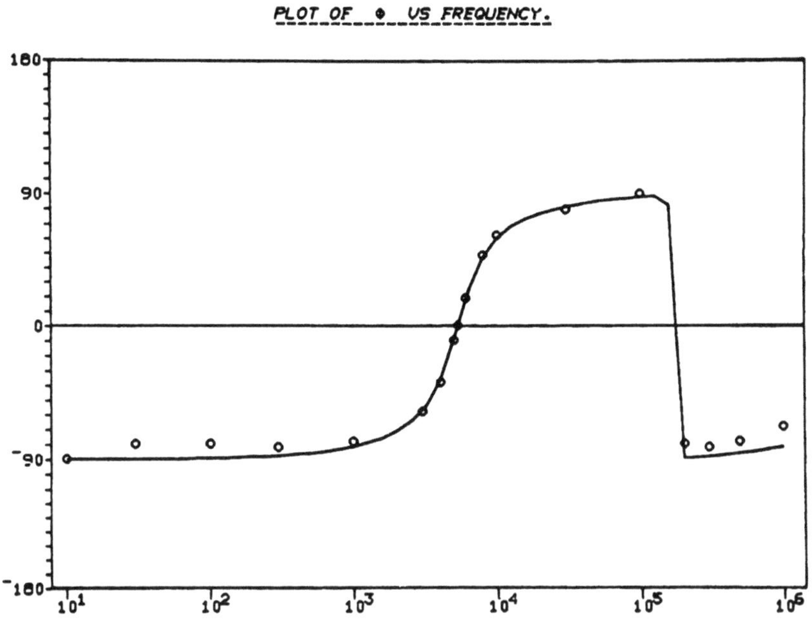

Fig. 11: Model confirmation

of series and parallel resonant circuits. The frequencies at which this curve passes through zero correspond to the resonance minima and maxima in Figure 10.

It is precisely when a model can be manipulated quickly enough that insight into the model can be gained. The student can then decide if there is any way in which the model can adequately describe the experimental situation or if there are experimental modifications that can be made which will allow the results to agree with the particular restricted model which one has chosen.

Two examples where the computer has been used to test models in the laboratory have been presented. Neither the experiments nor the progamming techniques are novel. The emphasis on models is pedagogically very important, and it is with computers that we can take advantage of the ability to investigate and manipulate models. It is important that we provide students with experimental apparatus having great enough precision so that models can be critically tested. The investigation of unexplainable bumps and glitches - unexplainable with present knowledge - is what often leads to the discovery of new and important phenomena.

APPENDIX

Example of the product of a working group

MISSING PERSON: EVERYDAY USES OF PROBABILISTIC REASONING

Alfred Bork, University of California, USA
Teresa Mendes, University of Coimbra, Portugal
Antonietta Pontrelli, C.S.A.T.A., Italy
Miriam Reiner, Technion, Israel
Lee Shulman, Stanford University, USA
Ronald Thornton, Tufts University, USA

NATO ASI Series, Vol. F 23
Designing Computer-Based Learning Materials
Edited by A. Bork and H. Weinstock

I - RATIONALE: PSYCHOLOGICAL RESEARCH

The purpose of this computer dialog is to teach strategies of probabilistic reasoning to high-school or college age students. It has been demonstrated in studies by the psychologists Amos Tversky and Daniel Kahneman that sophisticated adults, even those with formal instruction in statistics, make serious errors in situations that require them to estimate the likelihood of future events. Instead of combining prior likelihoods and new data systematically, with Bayes' Theorem, individuals are likely to ignore significant sources of relevant information as they estimate likelihoods.

Among the most frequently encountered errors is ignoring the importance of the prior probability of an event. Students ignore the base rate frequency of an event's occurrence, and focus on the representativeness or salience of the new information presented. For example, we may tell you a vivid story about a circus that has just come to town, and especially of the beautiful zebras in the animal acts. Later in the evening you hear the sound of hoofbeats outside your window; we ask you to guess what animals are running outside. Despite the fact you have just been thinking about zebras, and you know some are in town, the best guess is that you hear the sound of horses, because the prior probability (the base-rate frequency) of horses in your town is still far higher than that of zebras.

This lesson is one of a projected series of dialogs in which students improve their probabilistic reasoning. We use the research of Tversky and Kahneman (summarized and augmented in a recent book by Nisbett and Ross) to anticipate the heuristics, or probabilistic misconceptions, most likely to arise in the students' everyday reasoning.

This program is a Socratic interaction. Students are initially encouraged to employ the typical heuristics, thus falling into the trap we have set. We then demonstrate that a serious error has been made, help the students to see what form of heuristic has been employed and why it is deficient, and then engage them in a computer dialog to develop an understanding of the importance of including data on base rates, whether empirically gathered or generally estimated, as a first step in producing an estimate of an event.

II - PROGRAM DESCRIPTION

The user of this program is asked to find a missing person using incomplete information requiring accurate probalistic reasoning for success. A number of missing people may be found. The first person is a student at a university. The user is presented with an out-dated description of the missing person that contains unreliable information. The intuitive response of students to this information results in looking for the student in the wrong department. The student is encouraged to gather quantitative information that will allow the maximum likelihood of finding the person. Tutorial help is available from the program to guide the student to an eventual successful analysis of the problem.

The program structure is as follows:

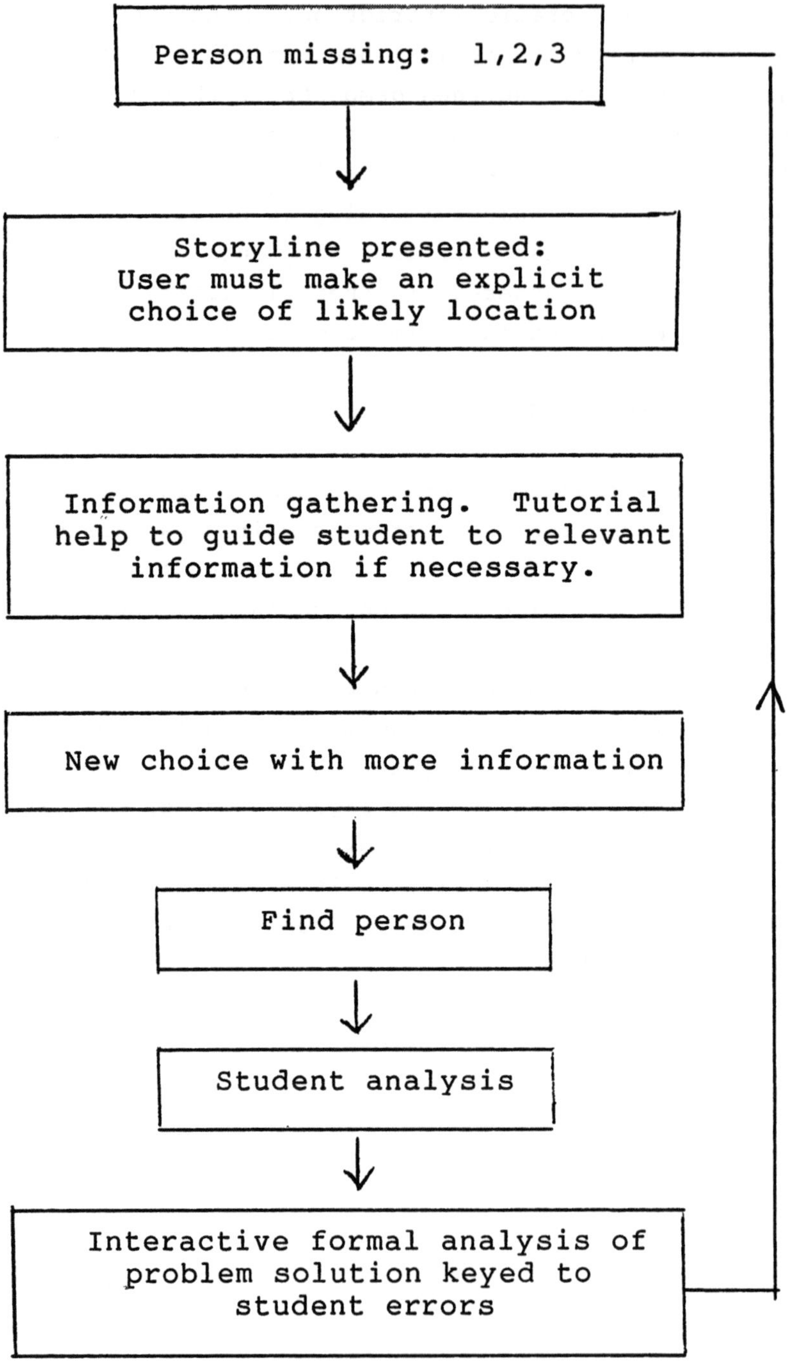
Person missing: 1,2,3
Storyline presented: User must make an explicit choice of likely location
Information gathering. Tutorial help to guide student to relevant information if necessary.
New choice with more information
Find person
Student analysis
Interactive formal analysis of problem solution keyed to student errors

The Missing Person

You are to find a person,

{Lee, Chris, Pat} {Johns, Smith}

delay two sec.

You know {name} is a student at

the University of {California, Texas, Michigan}

delay two sec.

You have a brief description from a high school friend

{Pick four of the following, display in random order}

delay two sec.

dreams of travelling to Italy

often visits museums

draws well

walks in the woods

{always pick these} (often visits museums, draws well, walks in the woods)

loves to read

won the school poetry prize

{wait for space-bar

clear the screen}

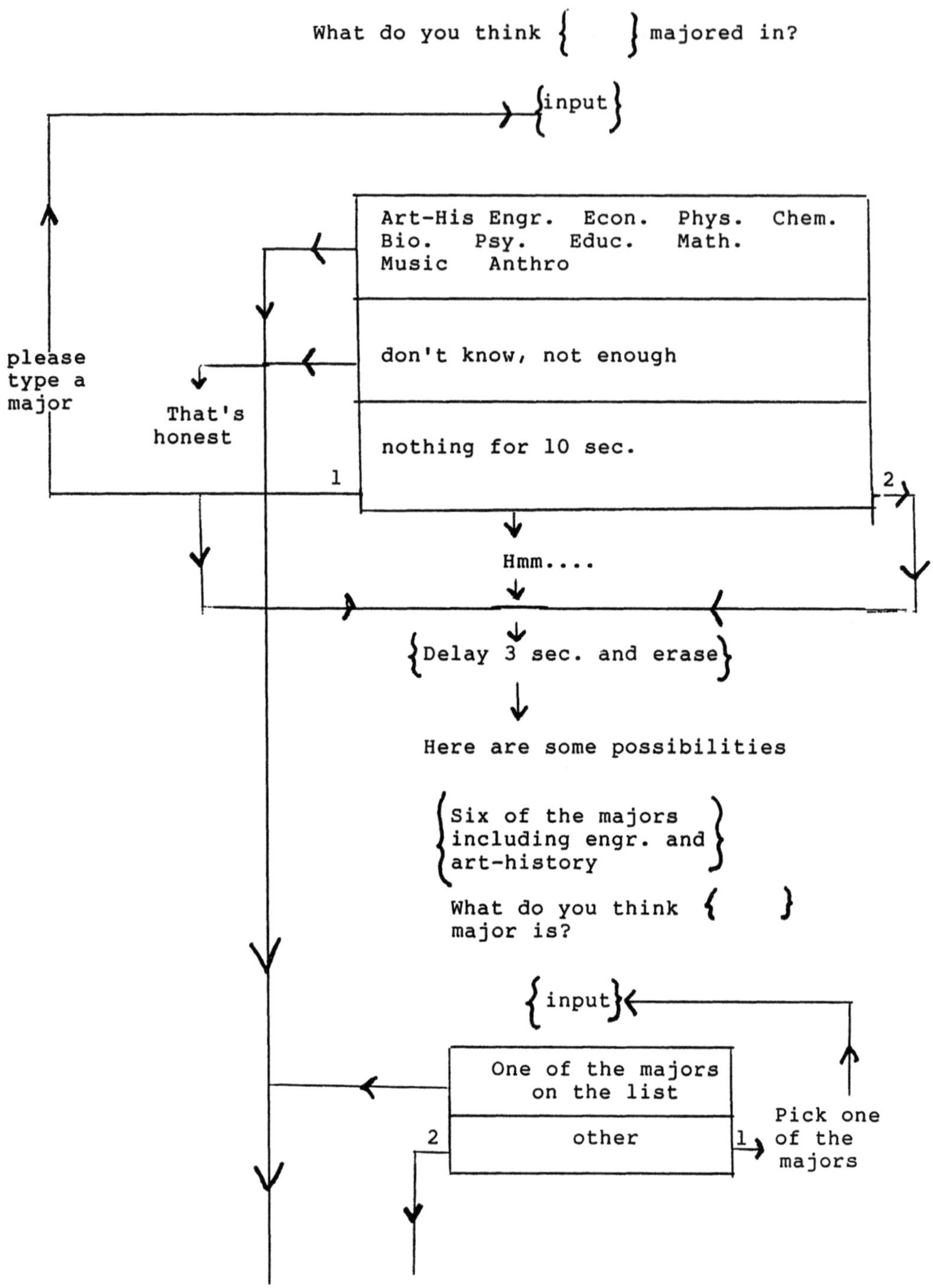
What do you think { } majored in?
{input}
Art-His Engr. Econ. Phys. Chem.
Bio. Psy. Educ. Math.
Music Anthro
don't know, not enough
nothing for 10 sec.
please type a major
That's honest
1
2
Hmm....
{Delay 3 sec. and erase}
Here are some possibilities
{Six of the majors including engr. and art-history}
What do you think { } major is?
{input}
One of the majors on the list
other
2
1
Pick one of the majors

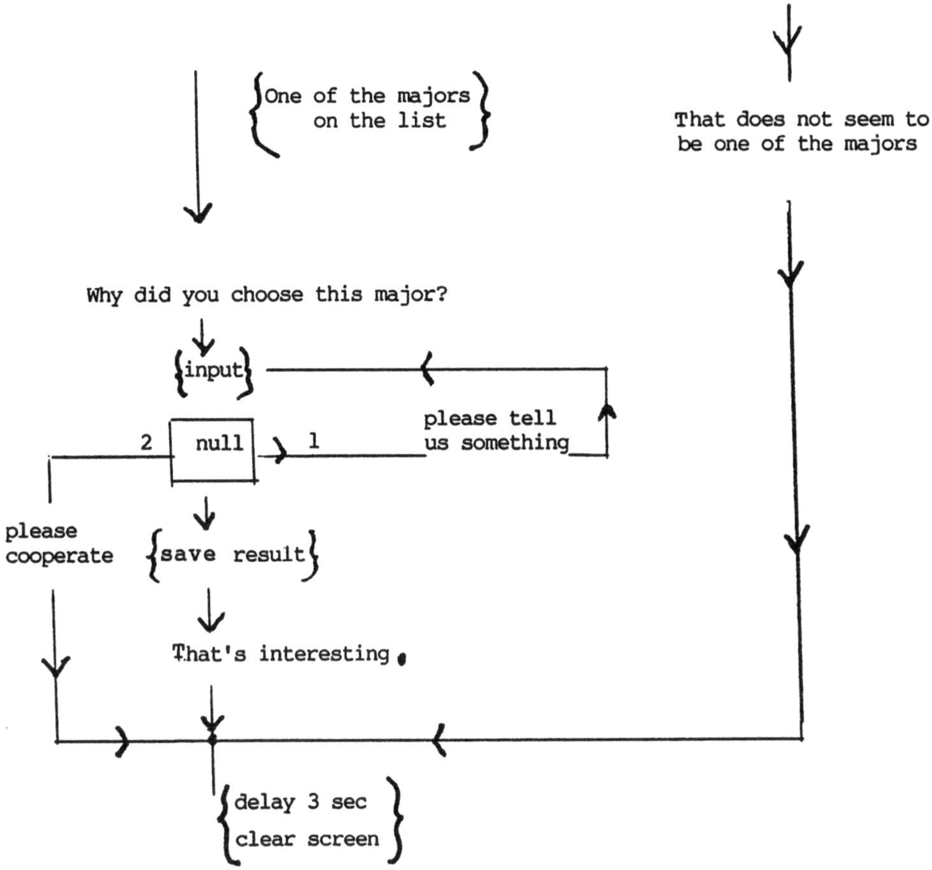

Let's continue the search.

A former high school teacher saw { } in one area of the campus, shown on the following map.

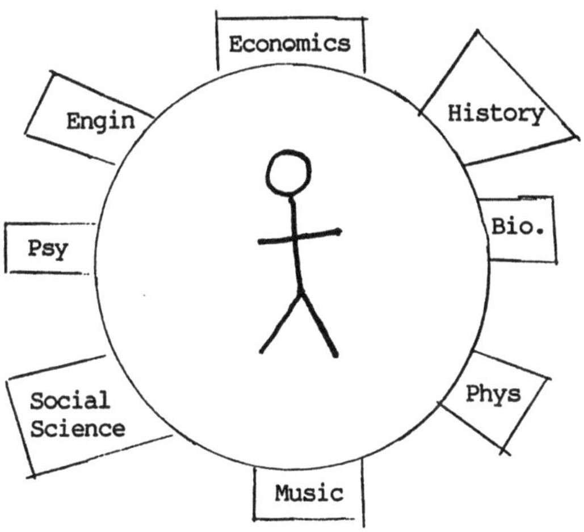

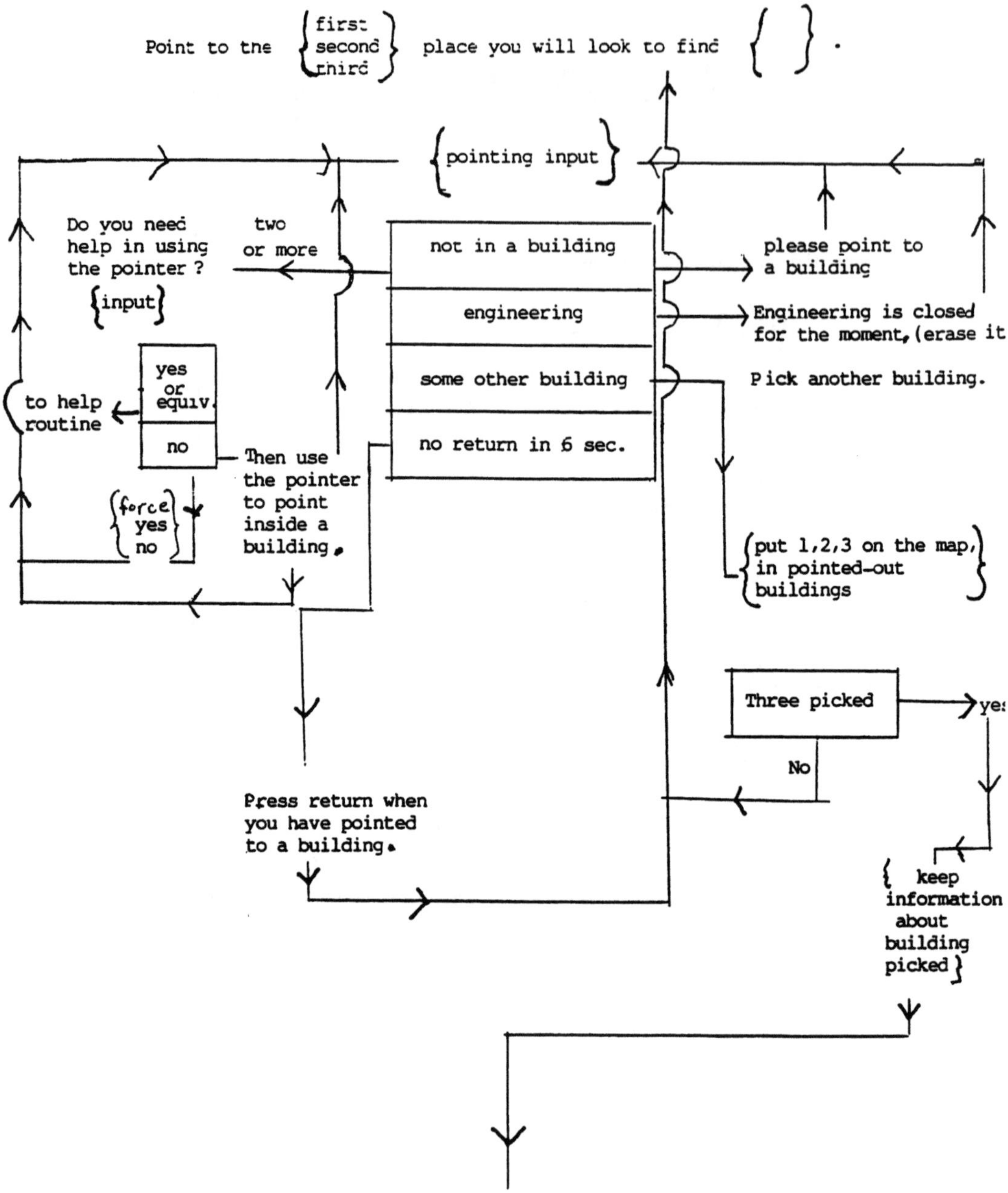
Point to the {first second third} place you will look to find { }.
{pointing input}
Do you need help in using the pointer ?
{input}
two or more
not in a building
engineering
some other building
no return in 6 sec.
please point to a building
Engineering is closed for the moment, (erase it
Pick another building.
yes or equiv.
no
to help routine
{force yes no}
Then use the pointer to point inside a building.
{put 1,2,3 on the map, in pointed-out buildings}
Three picked
yes
No
Press return when you have pointed to a building.
{ keep information about building picked }

wait for spacebar

clear everything but the picture

{ } is not in the three buildings

you picked!

delay 4 sec.
erase the screen

When you get back home, your uncle calls. You tell him you are trying to find { }. He says:

Suppose you know nothing about { } except that { } is a student at the university.

What information would be useful to you?

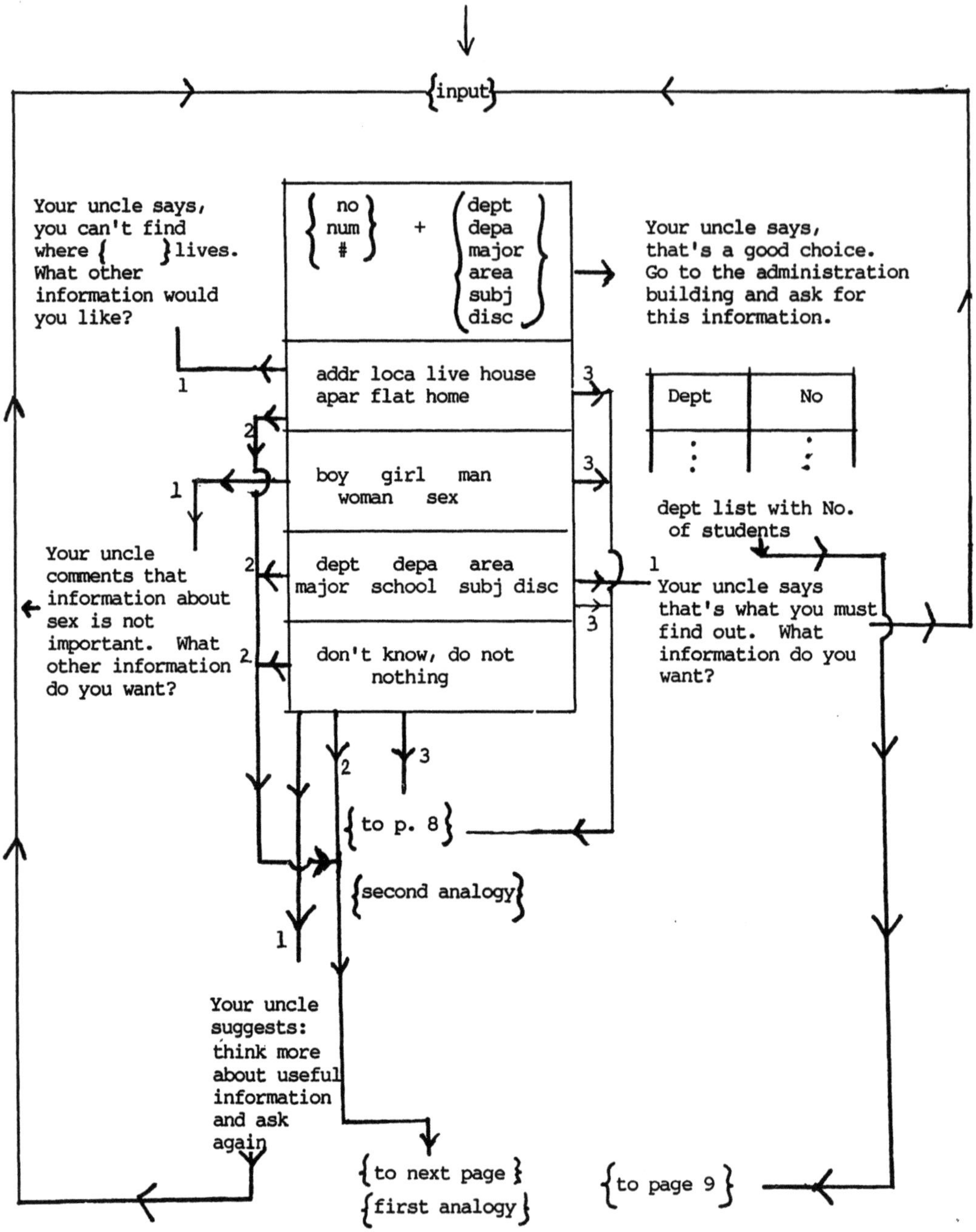
{input}
Your uncle says, you can't find where { } lives. What other information would you like?
{ no num # } + (dept depa major area subj disc)
Your uncle says, that's a good choice. Go to the administration building and ask for this information.
addr loca live house apar flat home
Dept
No
dept list with No. of students
boy girl man woman sex
Your uncle comments that information about sex is not important. What other information do you want?
dept depa area major school subj disc
Your uncle says that's what you must find out. What information do you want?
don't know, do not nothing
{to p. 8}
{second analogy}
Your uncle suggests: think more about useful information and ask again
{to next page}
{first analogy}
{to page 9}
1
2
3

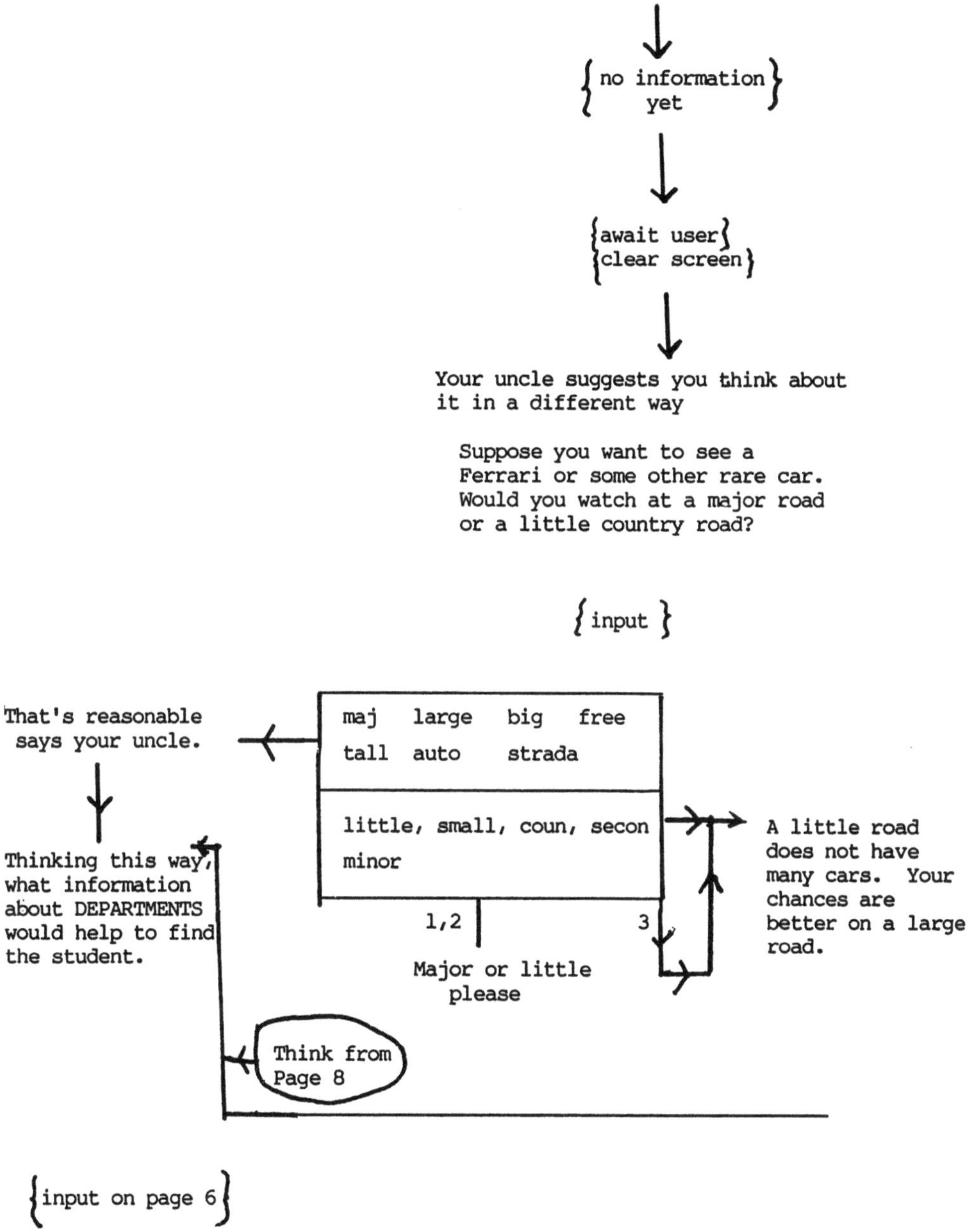
{no information yet}
{await user}
{clear screen}
Your uncle suggests you think about it in a different way
Suppose you want to see a Ferrari or some other rare car. Would you watch at a major road or a little country road?
{input}
maj large big free
tall auto strada
little, small, coun, secon
minor
That's reasonable says your uncle.
Thinking this way, what information about DEPARTMENTS would help to find the student.
1,2
Major or little please
3
A little road does not have many cars. Your chances are better on a large road.
Think from Page 8
{input on page 6}

{second analogy}

Your uncle says

Think about it this way.
You want to find a friend
in a camp on a lake. There are
two camps on the lake, one with
600 people, and one with 100
people. Which camp is the most
likely one to find your friend?

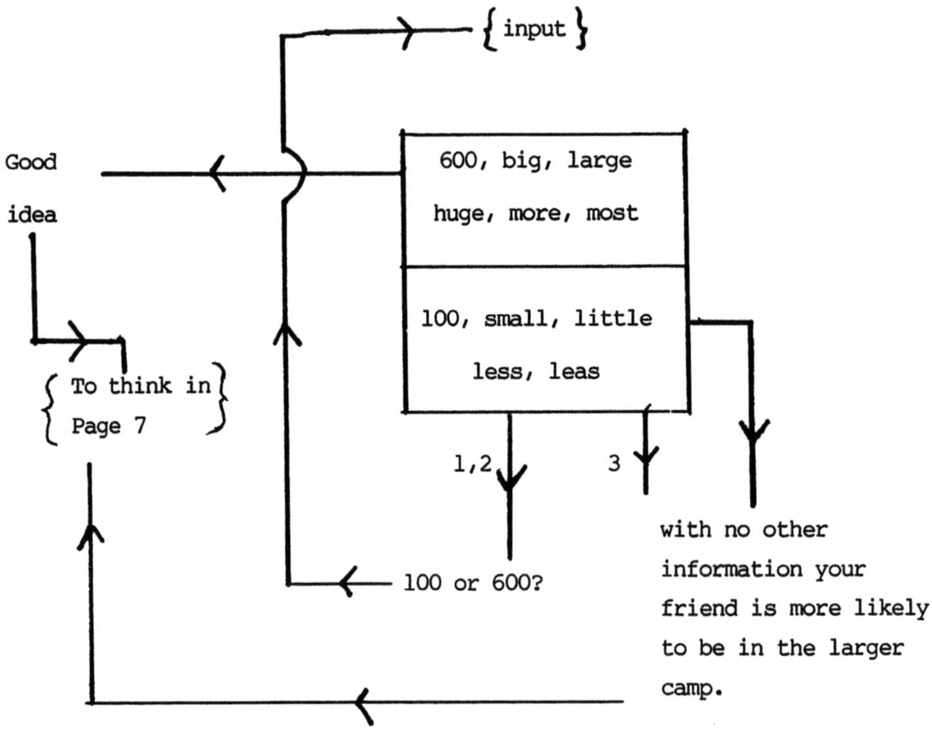

Here is the information you have so far.

{ put everything known on the screen }

{ initial description labeled high school friend's description, final map with no. of students in each department }

You meet on the campus a person who says, I am in class with { } and I'm sure { } is in art, history or engineering.

{ reduce inf. on screen so that only these two depts are represented. Keep description }

Which department is { } in?

{ input }

art, history, engin

{ record }

He is either in art history or engineering. Which?

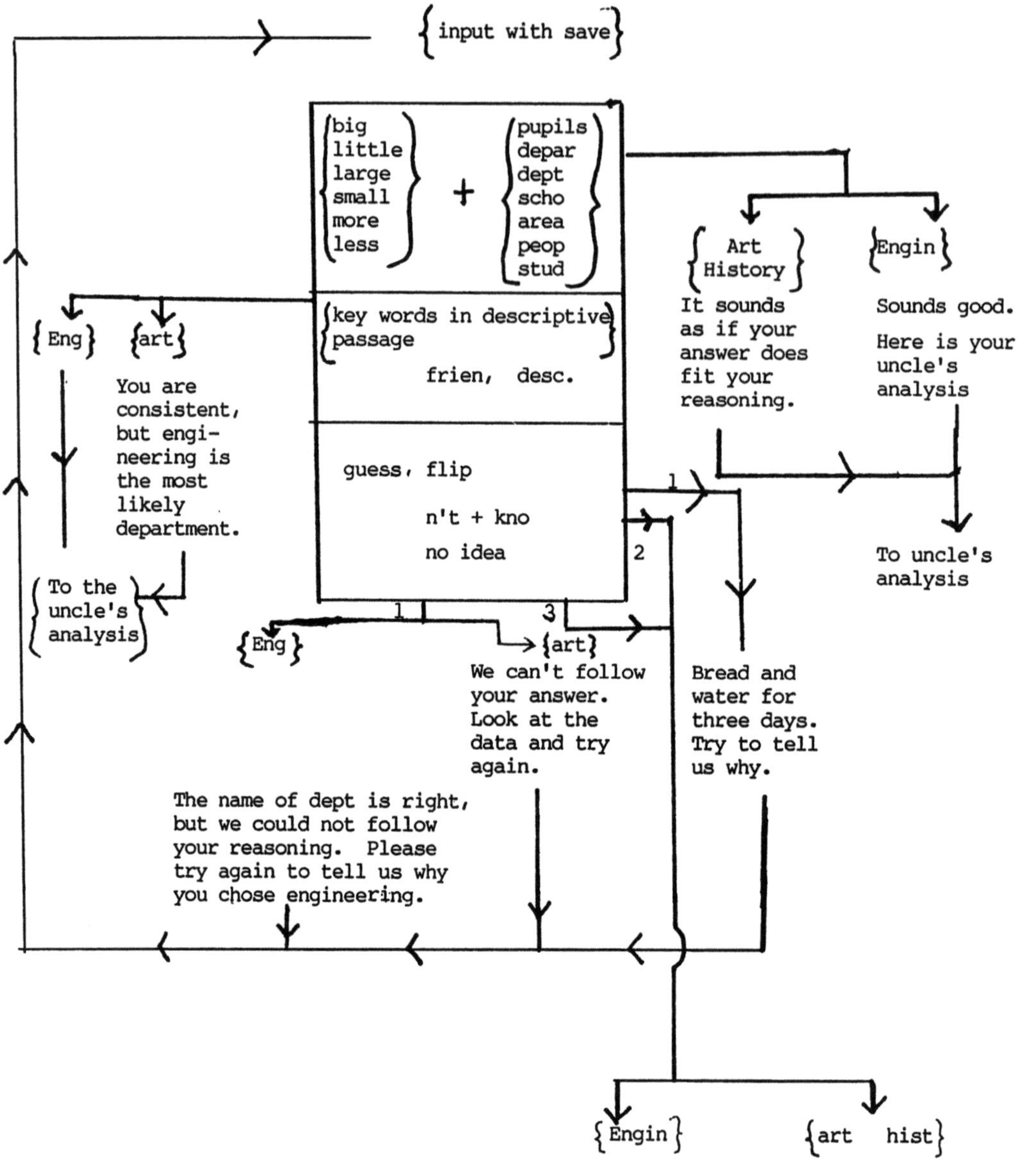

input with save
big
little
large
small
more
less
+
pupils
depar
dept
scho
area
peop
stud
key words in descriptive passage
frien, desc.
guess, flip
n't + kno
no idea
Art History
Engin
It sounds as if your answer does fit your reasoning.
Sounds good. Here is your uncle's analysis
To uncle's analysis
Eng
art
You are consistent, but engineering is the most likely department.
To the uncle's analysis
1
2
3
Eng
art
We can't follow your answer. Look at the data and try again.
Bread and water for three days. Try to tell us why.
The name of dept is right, but we could not follow your reasoning. Please try again to tell us why you chose engineering.
Engin
art hist

We accept your choice of department, but your reasoning still baffles us. Here is your uncle's analysis.

The most likely department is Engineering. Here is your uncle's analysis.

{To uncle's analysis}

Screen Layout

Uncle port - Labelled and boxed

Information port - sometime including graphic, long messages

Question port

Answer port

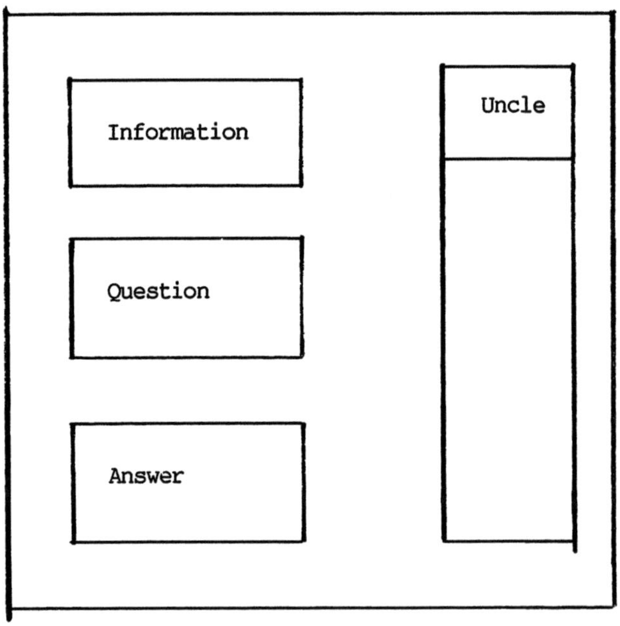

Port active only when needed.

FUTURE POSSIBILITIES FOR DEVELOPMENT

1. Fill in uncle's analysis. This analysis should depend on the errors of each student.

2. Two other missing persons are needed, with other storylines. These could depend also on students of different gender taking different majors.

3. Do we need the uncle?

4. Should we put more emphasis on the detective story?

5. The other storyline could include misleading evidence like comparing percentages instead of actual numbers.

6. The investigator might keep a notebook, available on request at any time.

7. Later cases might deal with the reliability and validity of old data.

LIST OF PARTICIPANTS

Mr. K. J. Adkins
College of Ripon & York
St. John
Lord Mayor's Walk
York YO3 7EX
UNITED KINGDOM

Professor Corrado Agnes
Dept. Fisica
Politecnico di Torino
24 Duca Degli Abruzzi
Torino 10129
ITALY

Ms. Mariarosa Allodi
Mathematics Department
Utica College of Syracuse University
Utica, NY 13502 USA

Dr. Daniel Amiguet
Ruelle du Croset 5
CH-1009 Pully
SWITZERLAND

Dr. J. Balderman
Department of Physics
Ben-Gurion University
84105 Beer Sheva
ISRAEL

Mr. Emilio Balzano
Dipartimento di Fisica
Universita di Napoli
Mostra d'Oltremare
Napoli 80125
ITALY

Professor Cipriano Barrio Alonso
Elorez Estrada 22-4
Oviedo, Asturias 33006
SPAIN

Ms. Jill Baxter
507 North, CERAS
Stanford University
Stanford, CA 94305 USA

Mr. Jean-Marie Brebec
8, Allee des Maoutouses
34890 Laverune
FRANCE

Professor D. J. Britten
Department of Mathematics
University of Windsor
401 Sunset Avenue
Windsor, Ontario N9B 3P4
CANADA

Mr. Paul Brna
Dept. of Artificial Intell.
University of Edinburgh
Edinburgh EH1 2OL
Scotland, UNITED KINGDOM

Professor Alex F. Burr
Department of Physics
New Mexico State University
P. O. Box 3D
Las Cruces, NM 88003 USA

Dr. Nigel H. Buttimore
Department of Mathematics
Trinity College
Dublin
IRELAND

Dr. Michel Caillot
LIRESPT-Universite Paris 7
Tour 23 - 5e Etage
2, Place Jussieu
75251 Paris Cedex 05
FRANCE

Professor Frans Cerulus
Departement Natuurkunde
Kath. Universiteit Leuven
Celstijnenlaan 200 D
B-3030 Heverlee
BELGIUM

Dr. Hubert Christiaen
Toegepaste Wetenschappen
Celestijnenlaan 200 A
B-3030 Heverlee
BELGIUM

Ms. Elizabeth Concannon
6 Ash St.
Room 302
Cambridge, MA 02138 USA

Professor E. Costa
Universidade de Coimbra
Dpt Engenharia Electrotecnica
Largo Marques de Pombal
Coimbra
PORTUGAL

Dr. Daniel Davidson
Microcomputer Center
Pima Community College
2202 W. Anklam Road
Tucson, AZ 85709 USA

Professor Joseph Depireux
Institut de Physique
Universite de Liege
BO-4000 Sart-Tilman (Liege 1)
BELGIUM

Ms. Martine Dujardin
Vrije Universiteit Brussel
Projekt EDUCO
Pleinlaan 2
1050 Brussel
BELGIUM

Professor Harold Ellenton
Department of Physics
University of Waterloo
Waterloo, Ontario N2L 3G1
CANADA

Mr. Augusto Fitas
Departamento de Fisica
Universidade di Evora
Evora
PORTUGAL

Professor Wolfgang Fraunholz
Erziehungswissenschaftliche Hochschul
Reinau 3-4
D-5400 Koblenz
WEST GERMANY

Mrs. Anna Maria Garcia Lleonart
Centre de Calcul de la Universitat
Politecnica de Catalunya
Av. Dr. G. Maranon, s/n
08028 Barcelona
SPAIN

Professor Ladnor Geissinger
Mathematics Dept.
376 Phillips
University of North Carolina
Chapel Hill, NC 27514 USA

Mr. Jorunn Grip
Institutt for Almen Fysikk
University of Trondheim
N-7034 Trondheim-NTH
NORWAY

Professor Raymond Guenther
Department of Physics
University of Nebraska at Omaha
Omaha, NE 68182-0266 USA

Mr. Sadettin Gunsoy
Dept. of Electrical Engineering
Middle Eastern Tech. University
Gaziantep Extension Campus
Gaziantep
TURKEY

Professor Joseph E. J. Habowsky
Biology Department
University of Windsor
Windsor, Ontario N9B 3P4
CANADA

Dr. Jacqueline Hellemans
Katholieke Universiteit Leuven
Centrum voor Didakische Fysika
Naamsestraat 61
B-3030 Leuven
BELGIUM

Professor Robert Hexter
Department of Chemistry
University of Minnesota
207 Pleasant St. SE
Minneapolis, MN 55455 USA

Willie Hols-Elders P/a
Open University
Media Department
P. O. Box 2960
6401 DL Heerlen
THE NETHERLANDS

Professor Barbara A. Hutson
Virginia Tech Graduate Center
2990 Telestar Court
Falls Church, VA 22042 USA

Mr. John Jensen
Norwegian Institute of Technology
Division of General Physics
N-7034 Trondheim-NTH
NORWAY

Professor Karen L. Johnston
Department of Physics
North Carolina State University
Box 8202
Raleigh, NC 27695-8202 USA

Dr. Mebius F. Kramer
Regentesselaan 9
Utrecht
NETHERLANDS

Prof. Dr. Guenther Kurz
Pojektgruppe CAT
Fachhochschule fuer Technik
Muehlstrasse 1
Esslingen D-7300
WEST GERMANY

Lektor Inger Larsen
Electrical Department
Danish Engineering Academy
Building 451
Lyngby DK 2800
DENMARK

Lektor Mogens O. Larsen
Chemical Department
Danish Engineering Academy
Building 375
Lyngby DK 2800
DENMARK

Dr. Mark Leiblum
Eikenlaan 23
6584 BT Molenhoek
NETHERLANDS

Professor Francis W. Lemire
Mathematics Dept.
University of Windsor
Windsor, Ontario N9B 3P4
CANADA

Ms. Ronnie Lowenstein
2998 Borge St.
Oakton, VA 22124 USA

Dr. S. A. Mariadoss
Department of Mathematics
St. Aloysius College
Mangalore - 575 003
INDIA

Professor Mario Martelli
510 Great Springs Road
Bryn Mawr, PA 19010 USA

Dr. J. M. Sune Martinsson
Barrkassvagen 26
S-86500 Alno
SWEDEN

Professor Teresa Mendes
Dept. Eng. Electrotecnica
Universidade de Coimbra
3000 Coimbra
PORTUGAL

Mme. Anne Michel-Pajus
10, Lot. Deguara
Rue de la Combe Caude
34100 Montpellier

Dr. Maria Milano
Via L. Giordano Cercola
Napoli 80040
ITALY

Professor Robert J. Munn
Department of Chemistry
University of Maryland
College Park, MD 20742 USA

Professor John Niman
Dept. of Mathematical Sciences
Hunter College of the CUNY
695 Park Avenue
New York, NY 10021 USA

Mr. Bjarne Nost
Institute of Physics
P. O. Box 1048
Blindern, Oslo,
NORWAY

Mr. Husnu Ozkan
Dept. of Physics
Orta Dogu Teknik Universitesi
Ankara
TURKEY

Prof. G. V. Palassopoulos
41 Blessa Street
Papagos
Athens 156-69
GREECE

Ms. Donatella Persico
Consiglio Nazionale delle Ricerche
Istituto per le Tecnol. Didattiche
Via All'Opera Pia, 11
16145 Genova
ITALY

Dr.Albert Pilot
Technische Hogeschool Twente
Onderwijskundig Centrum CDO
PB 217
7500 AE Enschede
NETHERLANDS

Ms. Antonietta Pontrelli
Euclide 23
74100 Taranto
ITALY

Professor Peter Ponzo
49 Margaret Ave. S.
Waterloo, Ontario N2J 2C8
CANADA

Professor Manfred Precht
Technical University, Munchen
Mathematics Department
Weihenstephan
8050 Freising 12
WEST GERMANY

Professor Floyd M. Read
Dept. of Science Education
East Carolina University
Greenville, NC 27834 USA

Dr. J. L. Redding
Department of Physics
Bishop's University
Lennoxville, Quebec J1M 1Z7
CANADA

Mr. Joseph Regev
Ben Gurion University
Computer Center
P. O. Box 653
84120 Beer Sheva
ISRAEL

Mrs. Miriam Reiner
48A Harofeh Street
Haifa 34367
ISRAEL

Dr. Tyson Rigg
Physics Department
Divine Mercy College
Henley on Thames
Oxfordshire RG9 3AE
UNITED KINGDOM

Professor Roger Rockefeller
Department of Physics
Utica College of Syracuse University
Utica, NY 13502 USA

Professor D. K. Saraswati
Physics Department
Athabasca University
Box 10,000
Athabasca, Alberta TOG 2R0
CANADA

Mr. Luigi Sarti
Consiglio Nazionale delle Ricerche
Istituto per le Tecnol. Didattiche
Via All'Opera Pia, 11
16145 Genova
ITALY

Mr. Arthur Schoeters
Populierenlaan 1 bus 13
B-2020 Antwerpen
BELGIUM

Dr. Gilberte Schuyten
H. Dunantlaan 1
9000 Gent
BELGIUM

Mr. Alain Senteni
235 Villeneuve O.
Montreal, Quebec H2T 1R8
CANADA

Professor Raymond Serway
Department of Physics
James Madison University
Harrisonburg, VA 22807 USA

Dr. Giovanna Sissa
Corso Magenta 29/3
Genova 16125
ITALY

Miss C. de Souza
12 A Westbury Road
Croydon CRO 2ES
Surrey
UNITED KINGDOM

Dr. Ron H. A. Staal
Technische Hogeschool Twente
Onderwijskundig Centrum CDO
PB 217
7500 AE Enschede
NETHERLANDS

Dr. Robert B. Teese
Physics Department
Muskingum College
New Concord, OH 43762 USA

Drs. Joseph-Marie Thijssen
Sophiaweg 306
Nijmegen
NETHERLANDS

Mr. Leo Thomas
Karel Druytslaan, 4
2350 Vosselaar
BELGIUM

Professor Ronald Thornton
Dept. of Education
Ctr. Math & Science Education
Tufts University
Medford, MA 02155 USA

Ms. Federica Velotti
Via Nazionale Cimitile
Napoli 80030
ITALY

Mrs. Pelagia Voutsa
American Farm School
P. O. Box 10140
Thessaloniki 54110
GREECE

Professor Alfred Warrinnier
Departement Wiskunde
K.U.L.
Celestijnenlaan 200B
B-3030 Heverlee
BELGIUM

Dean Samuel L. Wiley
College of Natural Science
California State University-Dominguez Hil
Carson, CA 90747 USA

Dr. Barry Wills
Assoc. Dean for Computing
Faculty of Engineering
University of Waterloo
Waterloo Ontario N2L 3G1
CANADA

LECTURERS

Professor Arnold Arons
Department of Physics
University of Washington
Seattle, Washington 98195 USA

Professor Alfred M. Bork, Director
Educational Technology Center
University of California
Irvine, California 92717 USA

Dr. Jef Moonen, Director
Centrum voor Onderwijs en
Informatietechnologie
Technische Hogeschool Twente
Enschede, THE NETHERLANDS

Dr. Giorgio Olimpo
Consiglio Nazionale della Ricerche
Istituto per le Tecnologie Didattiche
Via All'Opera Pia, 11
16145 Genova, ITALY

Dr. John M. Pitre
Department of Physics
University of Toronto
Toronto, Ontario M5S 1A7
CANADA

Dr. Peter Ross
Dept. of Artificial Intelligence
University of Edinburgh
Edinburgh EH1 1QL, UK

Dr. Elena Sassi
Istituto di Fisica Sperimentale
Universita di Napoli
Mostra d'Oltremare Pad. 20
80125 Napoli, ITALY

Professor Lee S. Shulman
School of Education
Stanford University
Stanford, California 94305 USA

Professor Harold Weinstock, Director
Educational Technology Center
Illinois Institute of Technology
Chicago, Illinois 60616 USA

Address as of July 1, 1986:

Dr. Harold Weinstock
AFOSR/NE
Bolling AFB, DC 20332-6448 USA

NATO ASI Series F

Vol. 1: Issues in Acoustic Signal – Image Processing and Recognition. Edited by C. H. Chen. VIII, 333 pages. 1983.

Vol. 2: Image Sequence Processing and Dynamic Scene Analysis. Edited by T. S. Huang. IX, 749 pages. 1983.

Vol. 3: Electronic Systems Effectiveness and Life Cycle Costing. Edited by J. K. Skwirzynski. XVII, 732 pages. 1983.

Vol. 4: Pictorial Data Analysis. Edited by R. M. Haralick. VIII, 468 pages. 1983.

Vol. 5: International Calibration Study of Traffic Conflict Techniques. Edited by E. Asmussen. VII, 229 pages. 1984.

Vol. 6: Information Technology and the Computer Network. Edited by K. G. Beauchamp. VIII, 271 pages. 1984.

Vol. 7: High-Speed Computation. Edited by J. S. Kowalik. IX, 441 pages. 1984.

Vol. 8: Program Transformation and Programming Environments. Report on an Workshop directed by F. L. Bauer and H. Remus. Edited by P. Pepper. XIV, 378 pages. 1984.

Vol. 9: Computer Aided Analysis and Optimization of Mechanical System Dynamics. Edited by E. J. Haug. XXII, 700 pages. 1984.

Vol. 10: Simulation and Model-Based Methodologies: An Integrative View. Edited by T. I. Ören, B. P. Zeigler, M. S. Elzas. XIII, 651 pages. 1984.

Vol. 11: Robotics and Artificial Intelligence. Edited by M. Brady, L. A. Gerhardt, H. F. Davidson. XVII, 693 pages. 1984.

Vol. 12: Combinatorial Algorithms on Words. Edited by A. Apostolico, Z. Galil. VIII, 361 pages. 1985.

Vol. 13: Logics and Models of Concurrent Systems. Edited by K. R. Apt. VIII, 498 pages. 1985.

Vol. 14: Control Flow and Data Flow: Concepts of Distributed Programming. Edited by M. Broy. VIII, 525 pages. 1985.

Vol. 15: Computational Mathematical Programming. Edited by K. Schittkowski. VIII, 451 pages. 1985.

Vol. 16: New Systems and Architectures for Automatic Speech Recognition and Synthesis. Edited by R. De Mori, C.Y. Suen. XIII, 630 pages. 1985.

Vol. 17: Fundamental Algorithms for Computer Graphics. Edited by R.A. Earnshaw. XVI, 1042 pages. 1985.

Vol. 18: Computer Architectures for Spatially Distributed Data. Edited by H. Freeman and G. G. Pieroni. VIII, 391 pages. 1985.

Vol. 19: Pictorial Information Systems in Medicine. Edited by K. H. Höhne. XII, 525 pages. 1986.

Vol. 20: Disordered Systems and Biological Organization. Edited by E. Bienenstock, F. Fogelman Soulié, G. Weisbuch. XXI, 405 pages. 1986.

Vol. 21: Intelligent Decision Support in Process Environments. Edited by E. Hollnagel, G. Mancini, D.D. Woods. XV, 524 pages. 1986.

Vol. 22: Software System Design Methods. The Challenge of Advanced Computing Technology. Edited by J.K. Skwirzynski. XIII, 747 pages. 1986.

Vol. 23: Designing Computer-Based Learning Materials. Edited by H. Weinstock and A. Bork. IX, 285 pages. 1986.

MIX
Papier aus verantwortungsvollen Quellen
Paper from responsible sources
FSC® C105338

If you have any concerns about our products,
you can contact us on
ProductSafety@springernature.com

In case Publisher is established outside the EU,
the EU authorized representative is:
Springer Nature Customer Service Center GmbH
Europaplatz 3, 69115 Heidelberg, Germany

Printed by Libri Plureos GmbH
in Hamburg, Germany